AF564752

Web Programming

WEB PROGRAMMING

Nishit Mathur

CENTRUM PRESS
NEW DELHI-110002 (INDIA)

CENTRUM PRESS
H.O.: 4360/4, Ansari Road, Daryaganj,
New Delhi-110002 (India)
Tel: 23278000, 23261597, 23255577, 23286875
B.O.: No. 1015, Ist Main Road, BSK IIIrd Stage,
IIIrd Phase, IIIrd Block, Bangalore-560085 (INDIA)
Tel: 080-41723429
Email: centrumpress@gmail.com
Visit us at: www.centrumpress.com

Web Programming

First Edition, 2011

PRINTED IN INDIA

Printed at Tarun Offset Printers, Delhi-110053

Contents

Preface

Just as there is a diversity of programming languages available and suitable for conventional programming tasks, there is a diversity of languages available and suitable for Web programming. There is no reason to believe that any one language will completely monopolize the Web programming scene, although the varying availability and suitability of the current offerings is likely to favor some over others. Java is both available and generally suitable, but not all application developers are likely to prefer it over languages more similar to what they currently use, or, in the case of non-programmers, over higher level languages and tools. This is OK because there is no real reason why we must converge on a single programming language for the Web any more than we must converge on a single programming language in any other domain.

The Web does, however, place some specific constraints on our choices: the ability to deal with a variety of protocols and formats (e.g. graphics) and programming tasks; performance (both speed and size); safety; platform independence; protection of intellectual property; and the basic ability to deal with other Web tools and languages. These issues are not independent of one another. A choice which seemingly is optimal in one dimension may be sub-optimal or worse in another.

Author

1

System Programming and Operating System

INTRODUCTION TO SYSTEM PROGRAMMING

System programming is the activity of programming system software. The primary distinguishing characteristic of systems programming when compared to application programming is that application programming aims to produce software which provides services to the user (*e.g.* word processor), whereas systems programming aims to produce software which provides services to the computer hardware. It also requires a greater degree of hardware awareness.

The architects of the earliest computer systems gave little thought to software. (The very word was still a decade in the future.) Building the machine itself was the serious intellectual challenge; converting mathematical formulas into program statements looked like a routine clerical task. The awful truth came out soon enough. Maurice V.Wilkes, who wrote what may have been the first working computer program, had his personal epiphany in 1949, when "the realization came over me with full force that a good part of the remainder of my life was going to be spent in finding errors in my own programs." Half a century later, we're still debugging.

The very first programs were written in pure binary notation: Both data and instructions had to be encoded in long, featureless strings of 1s and 0s. Moreover, it was up to the programmer to keep track of where everything was stored in the machine's memory. Before you could call a subroutine, you had to calculate its address. The technology that lifted these burdens from the programmer was assembly language, in which raw binary codes were replaced by symbols such as load, store, add, sub. The symbols were translated into binary by a program called an assembler, which also calculated addresses.

This was the first of many instances in which the computer was recruited to help with its own programming. Assembly language was a crucial early advance, but still the programmer had to keep in mind all the minutiae in the instruction set of a specific computer. Evaluating a short mathematical expression such as x2+y2 might require dozens of assembly-language instructions. Higher-level languages freed the programmer to think in terms of variables and equations rather than registers and addresses. In Fortran, for example, x2+y2 would be written simply as X** 2+Y**2. Expressions of this kind are translated into binary form by a program called a compiler.

With Fortran and the languages that followed, programmers finally had the tools they needed to get into really serious trouble. By the 1960s large software projects were notorious for being late, overbudget and buggy; soon came the appalling news that the cost of software was overtaking that of hardware. Frederick P. Brooks, Jr., who managed the OS/360 software program at IBM, called large- system programming a "tar pit" and remarked,"Everyone seems to have been surprised by the stickiness of the problem." One response to this crisis was structured programming, a reform movement whose manifesto was Edsger W. Dijkstra's brief letter to the editor titled "Go to statement considered harmful."

Structured programs were to be built out of subunits that have a single entrance point and a single exit (eschewing the goto command,which allows jumps into or out of the middle of a routine). Three such constructs were recommended: sequencing (do A, then B, then C), alternation (either do A or do B) and iteration (repeat A until some condition is satisfied). Corrado Böhm and Giuseppe Jacopini proved that these three idioms are sufficient to express essentially all programs.

Structured programming came packaged with a number of related principles and imperatives. Top-down design and stepwise refinement urged the programmer to set forth the broad outlines of a procedure first and only later fill in the details. Modularity called for self-contained units with simple interfaces between them.

Encapsulation, or data hiding,required that the internal workings of a module be kept private, so that later changes to the module would not affect other areas of the program. All of these ideas have proved their worth and remain a part of software practice today. But they did not rescue programmers from the tar pit.

SYSTEM PROGRAMMING LANGUAGE

System programming languages are higher level and they are strongly typed languages. The term "higher level" means that many details are handled automatically so that programmers can write less code to get the same job done. System programming languages are well suited to building components where the complexity is in the data structures and algorithms.

System programming support following features:

- Register allocation is handled by the compiler so that programmers need not write code to move information between registers and memory.
- Programmers can use simple keywords such as while and if for control structures; the compiler generates all the detailed instructions to implement the control structures.
- Procedure calling sequences are generated automatically: programmers need not worry about moving arguments to and from the call stack.

EMBEDDED SYSTEM PROGRAMMING

Embedded System Programming was first used in Apollo guidance computer to guide Apollo. Technological advancement brought the price of embedded system (ICs) lower making it possible to use them for commercial purpose.

Today embedded systems are widely used in various devices performing specific functions with drastic improvement in processing power. Embedded system programming has been derived from the word embedded system. An embedded system is nothing but a special purpose system in which the computer is fully encapsulated by the device it controls. Embedded software designs have advanced enough to produce widely used devices performing specific function devices such as ATM, PDA, mobile phones etc.

This widely used technological term in the field of Information Technology, is the combination of computer hardware and software which is either fixed in facility or programmable. In short it is purposely designed for a meticulous kind of application device. Systems that hosts this embedded systems are various industrial machines, automobiles, medical equipment, cameras, household appliances, and airplanes, vending machines, toys, cellular phone and PDA. Seeing its importance and worth embedded systems programming has gained lot popularity and people are looking for companies providing this service. If you are looking for a company providing embedded systems programming then your search is over as Softage is there for you. Softage is Russia's leading IT service provider providing best and advanced embedded systems programming. Embedded systems programming is specially dedicated to unequivocal tasks so that design engineers can optimize it by reducing the magnitude and cost of the product. In fact nowadays, embedded systems are frequently mass-produced. This has resulted in the cost savings that may be multiplied by millions of items. Apart from the other devices embedded systems also range from portable devices such as MP3 players, to large stationary installations like traffic lights or factory controllers. According to the experts embedded systems are easily programmable and are provided with a programming interface. Embedded system programming is a tough and professional work which is efficiently handled by Softage. Backed by years of experience Softage hosts some of the best and professional programmers those are experts in embedded system software programming. Embedded systems programming is basically done in various languages such as J2e, C/C++, x86 assembler, ADSP assembler, and SQL accessing appropriate language for specific devices. All these languages are supported and provided by Softage and that too easily affordable. Thus, what you are waiting for if you are looking for embedded systems programming then Softage is there for you.

WINDOWS SYSTEM PROGRAMMING

Introduction

In old days, the operating system program executes the program's instructions in sequence one instruction after another as they arranged by the programmer. When the program calls a function or interacts with the Operating System (OS) by calling one of the OS's service functions, the function's instructions executed in similar way and the execution continue sequentially until the end of the last instruction of the main program.

In this traditional way of programming the program only need one main function to start the execution. Nowadays, in event driven programming environment such as Windows, the interaction between the program and the OS is a message-based interaction. In this interaction the program start in a wait mode until the user create an event like for example, press a key or click a mouse button. The OS generates appropriate message and inserts it in application's message queue.

The program, when it ready, should dispatch the messages (read a message from the queue and send it back to the OS) one message after another for time scheduling purpose. After that, the OS then send the message again to the program and the program respond by taking appropriate actions. In this kind of interaction, a simple program need at least two functions, the main function that start the message loop

(WinMain ()) and the other called by the OS (Windows Function())and respond to the passed message. The following is a skeleton program for Windows operating system that can be used as a starter for studying and testing windows applications.

Windows Program

```
WinMain ()
{
Define a window structure
Register the windowstructure
Create the window
Display the window
Run the message loop
}
WindowFunc ()
{
Switch (message)
{
case message 1:
_ _ _
_ _ _
_ _ _
case message 2:
_ _ _
_ _ _
_ _ _
default:
_ _ _
_ _ _
_ _ _
}
}
/* A minimal windows skeleton program. */
#include <windows.h>
LRESULT CALLBACK WindowFunc(HWND, UINT, WPARAM,
LPARAM);
/* name of windows class */
char szWinName[] = "MyWin";
int WINAPI WinMain(HINSTANCE hThisInst, HINSTANCE
hPrevInst,LPSTR
```

```
lpszArgs, int nWinMode)
{
HWND hwnd;
MSG msg;
WNDCLASSEX wcl;
/* Define a window class.*/
wcl.cbSize = sizeof(WNDCLASSEX);
wcl.hInstance = hThisInst;/* handle to this
instance */
wcl.lpszClassName = szWinName;/* window class name
*/
wcl.lpfnWndProc = WindowFunc;/* window function*/
wcl.style = 0;/* default style */
wcl.hIcon = LoadIcon(NULL,IDI_APPLICATION);/*std
icon */
wcl.hIconSm = LoadIcon(NULL,IDI_WINLOGO);/*small
icon */
wcl.hCursor = LoadCursor(NULL,IDC_ARROW);/*cursor
style */
wcl.lpszMenuName = NULL;/* no menu */
wcl.cbClsExtra = 0;/* no extra */
wcl.cbWndExtra = 0;/* information needed */
/* Make the window background white. */
wcl.hbrBackground=                    (HBRUSH)
GetStockObject(WHITE_BRUSH);
/* Register the window class */
if(!RegisterClassEx(&wcl)) return 0;
/* Now that a window class has been registered,
** a window can be created. */
hwnd = CreateWindow(
szWinName,/* name of window class */
"Windows Skeleton Program",/* title */
WS_OVERLAPPEDWINDOW,/* window style:normal */
CW_USEDEFAULT,/* X coordinate-let windows decide
*/
CW_USEDEFAULT,/* Y coordinate-let windows decide
*/
CW_USEDEFAULT,/* width-let windows decide */
```

```
CW_USEDEFAULT,/* height- let windows decide */
HWND_DESKTOP,/* no parent window */
NULL,
hThisInst,/*handle of this instance of hte program
*/
NULL/* no additional arguments */
);
/* Display the window. */
ShowWindow(hwnd, nWinMode);
UpdateWindow(hwnd);
/* Create the message loop. */
while(GetMessage(&msg, NULL, 0, 0))
{
TranslateMessage(&msg);/* allow use of keyboard
*/
DispatchMessage(&msg);/*return control to windows
*/
}
return msg.wParam;
}
/* This function is called by Windows OS and
** is passed message from the message queue.
*********************************************/
LRESULT CALLBACK WindowFunc(HWND hwnd, UINT
message,WPARAM wParam,
LPARAM lParam)
{
switch(message) {
case WM_DESTROY:/* terminate the program */
PostQuitMessage(0);
break;
default:
/* Let Windows NT process any messages
** not specified in the preceding switch
** statement. */
return DefWindowProc(hwnd, message,
wParam,lParam);
}
```

```
return 0;
}
```

The WinMain function starts by creating a window since we need one to display the output. Unlike the old programming under DOS, there is no standard output. After a window created the function start the message loop. The second function usually called the Windows Function or Windows Procedure has a switch statement to handle different messages.

UNIX SYSTEMS PROGRAMMING

Introduction

The Unix systems programming API has been standardised by a large number of POSIX standards documents from the IEEE. For the majority of programmers the most important of these is POSIX 1003.1 which covers process primitives and environments, directories and files, I/O primitives and device specific functions. Later standards cover other issues, such as Shells and Utilities (POSIX 1003.2) and Administration (POSIX 1387.2).

One of the unusual characteristics of POSIX 1003.1 is its use of the C language throughout. Whereas IEEE standards would normally be expected to be language independent, the history of Unix is so bound up with C that this was the only feasible route. The document claims that it will be the basis for definitions that are independent of particular programming languages. In fact, new language dependent versions have arisen, such as Ada (POSIX 1003.5) and Fortran.

Irrespective of the formal standards mechanisms, designers of libraries for other languages have used POSIX 1003.1 as the specification for their own libraries. For example, tcl [Ousterhout] and Perl [Wall] have well-developed Unix bindings that copy the syntax, and rely on the semantics, of POSIX 1003.1.

Java [Arnold] is the latest flavour in programming languages for all sorts of excellent reasons, despite some serious shortcomings. It is a full O/O language (although not as pure as SmallTalk or Eiffel); it is based on C/C++, but avoids the worst of both languages (not completely, though); by use of a virtual machine it is cross-platform (although some vendors have variant versions); it has a rich set set of libraries that deal with, for example, graphics and networking. These are combining to produce the "Web programming" environment where applications or applets are written once to run on any platform. Java extends the open authoring environment of HTML to an open programming environment.

How do Unix and Java co-exist? Very well in general terms. A Java application can do exactly the same things in a Unix environment that it can do in a Mac or Windows environment. With care, applications can even be written that transparently handle such issues as forward- versus back-slashes for directory separators.

Java currently lacks the depth of hooks into the POSIX API that tcl and Perl have. The standard must continue to have this lack or it will lose its universal applicability. However, *extensions* by *non-standard* libraries can supply this depth, as long as they are done in an appropriate manner. This paper reports on a project to make the POSIX API available to Java applications or applets using a non-standard library. It encapulates POSIX calls within Java methods for a new set of classes in the posix package.

This project must be contrasted in aims and methods to the Microsoft policy with J++: their attempt is to make J++ the best environment for doing Windows programming in Java [J++], and this implicitly rejects the notion of a cross-platform environment. It may even turn out to be difficult for the programmer using J++ to be certain of how general their code is. The statements from Microsoft do not seem to dispel any uncertainty.

This project, on the other hand, makes it explicit about the introduction of non-standard features, by placing all the new classes in a package that is non-standard. No application using the posix package will ever pass the "Java Pure" tests. On the other hand, this package will develop by an open process method: the source code will be freely available to all, and can be freely modified. If interest is high enough, it can be divorced from individual control and given to a suitable co-ordinating authority.

What's in POSIX?

Most operating system APIs share common functionality. For example, both Unix and Windows have means to list the files in a directory and to change to that directory. Some of this common functionality has already been captured in the Java class File which can return a list of files in a directory. However, many useful methods are missing. For example, the ability to change directories does not appear to be there because it has different effects in DOS to Unix (in DOS it changes directories for all processes, but in Unix only for the calling process).

Some of the areas in which the POSIX API supplies extra functionality over the Java Core is given in the following (incomplete) table:

- Files
- Multiple links
- File status
- Access mode
- FIFOs
- Processes
- File creation mask
- Execution times
- User id
- Signals
- Process groups

POSIX Library

Java allows an application or applet to be built from application-specific files and from common libraries. The Java Core libraries supply a standard set of libraries that can be guaranteed in all environments with the Java logo (although at least one vendor is likely to lose this by non-compliance with this requirement). The Core libraries cover language features (java.lang), general I/O (java.io), useful utilities (java.util), networking (java.net), windowing (java.awt), *etc*, plus techniques such as remote method invocation (RMI) and Java Native Interface (JNI).

Any application or applet can add classes that are written in Java. These can be accessed from local copies or downloaded across the network. This is the principle behind the network computer, and is captured in the "Pure Java" certification. This validates that an aplication or applet should be able to run in any Java-conforming environment.

The key to all of this is that implementations of the Java Core classes must exist on all Java-conforming platforms. It is not often stated, but these Core classes are riddled with native, platform-dependent code. They have to be: the AWT relies on the native windowing system, and the network classes rely on the native TCP/IP stack. What Pure Java really means is: use no native code apart from that sanctioned by Sun.

The Java Virtual Machine interpreters are currently written in C. There is an interface between compiled Java and the interpreter which is formalised by a set of Java to native-code C functions. Regrettably, there are several sets of interface APIs: the original set from Java 1.0, which is still heavily used but not talked about anymore (*eg* in the AWT); the Java Native Interface (JNI) which is the new public standard [JNI]; the Microsoft set, which differs from JNI and is one of the points of contention between Sun and Microsoft.

This POSIX library is implemented using the Java Native Interface (JNI) API. It is a "thin" library, calling directly into the C API with very little extra work. It will need to be compiled for all native platforms, since it is written in C as well as Java. The intent is that it should run on all Posix platforms, but of course this has still to be tested.

Language Differences

Return Values

The POSIX system calls in C use the return value of functions for a variety of purposes. For example, in open() a "handle" to the file (a file descriptor) is returned for all future references to the file; in umask() the previous value of the mask is returned. In Java, these uses may be irrelevant or deprecated. Handles to structures are rarely needed since in Java one is dealing with *objects,* and the reference to an object is a handle to that object. Special integer values (for example) are not needed. Style issues may cause some problems. The Java Beans specification encourages the use of "getter" and "setter" methods. For example, the function umask()in C returns the old mask while also setting a new one. In Java Beans style, this would be two separate methods, getUmask() and setUmask().

Data Types

There are some data representation issues that are difficult to resolve. Java has a more limited set of integer types, and does not include the unsigned values. This is discussed in more detail later. Java does not allow mechanisms to perform address arithmetic. There does not seem to be any need to do this in the POSIX API, so this is not a problem.

Error handling

Systems calls may succeed or fail. There must be a way of signalling both cases. In C, the standard method to do this is by the function return value. For example, the function open() will return a non-negative integer (the file descriptor) if the call succeeds, or minus one if it fails.

In Java, errors are signalled by raising exceptions, and if no exception is raised then the method has succeeded.

Decisions

For a first cut at a Java/POSIX binding all decisions were made in favour of the C programmer. This was based on the fact that the design decisions for the API had already been made and it was relatively easy to take these decisions unchanged into Java. It also allowed concentration on the (initially) "harder" bits which involved using the JNI API to map Java into C.

However, the resulting code did not fit the Java coding styles or standards. Programs using this had an awkward feel. It was discarded in favour of a more Java-like solution, reworking the POSIX API. Some of the possibilities are discussed in the sequel as to why this decision was made.

Class Structure

Related to the language issue is the classification of POSIX calls into Java classes. C++ can adopt the C API unchanged since it is a mixed OO/procedural language that will accept C functions unchanged. In Java, all functions must belong to methods of classes. This means that some changes must be made to the API anyway. This section discusses some of the issues in this.

The POSIX specification chapter on "Files and Directories" contains function calls in a number of categories. There is a set of functions that merely take the name of a file: these include chmod() and access(). Another set refer to a file as object by using a *file descriptor*, such as open(), creat(), read() andwrite(). The C system calls stat() and fstat() take a structure and fill values in. The functions link() and unlink() really refer to file names within directories, and as such refer to directories rather than files, even though programmers tend to think of them as file rather than directory operations. The functionumask() sets file creation flags for the current process, and is unrelated to files except in their creation.

The other chapters in the POSIX 1003.1 specification contain an equal mixture of categories. In other words, this specification is not drawn up on lines that are suitable for OO languages. Categorisation of C functions into OO classes and methods is not clear-cut.

Class Stat

A set of functions that map well into Java are the functions stat() and fstat() as they deal with the stat structure. The C stat structure has a number of fields and a set of C macros that act on one of these fields:

```
struct stat {
```

```
mode_t st_mode;
ino_t st_ino;
...
}
/* constants */
#define S_IRUSR...
#define S_IWUSR...
/* macros */
#define S_ISDIR(mode)...
#define S_ISCHR(mode)...
```

This displays a number of characteristics of POSIX:

- Structure field names have a prefix st_ to label them as belonging to structure stat
- Native data types are hidden by typedef definitions, such as mode_t
- To reduce name clashes, defined constants have a prefix S_
- To reduce name clashes, macros have a prefix S_

The functions that manipulate this structure are stat() and fstat(). These fill in the fields with values that can be queried by a program. These system calls cannot be used to set values.

In Java terms, many of these devices for avoiding namespace problems can be dropped, since Java has its own mechanisms. The read-only nature of the fields can also be specified. The difference between the two system calls that fill in the stat structure correspond to two different constructors. However, the type synonym problem is not handled well, and may need to revert to base types. A Java class for this structure and its functions could be

```
public class Stat {
//constants
public final int RWXU;
public final int RUSR;
public final int WUSR;
//etc
//constructors
public Stat(String fileName) throws
PosixException;//stat()
```

```
public Stat(posix.File file) throws
PosixException;//stat()
public Stat(posix.OpenFile fd) throws
PosixException;//fstat()
//public field access
public int getMode();
public int getIno();
public int getDev();
//etc
public boolean isDir();
public boolean isChr();
//etc
}
```

Note also that the constants such as RUSR are not assigned their "well known" values (such as 0400) in these definitions. The actual values are not part of POSIX and so should not be part of the Java class definitions. The technique of "blank finals" is used here, and is discussed later in implementation issues.

Class Pipe

Posix uses the un-named pipe as primary means of inter-process communication, although there are plenty of other methods: named pipes, streams, shared memory, ports, *etc.* A pipe creates a pair of I/O channels, one used for read and one for write. A C pipe returns an array of two file descriptors. The programmer has to remember that index zero is used for reads, in analogy to file descriptor zero being the read descriptor. Similarly for index one, used for writes.

A Java version of pipe() can define a class that avoids the potential problem of poor programmer memory by making type-safe versions in a class Pipe:

```
public Class Pipe {
  public Pipe();
  public ReadFile in();
  public WriteFile out();
}
```

The two public methods are both "getter" methods that return the appropriate OpenFile. However, by returning a subclass, it is only possible to use "read" methods on in() and "write" methods on out().

System call dup2()

A typical systems programming activity is to create a pipeline of two separate processes, such as

```
ls | wc
```

In order to do this in C, it is necessary to create a pipe, perform a fork(), and then map the ends of the pipe onto the standard file descriptors using dup() or preferably dup2(). The dup2() C function call takes two parameters, the current file descriptor and the file descriptor it would "like to be". Typically one of the desired file descriptors is zero (for standard input) or one (for standard output). The "current file descriptor" will be an OpenFile object. The desired file descriptor could be an integer as in the C call, or could be another OpenFile object, since this binding is deprecating the need for an integer file descriptor. After the dup2(), reads/ writes to either object should have the same effect.

For this to function seamlessly, there will need to be existing objects corresponding to file descriptors 0, 1 and 2. These can be done in a similar manner to the Core streams System.in and System.out.

These all give further fields and methods of class OpenFile:

```
public class OpenFile {
  protected native void dup2(int fd);
  public void dup2(OpenFile f);
  ....
}
with the standard files in a general Posix class
public class Posix {
  static public InputFile stdin;
  static public OutputFile stdout;
  static public OutputFile stderr;
}
This means that we can now perform operations
```

```
such as
ReadFile f = new ReadFile("/etc/passwd");
f.dup2(stdin);
f.read(buf, 128);//reads from/etc/passwd
stdin.read(buf, 128);//reads more from/etc/passwd
```

Class Process

Java already has threads, and in practice they sit on top of a threads package which may be supplied from the O/S or be a separate package. These allow multiple Java threads to share memory and objects, but otherwise run disjointly.

The traditional multi-tasking model in Unix has been *via* processes, which are more heavyweight and do not share memory (although they share some things, such as file descriptors). Processes are identified by a "process id" which is an unsigned integer. Each process has its own process id, and all but the initial process will have a parent process id.

There are a host of functions that work on the current process, such as getpid() and getuid(). Functions that work on *other* processes, such as kill(), can only use the process id since that is all the information that will typically be available.

In any running Java application there can only be one process (although there may be many threads). It hardly seems worthwhile creating an object of typeProcess if there can only be one of them. So instead of being able to create objects of this class, it is easier to define them as all being static methods of the class.

This binding is not complete for this class. A partial definition is.

```
public class Process {
  public static int execvp(String file, String
  args[]);
  public static int fork();
}
```

Class PosixException

A PosixException is raised when an error occurs. This contains an error message as produced by strerror().

Examples

Copying input to output

Copying from standard input to standard output may be done by

```
final int SIZE = 1024;
byte buf[SIZE];
int nread;
try {
    while ((nread = Posix.stdin.read(buf, SIZE))
!= 0)
      Posix.stdout.write(buf, nread);
} catch(PosixException e) {
   System.err.println("Error in copy " +
   e.toString());
}
```

The while loop terminates on end of file. Any error is caught by the exception handler. This separates the two possibilities which are often combined in the C code of while ((nread = read(...)) > 0)

File information

Check read permissions to current directory:

```
Stat currDir;
try {
    currDir = new Stat(".");
} catch(PosixException e) {
System.out.println("Stat failed on. " +
e.toString());
System.exit(1);
}
int mode = currDir.getMode();
if (mode & Stat.ROTH)
System.out.println(". is world readable");
```

A Pipeline

It is common in Posix systems programming to set up a pipeline, to fork and to execute another program within one or both of the processes.

To perform the pipeline,

```
ls | wc
```

in C can be done by (with no error checking)

```
int pfd[2];
pipe(pfd);
if (fork() == 0) {
  close(pfd[1]);
  dup2(pfd[0], 0);
  close(pfd[0]);
  char *args[] = {"wc", NULL};
  execvp("wc", args);
} else {
   close(pfd[0]);
   dup2(pfd[1], 1);
   close(pfd[1]);
   char *args[] = {"ls", NULL};
   execvp("ls", args);
}
```

The classes given in this binding allow this to be done in Java by

```
Pipe p = new Pipe();
if (Process.fork() == 0) {
   p.out().close();
   p.in().dup2(Posix.stdin);
   p.in().close();
   String args[] = new String[] {"wc"};
   Process.execvp("wc", args);
} else {
   p.in().close();
   p.out().dup2(Posix.stdout);
   p.out().close();
   String args[] = new String[] {"ls"};
   execvp("ls", args);
}
```

Implementation

Constants

POSIX defines all constants symbolically. For example,

although "everybody knows" that the file mode "readable by user" has the value 0400, POSIX does not define it as such, but only by the symbolic value S_IRUSR. This is entirely correct: the actual value may depend on the platform and should not be pinned down in this standard.

This means that constants should not be hard-coded in the Java binding, but instead picked up from the local environment. In Java 1.0 this would only be possible for *variables,* and allowing constants to be variable would not be a good idea. From Java 1.1, constants (declared as final) need not have their value statically defined, but can be assigned to *once,* in an initialisation section such as a constructor. This allows a native code call to assign a value.

Alas, things are not quite straightforward. The Java compiler must *ensure* that the constants are assigned a value, and this cannot be hidden in native code inaccessible to the compiler.

A dummy value must be used:

```
public static final int RUSR;
private static int rusr;//dummy vbl
protected static native void
initialiseConstants();
static {
  initialiseConstants();//sets rusr, etc
    RUSR = rusr;//yuk
...
}
```

Types

In a similar vein, POSIX uses typedef's to hide native data types. For example, mode_t is usually a synonym for unsigned short. This could be a different type (although it is unlikely). Java does not have a mechanism for typedefs.

In version 1.0 of this binding, common assumptions were made about what the types resolve to, to give common code across all versions of Unix. However, in version 2 this is being rewritten to allow for different implementations and also to allow for different sizes of basic data types, such as 64-bit versus 32-bit integers. In this new version, a method such as getMode() is defined to return an interface value,

```
interface ModeT {
}
```

where the type is implemented in a variety of ways. For example,

```
class ModeT_32bit_signed {
   int mode;
}
```

The correct version is selected at compile time of the C library using a Perl script used by autoconf.

Varargs

C allows functions to have a variable number of arguments, such as printf(). This is not allowed in Java. This affects a few Posix functions such as execl()which cannot be implemented in Java. Fortunately, there are alternatives such as execvp() which replace the varargs with an array of args.

LINUX SYSTEM PROGRAMMING

Sample Program

Make sure the C compiler is installed in your system

```
type in this program, save it as hello.
#include<stdio.h>
int main()
{
printf("Hello World\n");
exit(0);
}
type in the two lines of commands, to see the
result.
gcc -o hello hello.c
./hello
```

Header Files:

- Header _les are normally located in/usr/include. Depends on the particular form of Unix or Linux, they can run in/usr/include/sys,/usr/include/linux.

- Use header _les in non standard place. For example, you would like compiler to look in the speci_c directory, as well as the standard places for header _les, which are included in fred.c. gcc -I/usr/openwin/ include fred.c
- Search for header _le by using \grep" command. For example, you don't remember a function call for exit status cd/usr/include grep EXIT_ *.h

On the command line, it appears as following:

- Stdlib.h:#define EXIT_FAILURE 1
- Stdlib.h:#define EXIT_SUCCESS 0

Libraries

- Standard libraries are usually stored in/lib and/usr/ lib. The C compiler has to be told explicitly which libraries to search, as by default, it searches only the standard C library.

```
-A simple example:
a.cc -o fred fred.c/usr/lib/libm.a
 or
b.cc -o fred fred.c -lm
c.Search for a specific library
d.cc -o x11fred -L/usr/opendwin/lib
x11fred.c -lX11
```

where -L indicates the location of libX11.

- Static libraries and Shared libraries Library is a collection of object _les kept together in a ready-to-use form. The compiler and linker take care of combining the program code and the library into a single executable program. You must use the -l option to indicate which libraries.
- *Static Libraries*:.a
- *Shared Libraries*:.so

When a program uses a shared library, it is linked in such a way that it doesn't contain function code itself, but reference to shared code that will be made available at run time. When the program is executed, the function references are resolved and calls are made to the shared library, which will be loaded into memory if needed.

- Try it out(build a library)

```
/* This is fred.c */
#iclude <stdio.h>
void fred(int arg)
{
printf("fred: you passed%d\n", arg);
}
/* This is bill.c*/
#include <stdio.h>
void bill(char *arg)
{
printf("bill: you passed%s\n", arg);
}
/* compile the functions */
cc -c bill.c fred.c
ls *.o
/* This is lib.h. It declares the function
fred and bill*/
void bill(char *arg);
void fred(int);
/* This is program.c */
#include "lib.h"
int main()
{
bill("Hello World");
exit(0);
}
/* compile the function separately, test it */
cc -c program.c
cc -o program program.o bill.o
./program
/* create our own library called libfoo.a */
ar crv libfoo.a bill.o fred.o
/* create a table contents for the library,
make the library ready to use */
ranlib libfoo.a
/* use this library to link to program.o */
cc -o program program.o libfoo.a
```

```
./program
/* a shorthand */
cc -o program program.o -L. -lfoo
```

Shell Programming

Shell is a program that acts as the interface between you and Unix system, allowing you to enter commands for the operating system. Shell is not suitable for time-critical and processor-intensive tasks.

This section on shell programming is a brief introduction to shell programming, and only talks about the bash shell.

Linux Variables

When variables are used they are referred to with the $ symbol in front of them. There are several useful variables available in the shell program.

Here are a few:

- $$ = The PID number of the process executing the shell.
- $? = Exit status variable.
- $0 = The name of the command you used to call a program.
- $1 = The first argument on the command line.
- $2 = The second argument on the command line.
- $n = The nth argument on the command line.
- $* = All the arguments on the command line.
- $# The number of command line arguments.

The "shift" command can be used to shift command line arguments to the left, ie $1 becomes the value of $2, $3 shifts into $2, etc. The command, "shift 2" will shift 2 places meaning the new value of $1 will be the old value of $3 and so forth.

Iteration, control and if statements

```
if-Used to execute one or more statements on a
condition. An example:
if [! -d/mnt] # be sure the directory/mnt exists
then
mkdir/mnt
```

```
fi
case-Used to execute specific commands based on
the value of a variable. An example:
case $NUM of
echo The number is 1
;;
echo The number is 2
;;
*)
echo The number is not 1 or 2
;;
esac
```

- for-Used to loop for all cases of a condition. In the example below, it is used to copy all files found in/ mnt/floppy to the/etc directory.

The lines were numbered for reference with descriptions:

- The for loop statement will loop until all files have been found.
- A test to be sure the file is a normal file and not a directory.
- A comment line.
- This line extracts the name of the file from its full path pointed to by the variable $i and puts it in the variable $filename. The method used here is called parameter expansion and is documented in the bash man page. For more information on parameter expansion read the "Linux Programmer's Guide".
- This line sends a statement to the standard output, telling what file is being copied.
- This line performs the copy command using the -p option to preserve file attributes. Note: Much ability to perform script programming is couched in the ability to know and use the various commands, programs and tools available in Linux rather than a strict understanding of syntax. This is obvious to anyone who reads the system startup script files in/ etc/rc.d and associated directories.
- This line ends the if statement.
- This line ends the for statement.

```
for i in/mnt/floppy/*; do
if [-f $i]; then
# if the file is there
filename=${i#/mnt/floppy/}
echo copying $i to/etc/$filename
cp -p $i/etc/$filename
fi
done
```

until-Cycles through a loop until some condition is met. The syntax for the command is shown below:

```
until [expression]
do
statements
done
```

while-Cycles through a loop while some condition is met. The below example will cycle through a loop forever:

```
while [1]
do
statement(s)
done
```

Tests

There is a function provided by bash called test which returns a true or false value depending on the result of the tested expression.

Its syntax is: Test expression

It can also be implied as follows: [expression]

The tests below are test conditions provided by the shell:

- -b file = True if the file exists and is block special file.
- -c file = True if the file exists and is character special file.
- -d file = True if the file exists and is a directory.
- -e file = True if the file exists.
- -f file = True if the file exists and is a regular file
- -g file = True if the file exists and the set-group-id bit is set.

- -k file = True if the files' "sticky" bit is set.
- -L file = True if the file exists and is a symbolic link.
- -p file = True if the file exists and is a named pipe.
- -r file = True if the file exists and is readable.
- -s file = True if the file exists and its size is greater than zero.
- -s file = True if the file exists and is a socket.
- -t fd = True if the file descriptor is opened on a terminal.
- -u file = True if the file exists and its set-user-id bit is set.
- -w file = True if the file exists and is writable.
- -x file = True if the file exists and is executable.
- -O file = True if the file exists and is owned by the effective user id.
- -G file = True if the file exists and is owned by the effective group id.
- file1 –nt file2 = True if file1 is newer, by modification date, than file2.
- file1 ot file2 = True if file1 is older than file2.
- file1 ef file2 = True if file1 and file2 have the same device and inode numbers.
- -z string = True if the length of the string is 0.
- -n string = True if the length of the string is non-zero.
- string1 = string2 = True if the strings are equal.
- string1 != string2 = True if the strings are not equal.
- !expr = True if the expr evaluates to false.
- expr1 –a expr2 = True if both expr1 and expr2 are true.
- expr1 –o expr2 = True is either expr1 or expr2 is true.

The syntax is: arg1 OP arg2 where OP is one of –eq, -ne, -lt, -le, -gt, or –ge. Arg1 and arg2 may be positive or negative integers or the special expression "–l string" which evaluates to the length of string.

Example Script

The file below is an example file which demonstrates some of the testing as talked above along with several looping and control statements.

```
#!/bin/bash
# Use the bash shell to run the script
# This is an example file to take entries from
the user
# entries Version 1.0 May 22, 2000
DONE=no
ENTRIES="hello bye ls 1"
while [$DONE = no]
do
  echo Valid entries are: $ENTRIES
  read ENTRY # Read the variable ENTRY
 from the user
  case $ENTRY in
1)
  pwd
  ;;
hello)
  echo How are you?
  ;;
bye)
  echo exiting...
  DONE=yes
  ;;
ls)
  ls -al |more
  ;;
*)
  echo $ENTRY is an unrecognized command.
  ;;
  esac
done
```

GDB debugger commands

See the gdb(1) man page for more information on the gdb program.

Below are Listed Some Commands:

- *File:* Loads the exe file.
- *Kill:* Terminates the program being debugged.

- *List:* List sections of the source code.
- *Next:* Advances one line of source code in the Current function and steps into other functions.
- *Run:* Executes the program that is being debugged.
- *Quit:* Ends gdb.
- *Watch:* Enables you to tell the value of a variable When it changes.
- *Break*: Set a break point.
- *Make:* Remake the exe program without quitting Gdb.
- Shell-Run a UNIX shell command without leaving Gdb.

LINKERS

DEFINITION

In computer science, a linker is a program that takes one or more objects generated by a compiler and assembles them into a single executable program. In IBM mainframe environments such as OS/360 this program is known as a "linkage editor". On Unix variants the term loader is often used as a synonym for linker. Because this usage blurs the distinction between the compile-time process and the run-time process, this article will use "linking" for the former and "loading" for the latter. However, in some operating systems the same program handles both the jobs of linking and loading a program; see "dynamic linking".

Computer programs are typically comprised of several parts or modules; these parts, if not all contained within a single object file, refer to each other by means of symbols.

Typically, an object file can contain three kinds of symbols:

- Defined symbols, which allow it to be called by other modules,
- Undefined symbols, which call the other modules where these symbols are defined, and
- Local symbols, used internally within the object file to facilitate relocation.

When a program comprises multiple object files, the linker combines these files into a unified executable program, resolving the symbols as it goes along. Linkers can take objects from a collection called a "library". Some linkers do not include the whole library in the output; they only include its symbols that are referenced from other object files or libraries. Libraries exist for diverse purposes, and one or more system libraries are usually linked in by default.

The linker also takes care of arranging the objects in a program's address space. This may involve "relocating" code that assumes a specific base address to another base. Since a compiler seldom knows where an object will reside, it often assumes a fixed base location (for example, zero). Relocating machine code may involve re-targeting of absolute jumps, loads and stores.

The executable output by the linker may need another relocation pass when it is finally loaded into memory (just before execution). This pass is usually omitted on hardware offering virtual memory — every program is put into its own address space, so there is no conflict even if all programs load at the same base address. This pass may also be omitted if the executable is a position independent executable.

CONCEPT

The basic job of any linker is simple: it binds more abstract names to more concrete names, which permits programmers to write code using the more abstract names. That is, it takes a name written by a programmer such as get line and binds it to "the location 612 bytes from the beginning of the executable code in module iosys." Or it may take a more abstract numeric address such as "the location 450 bytes beyond the beginning of the static data for this module" and bind it to a numeric address.

A linkers is used in the development of computer programming in systems. The earliest computers were programmed entirely in machine language. Programmers would write out the symbolic programs on sheets of paper, hand assemble them into machine code and then toggle the machine code into the computer, or perhaps punch it on paper tape or cards. If the programmer used symbolic addresses at all, the symbols were bound to addresses as the programmer did his or her hand translation. If it turned out that an instruction had to be added or deleted, the entire program had to be hand-inspected and any addresses affected by the added or deleted instruction adjusted.

The problem was that the names were bound to addresses too early. Assemblers solved that problem by letting programmers write programs in terms of symbolic names, with the assembler binding the names to machine addresses. If the program changed, the programmer had to reassemble it, but the work of assigning the addresses is pushed off from the programmer to the computer. Libraries of code compound the address assignment problem. Since the basic operations that computers can perform are so simple, useful programs are composed of subprograms that perform higher level and more complex operations.

Computer installations keep a library of pre-written and debugged subprograms that programmers can draw upon to use in new programs they write, rather than requiring programmers to write all their own subprograms. The programmer then loads the subprograms in with the main program to form a complete working program. Programmers were using libraries of subprograms even before they used assemblers. By 1947, John Mauchly, who led the ENIAC project, wrote about loading programs along with subprograms selected from a catalog of

programs stored on tapes, and of the need to relocate the subprograms' code to reflect the addresses at which they were loaded. Perhaps surprisingly, these two basic linker functions, relocation and library search, appear to predate even assemblers, as Mauchly expected both the program and subprograms to be written in machine language.

The relocating loader allowed the authors and users of the subprograms to write each subprogram as though it would start at location zero, and to defer the actual address binding until the subprograms were linked with a particular main program.

With the advent of operating systems, relocating loaders separate from linkers and libraries became necessary. Before operating systems, each program had the machine's entire memory at its disposal, so the program could be assembled and linked for fixed memory addresses, knowing that all addresses in the computer would be available.

But with operating systems, the program had to share the computer's memory with the operating system and perhaps even with other programs, This means that the actual addresses at which the program would be running weren't known until the operating system loaded the program into memory, deferring final address binding past link time to load time.

Linkers and loaders now divided up the work, with linkers doing part of the address binding, assigning relative addresses within each program, and the loader doing a final relocation step to assign actual addresses. As systems became more complex, they called upon linkers to do more and more complex name management and address binding. Fortran programs used multiple subprograms and common blocks, areas of data shared by multiple subprograms, and it was up to the linker to lay out storage and assign the addresses both for the subprograms and the common

blocks. Linkers increasingly had to deal with object code libraries. Including both application libraries written in Fortran and other languages, and compiler support libraries called implicitly from compiled code to handle I/O and other high-level operations. Programs quickly became larger than available memory, so linkers provided overlays, a technique that let programmers arrange for different parts of a program to share the same memory, with each overlay loaded on demand when another part of the program called into it.

Overlays were widely used on mainframes from the advent of disks around 1960 until the spread of virtual memory in the mid-1970s, then reappeared on microcomputers in the early 1980s in exactly the same form, and faded as virtual memory appeared on PCs in the 1990s. They're still used in memory limited embedded environments, and may yet reappear in other places where precise programmer or compiler control of memory usage improves performance. With the advent of hardware relocation and virtual memory, linkers and loaders actually got less complex, since each program could again have an entire address space. Programs could be linked to be loaded at fixed addresses, with hardware rather than software relocation taking care of any load-time relocation.

But computers with hardware relocation invariably run more than one program, frequently multiple copies of the same program. When a computer runs multiple instances of one program, some parts of the program are the same among all running instance (the executable code, in particular), while other parts are unique to each instance. If the parts that don't change can be separated out from the parts that do change, the operating system can use a single copy of the unchanging part, saving considerable storage.

Compilers and assemblers were modified to create object code in multiple sections, with one section for read only code and another section for writable data, the linker had to be able to combine all of sections of each type so that the linked program would have all the code in one place and all of the data in another. This didn't delay address binding any more than it already was, since addresses were still assigned at link time, but more work was deferred to the linker to assign addresses for all the sections.

LINKER ACTION

Program Loading

Copy a program from secondary storage (which since about 1968 invariably means a disk) into main memory so it's ready to run. In some cases loading just involves copying the data from disk to memory, in others it involves allocating storage, setting protection bits, or arranging for virtual memory to map virtual addresses to disk pages.

Relocation

Compilers and assemblers generally create each file of

object code with the program addresses starting at zero, but few computers let you load your program at location zero. If a program is created from multiple subprograms, all the subprograms have to be loaded at non-overlapping addresses. Relocation is the process of assigning load addresses to the various parts of the program, adjusting the code and data in the program to reflect the assigned addresses.

In many systems, relocation happens more than once. It's quite common for a linker to create a program from multiple subprograms, and create one linked output program that starts at zero, with the various subprograms relocated to locations within the big program. Then when the program is loaded, the system picks the actual load address and the linked program is relocated as a whole to the load address.

Symbol Lesolution

When a program is built from multiple subprograms, the references from one subprogram to another are made using symbols; a main program might use a square root routine called sqrt, and the math library defines sqrt. A linker resolves the symbol by noting the location assigned to sqrt in the library, and patching the caller's object code to so the call instruction refers to that location.

Although there's considerable overlap between linking and loading, it's reasonable to define a program that does program loading as a loader, and one that does symbol resolution as a linker.Either can do relocation, and

there have been all-in-one linking loaders that do all three functions. The line between relocation and symbol resolution can be fuzzy. Since linkers already can resolve references to symbols, one way to handle code relocation is to assign a symbol to the base address of each part of the program, and treat relocatable addresses as references to the base address symbols.

TWO-PASS LINKING PROCESS

Now we turn to the general structure of linkers. Linking, like compiling or assembling, is fundamentally a two pass process. A linker takes as its input a set of input object files, libraries, and perhaps command files, and produces as its result an output object file, and perhaps ancillary information such as a load map or a file containing debugger symbols as shown in Figure.

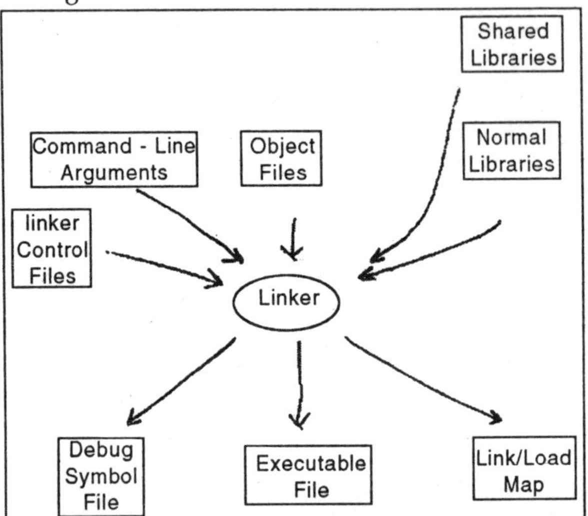

Each input file contains a set of *segments,* contiguous chunks of code or data to be placed in the output file. Each input file also contains at least one *symbol table.* Some symbols are exported, defined within the file for use in other files, generally the names of routines within the file that can be called from elsewhere. Other symbols are imported, used in the file but not defined, generally the names of routines called from but not present in the file. When a linker runs, it first has to scan the input files to find the sizes of the segments and to collect the definitions and references of all of the symbols It creates a segment table listing all of the segments defined in the input files, and a symbol table with all of the symbols imported or exported.

Using the data from the first pass, the linker assigns numeric locations to symbols, determines the sizes and location of the segments in the output address space, and figures out where everything goes in the output file. The second pass uses the information collected in the first pass to control the actual linking process. It reads and relocates the object code, substituting numeric addresses for symbol references, and adjusting memory addresses in code and data to reflect relocated segment addresses, and writes the relocated code to the output file. It then writes the output file, generally with header information, the relocated segments, and symbol table information. If the program uses dynamic linking, the symbol table contains the info the runtime linker will need to resolve dynamic symbols.

In many cases, the linker itself will generate small amounts of code or data in the output file, such as "glue code" used to call routines in overlays or dynamically linked libraries, or an array of pointers to initialization routines that need to be called at program startup time. Whether or not the program uses dynamic linking, the file may also contain a symbol table for relinking or debugging that isn't used by the program itself, but may be used by other programs that deal with the output file.

Some object formats are relinkable, that is, the output file from one linker run can be used as the input to a subsequent linker run. This requires that the output file contain a symbol table like one in an input file, as well as all of the other auxiliary information present in an input file. Nearly all object formats have provision for debugging symbols, so that when the program is run under the control of a debugger, the debugger can use those symbols to let the programmer control the program in terms of the line numbers and names used in the source program.

Depending on the details of the object format, the debugging symbols may be intermixed in a single symbol table with symbols needed by the linker, or there may be one table for the linker and a separate, somewhat redundant table for the debugger. A few linkers appear to work in one pass. They do that by buffering some or all of the contents of the input file in memory or disk during the linking process, then reading the buffered material later. Since this is an implementation trick that doesn't fundamentally affect the two-pass nature of linking, we don't address it further here.

RELOCATION AND CODE MODIFICATION

The heart of a linker or loader's actions is relocation and code modification. When a compiler or assembler generates and object file, it generates the code using the unrelocated addresses of code and data defined within the file, and usually zeros for code and data defined elsewhere. As part of the linking process, the linker modifies the object code to reflect the actual addresses assigned. For example, consider this snippet of x86 code that moves the contents of variable a to variable b using the eax register.

- Mov a,%eax
- Mov%eax,b

If a is defined in the same file at location 1234 hex and b is imported from somewhere else, the generated object code will be: A1 34 12 00 00 mov a,%eax A3 00 00 00 00 mov%eax,b Each instruction contains a one-byte operation code followed by a fourbyte address. The first instruction has a reference to 1234 (byte reversed, since the x86 uses a right to left byte order) and the second a reference to zero since the location of b is unknown. Now assume that the linker links this code so that the section in which a is located is relocated by hex 10000 bytes, and b turns out to be at hex 9A12.

The linker modifies the code to be:

- A1 34 12 01 00 mov a,%eax
- A3 12 9A 00 00 mov%eax,b

That is, it adds 10000 to the address in the first instruction so now it refers to a's relocated address which is 11234, and it patches in the address for b. These adjustments affect instructions, but any pointers in the data part of an object file have to be adjusted as well. On older computers with small address spaces and direct addressing, the modification process is fairly simple, since there are only only one or two address formats that a linker has to handle. Modern computers, including all RISCs, require considerably more complex code modification.

No single instruction contains enough bits to hold a direct address, so the compiler and linker have to use complicated addressing tricks to handle data at arbitrary addresses. In some cases, it's possible to concoct an address using two or three instructions, each of which contains part of the address, and use bit manipulation to combine the parts into a full address. In this case, the linker has to be prepared to modify each of the instructions appropriately, inserting some of the bits of the address into each instruction.

In other cases, all of the addresses used by a routine or group of routines are placed in an array used as an "address pool", initialization code sets one of the machine registers to point to that array, and code loads pointers out of the address pool as needed using that register as a base register. The linker may have to create the array from all of the addresses used in a program, then modify instructions that so that they refer to the appropriate address pool entry.

LINKER COMMAND LANGUAGES

Every linker has some sort of command language to control the linking process. At the very least the linker needs the list of object files and libraries to link. Generally there is a long list of possible options: whether to keep debugging symbols, whether to use shared or unshared libraries, which of several possible output formats to use. Most linkers permit some way to specify the address at which the linked code is to be bound, which comes in handy when using a linker to link a system kernel or other program that doesn't run under control of an operating system.

In linkers that support multiple code and data segments, a linker command language can specify the order in which segments are to be linked, special treatment for certain kinds of segments, and other application-specific options.

There are four common techniques to pass commands to a linker:

- *Command Line:* Most systems have a command line or the equivalent, via which one can pass a mixture of file names and switches. This is the usual approach for Unix and Windows linkers. On systems with limited length command lines, there's usually a way to direct the linker to read commands from a file and treat them as though they were on the command line.

Intermixed with Object Files

Some linkers, such as IBM mainframe linkers, accept alternating object files and linker commands in a single input file. This dates from the era of card decks, when one would pile up object decks and hand-punched command cards in a card reader.

Embedded in Object Files

Some object formats, notably Microsoft's, permit linker commands to be embedded inside object files. This permits a compiler to pass any options needed to link an object file in the file itself. For example, the C compiler passes commands to search the standard C library.

Separate Configuration Language

A few linkers have a full fledged configuration language to control linking. The GNU linker, which can handle an enormous range of object file formats, machine architectures, and address space conventions, has a complex control language that lets a programmer specify the order in which segments should be linked, rules for combining similar segments, segment addresses, and a wide range of other options. Other linkers have less complex languages to handle specific features such as programmer-defined overlays.

LOADER

INTRODUCTION

It is the Loader's function to fix absolute addresses for the relocated values in a relocatable module, thereby converting a relocatable module into an "executable" output file. The Loader is usually called automatically by the Linker but it may also be called separately by the user. As indicated below, several different Loaders are (optionally) available for use with Introl-C and, if the user has elected to obtain such optional Loaders, a variety of executable output file formats can be generated, depending on the Loader being used. Each resident Introl-C compiler package, and each Introl-C cross-compiler package, nominally includes a single, specific type of Introl Loader which is considered as being the "standard" Loader for that compiler's particular host system configuration. For resident Introl-C Compiler packages, the 'standard' Loader that is furnished is an "operating system dependent" type of Loader which generates an output file that is executable on that particular Compiler's host system.

For cross-compiler versions of Introl-C, the "standard" Loader furnished is typically a "hex" type Loader that generates a file of output load records, which can be either Motorola S-Records, intel Hex, Tektronix Hex, or Tektronix Extended Hex at user option. Besides the "standard" Loader that accompanies any given Compiler type, it is also possible for the user to optionally obtain and use other compatible "cross-Loaders" which generate output formats unrelated to the Compiler's host operating system.

For example, "hex-type" Loaders are optionally available for use with resident versions of Introl-C; "operating system dependent" type Loaders are optionally available for use with cross-compiler versions; etc. There are, therefore, several different species of Loaders, (as well as several different types of related Standard Libraries) that may potentially be used under Introl-C. The "standard" Loader supplied with your Introl-C package, as well as any other Loaders that may have been optionally ordered, are described in detail in the Loader Appendix of this Linker Reference Manual.

This Loader section describes the general features that are common to all Loader types. Normally the input to the Loader is expected to be a relocatable file which has no unresolved external references; if unresolved references do exist in its input, loading will normally not be successful. A Loader option is provided, however, to force a file to be loaded even if it contains unresolved references. Usually a relocatable file has to be linked before it can be used as input to the Loader. It is also possible, of course, to assemble a file which makes no external references and then use the relocatable output file produced by the Assembler directly as input to the Loader (ie without having actually linked it)

FUNCTIONS OF LOADER

- Allocate space in memory for the program (allocation).
- Resolve symbolic references between object programs (linking).
- Adjust all address dependent locations, such as address constraints, to correspond to the allocated space (relocation).
- Physically place the machine instruction and data into memory(loading) for execution.
- *Loader:* System program that performs the loading function.
- *Linker (or linkage editor):* System program that performs the linking operations (*i.e.* linking and relocation).

KINDS OF LOADER

Absolute Loader

- *Object Program Contains:*
  - H card (or record)
  - T cards (or record)
  - E card (or record)
- Check the starting address and memory size required (*i.e.* specified in H record), load Text records into memory sequentially, and then jump to the starting address specified by End record.

Absolute loader Algorithm

- Begin
  - Read Header Record
  - Verify program name and Length
  - Read first Text Record
- While Record type '" 'E' do
- Begin
  - {if object code is in character form, convert into
  - Internal representation}
  - Move object code to specified location in memory

  - Read next object program record
- End
  - Jump to address specified in End record
- End

Relocatable Loader

Perform Allocation, Relocation, and Loading:

- *Modification Record:* Used to describe the starting address and length of code to be modified.
- *SIC Computer:* Most instructions use direct addressing. à Too many modification records are needed.
- *Another Approach:* Use relocation bit to indicate that the word should be modified or not.

Linkage Editor

Performing Linking Only:

- Produce a linked version of the program (called load module, executable image, or image program).
- Solve external reference and library search, and perform relocation of all sections relative to the start of the linked program.
- Although all linking has been performed, information concerning external reference is retained in the linked program for further re-linking if necessary.

Linkage Editor Commands:

- *Example 1:* New version of library routine
  - INCLUDE PLANNER (PROGLIB)
  - DELETE PROJECT
  - INCLUDE PROJECT (NEWLY)
  - REPLACE PLANNER (PROGLIB)
- *Example 2:* Combine subroutines into a package
  - INCLUDE READR(FINLIB)
  - INCLUDE WRITER(FIN LIB)
  - INCLUDE BLOCK(FINLIB)
  - SAVE FINIO(SUBLIB)

→ The linked module name FINIO could be indexed in the directory of SUBLIB under the same name as the original subroutines.

- Linkage editor performs linking operation before the program is loaded for execution. Linking loader perform linking operation at load time.
- Dynamic linking (or dynamic binding, load on call) perform linking operation until execution.
  - When a subroutine call is encountered and the subroutine is not resident in memory, load the subroutine into memory, perform linking, and finally jump to the subroutine.
  - *Advantages:* Load the routines when they are needed, the memory space will be saved.

Linking loader

Perform Allocation, Linking, Relocation, and Loading:

- *Modification Record:* Used to describe the starting address and length of code to be modified.
- *SIC Computer:* Most instructions use direct addressing. →Too many modification records are needed.
- Another approach: use relocation bit to indicate that the word should be modified or not.

LOADER COMMAND LINE

The "standard" Loader supplied with your Introl-C package is normally automatically called by the Linker when the Linker pass finishes. However, linker command line options exist (see Linker Section of this manual) that mav be used to alternatively force the Linker to automatically call other optional Loaders. Situations also arise when it is desirable to explicitly call the Loader alone, without first executing the Linker. When such situations arise, the Loader may be independently called by the user with a loader command line of the general form:

- <c>ld <file> {<option>}

where <c>ld represents the Introl filename of the specific Loader being called, <file> is the name of the (linked) relocatable module which is to be loaded, and (<option>) represents zero or more Loader option specifiers. Each of the potentially usable Introl Loaders is uniquely identified by a 3-letter Loader filename, the last two letters of which are always "ld". The <c> designator indicated in the "<c>ld" loader call on the command line therefore represents the first letter in the three-letter Loader name.

For example, to call the Introl hex type of Loader, which has the filename "hld", the "<c>ld" entry on the command line would actually become "hld". For further specifics on the names of the loaders which can be legally accessed. The relocatable file that is input to the Loader is expected to have a filenarne extension; if none is specified, the default filename extension ".RL" is assumed. Normally the name of the executable output file will be identical to the name of the input file, but with a filename extension typically added by the Loader. The filename extensions each Loader appends are discussed in the Loader Appendices to this manual.

Loader Options

Each type of Loader available for use with the Introl-C has its own, generally unique set of options. When the Loader is being called separately, Loader options are specified directly on the loader command line when the Loader is being automatically called by the Linker, Loader options are specified on the link command line, together with the Linker options. If Loader options are specified on the link command line, any such options (ie those that do not apply to the Linker) will be automatically sent on to the Loader. For the most part Linker and. Loader option specifiers tend to be distinct, so that there is little ambiguity when Loader options are specified on the link command line.

Library Files

A library file is a file which contains one or more linkable object modules of the type produced by the Introl Assembler. When a file is compiled and assembled, the result is exactly one linkable module which is placed into a file.

This file is actually a library which happens to contain only a single module. When the user links a program, one or more of these "libraries" are specified on the link command line. Usually the "libraries" are those produced as a result of a compilation and contain only a single module, however, they may also contain several modules.

The Library Manager, "libman", is a program which allows the user to place several modules into a single library file. When the user has a large set of modules which are commonly used in programs, it is usually convenient to place them all in one library and then simply specify the library once on the link command line.

The Linker will extract only those modules it requires in order to satisfy the external references of the program. The Linker is designed to automatically search the "Standard Library", libc.R, if it still has external references to satisfy after it has exhausted all the alternatives provided by the modules specified an the link command line. For many C programs, the Standard Library is usually where most of the external references are satisfied. Many users find it useful to add to, or modify routines in, the Standard Library. The Library Manager is the utility program which allows the user to create new libraries and also to maintain existing ones.

Modes of Operation

The Library Manager has three modes of operation: Direct Mode, Interactive Mode, and Command File Mode. The most convenient to use for simple additions and deletions to the library is the Direct Mode. For more extensive modifications the user may instead wish to use Interactive mode. The third mode is the Command File mode which causes the Library Manager to read its commands from a file rather than getting them from the user terminal.

Direct Mode: In Direct Mode the user is permitted to specify a single command on the library manager command line. When the Library Manager is called, it executes this single command function and then immediately exits from the Library Manager. When modifying libraries, however, a single command function is often all that is necessary to accomplish the change desired by the user. When Direct Mode is being used, the desired command is specified right on the command line, following the <lib> library. specification.

Any Library Manager command may be used in the Direct Mode. Interactive Mode: if no command is specified on the Library Manager call line, the Library Manager will enter its Interactive Mode of operation. In Interactive Mode the Library Manager will print a colon (".") as a promet and will accept a succession of commands directly from the user terminal. Interactive Mode is useful when the user must make extensive changes to a library, or when the user wishes to step through the library checking and/or changing modules in an "interactive" manner. Once selected, the Interactive Mode will remain in effect until the user enters a "quit" or "omit" command. Command File Mode: One of the commands which the user can specify as an Interactive code or a Direct Mode command entry is the "Comfile" command. This command instructs the Library Manager to read subsequent instructions from a command file. When a "Comfile command is entered, the Library Manager will read from the file specified until it reads a "quit" or "omit" command or, alternatively, until it reaches the end of the file. when exiting the Command File Mode, the Library Manager will return to whatever mode it was in before the Command File Mode was entered. If the Command File Mode was entered as the result of a Direct Mode command, then the Library Manager will terminate when Command File Mode is exited. If entered from the Interactive Mode, it will return to the Interactive Mode.

ASSEMBLER

DEFINITION

An assembler is a program that converts simple commands into machine code. The simple commands, written in an assembly language, are used in groups to perform more complicated tasks.

FUNCTION

The function of the assembler is to translate programs

written in the assembler language into object modules. The code will then be in a suitable form for processing by the Linkage Editor. The assembler language is a symbolic representation of machine language. The correspondence between the two can be best understood by examining the listings produced by an assembler. The assembler, like the linkage editor, is supplied as part of VSE, CMS, and MVS, and executes under control of the appropriate control program. It accepts, as input, a source program written in the Assembler Language.

This consists of three types of instructions:

1. Machine instructions.
2. Assembler instructions.
3. Macro instructions.

As expected with an IBM language, code can also be copied in from a source statement library (VSE) or a pds (MVS) or MACLIB (CMS).

SEGMENTS AND OFFSETS IN ASSEMBLER

The original designers of the 8088, decided that nobody will every need to use more that one megabyte of memory. So they built the machine so it couldn't access above that. The problem is to access a whole megabyte 20 bits are needed (one bit being either a one or a zero). Registers only have 16 bits, and they didn't want to use two because that would be 32 bits and that was too much for anyone. They decided to do the addressing with two registers but not 32 bits. Is this confusing? *Blame the designers of the 8088:*

OFFSET = SEGMENT * 16
SEGMENT = OFFSET/16 (the lower 4 bits are lost)
SEGMENT * 16 |0010010000010000— —| range (0 to 65535) * 16
+OFFSET |— —0100100000100010| range (0 to 65535)
=20 bit address |00101000100100100010| range 0 to 1048575 (1 MEG)
====== DS ======
====== SI =====

(note DS and SI overlap). This is how DS:SI is used to make a 20 bit address. The segment is in DS and the offset is in SI.

Segment registers are: CS, DS, ES, SS. On the 386+ there are also FS & GS Offset registers are: BX, DI, SI, BP, SP, IP. In 386+ protected mode, ANY general register (not a segment register) can be used as an Offset register. (Except IP, which you can't access.)

REGISTERS

- *AX:* This is split into half-into AL and AH (for low and high). They store the high part and the low part of the number in ax.
- *BX (BH/BL):* Same as AX
- *CX (CH/CL):* Same as AX (used for loops)
- *DX (DH/DL):* Same as AX (used for multiplication/ division)
- *DI and SI:* are index registers and can be used as offset registers.
- *SP:* Stack Pointer. Does just that. Points to the current position in the stack. *Don't* alter unless you REALLY know what you are doing.

THE STACK

This is and area of memory that is like a stack of plates. The first one you put on is the first one that you take off. If another piece of data is put on the stack it grows downwards.

PUSH AND POP

Push puts a value onto the stack and pop takes it back off. Here's some code.

(you can't compile this-yet.)

- Push cx;put cx on the stack
- Push ax;put ax on the stack

;this is going to pop them back in the wrong order so they're reversed.

- Pop cx;put value from stack into cx
- Pop ax;put value from stack into ax

This means that cx is equal to what ax is and ax is equal to what cx was.

INSTRUCTIONS

- *MOV:* This moves a value from one place to another, here's some examples:
- MOV ax,10;moves an immediate value into ax
- ;(same as ax=5)
- MOV bx,cx;moves value from cx into bx
- *INT:* Calls a DOS interrupt, mainly to do somthing you would rather not write a function for *e.g.* change video mode, open a file etc.
- INT 21h;Calls DOS standard interrupt 21h (h meaning hex)
- INT 10h;Calls the Video BIOS interrrupt

All interrupts need a value to specify what subroutine to use. This is usually in AH.

To print a message on the screen all you need to do is this:

- MOV ah,9;subroutine number 9
- INT 21h;call the interrupt

But first you have to specify what to print. This function eeds DS:DX to be a far pointer to where the string is.

The string has to be terminated with a dollar sign ($).

- MyMessage db "This is a message!$"
  - mov dx,OFFSET MyMessage
  - mov ax,SEG MyMessage
  - mov ds,ax
  - mov ah,9

  int 21h
- DB declares a piece of data (like in basic 'LET MyMessage$ = "This is a message!"). DB declares a byte, DW declares a word and DD declares a Dword. You don't have to worry about this for now.

FIRST ASSEMBLY PROGRAM

Type this in and then assemble it. By typing A86 {name of file}.

Remove the line DOSSEG if you're using A86.

- THIS IS A SIMPLE PROGRAM TO DISPLAY A
- MESSAGE
- DOSSEG;REMOVE THIS LINE IF

- USING A86.
- MODEL SMALL;Ignore the first 4 four lines
- STACK 200h;I'll explain what this means later.
- CODE;starts code segment
- *ASSUME CS:* @CODE, DS:@CODE;don't worry about this for now
- *START:*;generally a good name to use as ;an entry point
- JMP BEGIN;jump to BEGIN: (like goto)
- MyMessage db "This is a message!$"
- *BEGIN:*;code starts here mov dx,OFFSET My Message; display a message on screen
- mov ax,SEG MyMessage
- mov ds,ax
- mov ah,9
- int 21h
- MOV ax,4c00h;move the value of 4c00 hex into AX
- INT 21h;call interrupt 21h, subroutine
- 4C which;returns control to dos END START;end here

The end. This is the first part in my programming assembly series. I hope you learned something. For your homework experiment with different strings. Try and display two different strings.

INTERPRETER

DEFINITION

An interpreter runs program code by converting it to machine code on the fly. You save some time in the front by avoiding the compiling and linking steps, but interpreters generally run slower because they have to convert the same code (in a loop, say) again and again. An example of a common interpreter is the one that executes.bat files.

An *interpreter* is also a program that translates a high-level language into a low-level one, but it does it at the moment the program is run.

You write the program using a text editor or something

similar, and then instruct the interpreter to run the program. It takes the program, one line at a time, and translates each line before running it: It translates the first line and runs it, then translates the second line and runs it etc.

The interpreter has no "memory" for the translated lines, so if it comes across lines of the program within a loop, it must translate them afresh every time that particular line runs.

Consider this simple Basic program:

- 10 FOR COUNT = 1 TO 1000
- 20 PRINT COUNT * COUNT
- 30 NEXT COUNT

Line 20 of the program displays the square of the value stored in COUNT and this line has to be carried out 1000 times. The interpreter must also translate that line 1000 times, which is clearly an inefficient process.

However, interpreted languages do have their uses, as we will see in a later section.

Examples of interpreted languages are Basic, JavaScript and LISP The Interpreter pattern discusses: defining a domain language (*i.e.* problem characterization) as a simple language grammar, representing domain rules as language sentences, and interpreting these sentences to solve the problem. The pattern uses a class to represent each grammar rule. And since grammars are usually hierarchical in structure, an inheritance hierarchy of rule classes maps nicely.

An abstract base class specifies the method interpret(). Each concrete subclass implements interpret() by accepting (as an argument) the current state of the language stream, and adding its contribution to the problem solving process.

STRUCTURE

Interpreter suggests modeling the domain with a recursive grammar.

Each rule in the grammar is either a "composite" (a rule that references other rules) or a terminal (a leaf node in a tree structure). Interpreter relies on the recursive traversal of the Composite pattern to interpret the "sentences" it is asked to process.

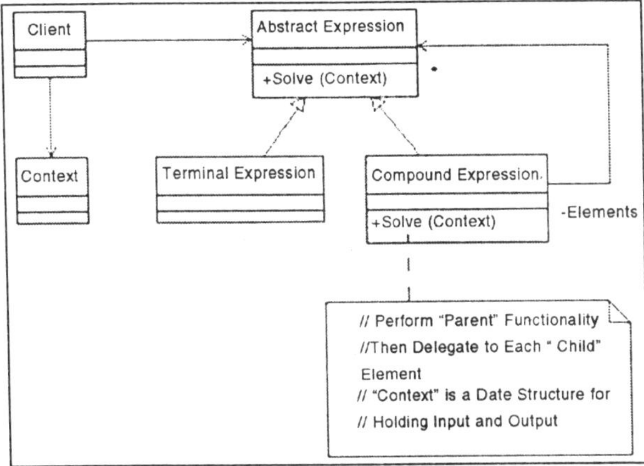

Example: The Interpreter pattern defines a grammatical representation for a language and an interpreter to interpret the grammar. Musicians are examples of Interpreters. The pitch of a sound and its duration can be represented in musical notation on a staff. This notation provides the language of music. Musicians playing the music from the score are able to reproduce the original pitch and duration of each sound represented.

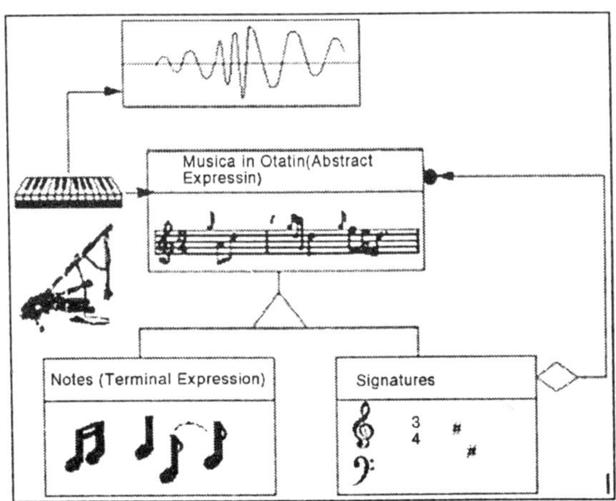

BEFORE AND AFTER

```
Before
//This is an adaptation of a design that appeared
```

```
in a Pascal
//data structures book. The intent was to use
stacks to convert
//normal "infix" syntax into "postfix" notation
with operator
//precedence already handled.
public class InterpreterDemo {
public static boolean precedence(char a, char b)
{
String high = "*/", low = "+-";
if (a == '(') return false;
if (a == ')' && b == '(') {
System.out.println(")-(");
return false;
}
if (b == '(') return false;
if (b == ')') return true;
if (high.indexOf(a) > -1 && low.indexOf(b) > -1)
return true;
if (high.indexOf(a) > -1 && high.indexOf(b) > -
1)
return true;
```

COMPILER

DEFINITION

A compiler completely converts program code to machine code once. The computer user runs the machine code in the form of an executable command, ending in.exe say. Because the translation is complete before execution, compiled code is much faster.

The Translation Process Should also Report the Presence of Errors in the Source Program.

Source Program	→	Compiler	→	Target Program
		↓		
		Error Messages		

There are two parts of compilation:

- The analysis part breaks up the source program into constant piece and creates an intermediate representation of the source program.
- The synthesis part constructs the desired target program from the intermediate representation.

Compilers were the first sort of translator program to be written. The idea is simple: You write the program, then hand it to the compiler which translates it.

Then you run the result. The compiler takes the file that you have written and produces another file from it. In the case of Pascal programs, for instance, you might write a program called my Prog.pas and the Pascal compiler would translate it into the file myProg.exe which you could then run. If you tried to examine the contents of myProg.exe using, say, a text editor, then it would just appear as gobbledy-gook. The compiler has another task apart from translating your program. It also checks it to make sure that it is grammatically correct.

Only when it is sure that there are no grammatical errors does it do the translation. Any errors that the compiler detects are called compile-time errors or syntax errors. If it finds so much as one syntax error, it stops compiling and reports the error to you.

Here is an example of the C++ compiler reporting a whole list of errors:

```
Message
Compiling C:\My Documents\Richard\web site\ca\spont1.cpp
spont1.cpp(149,1):Functions containing for are not expanded inline
spont1.cpp(230,4):Declaration syntax error
spont1.cpp(978,1):Declaration missing ;
spont1.cpp(978,1):Compound statement missing }
spont1.cpp(978,1):'input_pattern' is declared but never used
spont1.cpp(978,1):'best_num_inp_conn' is declared but never used
spont1.cpp(978,1):'best_num_conn' is declared but never used
spont1.cpp(978,1):'best_ratio' is declared but never used
spont1.cpp(978,1):'entered_input' is declared but never used
spont1.cpp(978,1):'average' is declared but never used
spont1.cpp(978,1):'weight_file' is assigned a value that is never used
spont1.cpp(978,1):'CA_activity_file' is assigned a value that is never used
spont1.cpp(978,1):'CA_pattern_file' is assigned a value that is never used
spont1.cpp(978,1):'write_CAs_to_file' is assigned a value that is never used
spont1.cpp(978,1):'option' is assigned a value that is never used
```

COMPILER PHASES

The Cousins of the Compiler are:

- Preprocessor.

- Assembler.
- Loader and Link-editor.

The Compiler has a Number of Phases Plus Symbol Table Manager and an Error Handler.

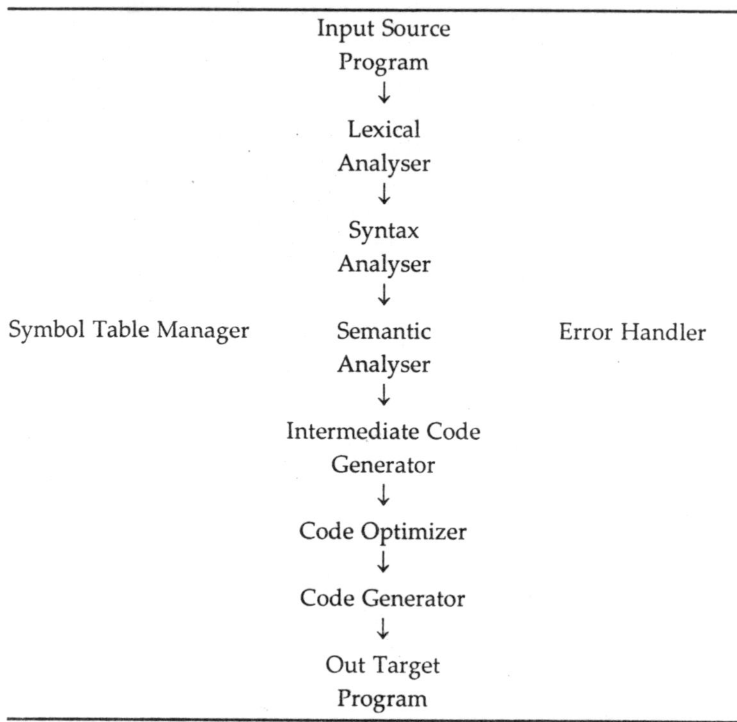

Front End vs Back End of a Compilers. The phases of a compiler are collected into front end and back end. The front end includes all analysis phases end the intermediate code generator. The back end includes the code optimization phase and final code generation phase. The front end analyses the source program and produces intermediate code while the back end synthesizes the target program from the intermediate code.

A naive approach (front force) to that front end might run the phases serially.

- Lexical analyser takes the source program as an input and produces a long string of tokens.

- Syntax Analyser takes an out of lexical analyser and produces a large tree.
- Semantic analyser takes the output of syntax analyser and produces another tree.
- Similarly, intermediate code generator takes a tree as an input produced by semantic analyser and produces intermediate code.

Minus Points

- Requires enormous amount of space to store tokens and trees.
- Very slow since each phase would have to input and output to and from temporary disk

Remedy

- Use syntax directed translation to inter leaves the actions of phases.
- Compiler construction tools.

Parser Generators

- The specification of input based on regular expression. The organization is based on finite automation.

Scanner Generator

- The specification of input based on regular expression. The organization is based on finite automation.

Syntax-Directed Translation

- It walks the parse tee and as a result generate intermediate code.

Automatic Code Generators

- Translates intermediate rampage into machine language.

Data-Flow Engines

- It does code optimization using data-flow analysis.

WORKING OF COMPILER

Compiling a program takes several stages of processing, which I have outlined below. The principles which are explained below also apply to interpreters, with the exception that the interpreters translate each program one line at a time before running it, and then moving on to the next line.

The process may be summarised in this diagram:

- Tokenising ? Syntax analysis ? Semantic analysis ? Translation

Tokenising

This part of the process is also sometimes called *Lexical Analysis*. It involves turning the program from a series of characters into a series of *tokens* that represent the building blocks of a program. The tokens are keywords of the language *i.e.* important words such as *if, print* or *repeat*), variable names and mathematical operators (+, *, brackets etc.).

The tokeniser takes each of the characters in turn, and as soon as it recognises a legitimate token, it reports it to the next stage of the process. Each token has a label and a type, so a variable "count" in a program would have the label corresponding to its name ("count") and the type "variable name". The tokeniser is also responsible for ignoring comments in the program-these are words and phrases inserted purely for the benefit of any human reading the program, and they have no function.

Syntax Analysis

Syntax means "grammar" and the syntax analyser in a compiler checks that the right tokens appear in the right order to make grammatically correct instructions. For instance, in C++, the instruction xyz++; is syntactically correct, but the instruction +;xyz+is not-the order of the tokens is wrong.

Semantic Analysis

The word "semantics" refers to *meaning*, and the semantic analyser checks the meaning of the program. This refers to aspects such as whether the variables have been declared, *e.g.*

xyz++; may be syntactically correct, but if the variable xyz has not been declared, then it is semantically incorrect!

The semantic analyser checks not only variable declarations and scope, but whether the program has entered or left loops, or subroutines, whether classes are accessed correctly etc.

ADVANTAGES

Choosing the right C compiler for your embedded-system projects may be a bigger challenge than you expect. The embedded-system-industry trend is moving from using assembly to using the higher level languages. Assembly language gives you more control over your code size and execution speeds. However, embedded C is easy to understand and portable from platform to platform. Another benefit is that developing code in C generally improves your product time to market. These features are advantageous if you expect your firmware to have longevity or if your staff changes periodically. A variety of embedded-C compilers is available in the market today. Embedded-C compilers are available as shareware from controller- or processor-IC vendors; or from high-end, reputable software companies whose selling prices often reflect the sophistication of the software. Some compiler-software companies have great advertisements and competitive prices but inferior products. So, how do you choose your compiler software for now and for the future?

There are many issues to consider when choosing your compiler. The most important are ANSI compliance, size and speed optimizations, portability, and supporting tools.

Adherence to the ANSI standard for the C language is critical for about 80 to 85% of code. This feature facilitates portability from part to part, as well as from software platform to software platform. ANSI-compliant software also integrates easy-to-understand code into your library. This type of code—if it is well-written—will have a shelf life like a good red wine. Even if portability is not an issue, it is important to understand how the compiler differs from ANSI and whether those differences will impact your development.

If the compiler of interest is ANSI-compliant, you should then examine the software's machine-code-generation capability. You might ask whether the compiler output code is optimized for small code (because memory is precious in controllers or processors) or whether the application executes in a timely or time-accurate manner. These features are somewhat mutually exclusive, but the compiler software should be able to optimize one or the other.

Portability between platforms is critical in larger companies that have a diverse range of products. However, it can also be convenient in smaller companies that may want the flexibility to quickly change controllers during development. Portability allows you to change quickly from one controller to another during application development. It also makes your code libraries more valuable over time.

If you want to easily complete your programming projects, the compiler cannot stand on its own. Every compiler needs an integrated suite of other tools. This tool suite should have, at a minimum, an integrated development environment that comes complete with a simulator and a hardware-debugging interface. Sometimes, you can mix and match these tools from other vendors, but use the vendor for your compiler as a first source. It can be difficult and frustrating to mix and then match tools from various vendors.

Some other characteristics that make up a good compiler are the availability of code libraries and library support. This concept does not fit into organizations with the NIH (not-invented-here) philosophy. An NIH organization deserves everything it gets (or doesn't get). Libraries with code that implements useful functions help expedite your projects to completion. Many times, these libraries have gone through evaluations and debugging to ensure their value.

Some of the final details in your compiler evaluation have to do with customer service. You need to ask whether your compiler company supports your questions and helps with its software bugs. You will find this information in the company's application-notes library, discussion forums, and software-release history. Although frequent releases can be a sign of responsiveness, they can also be an indication of serious stability concerns. The ideal compiler vendor has more support than you'll ever need.

In the past, most firmware designers would write embedded-firmware programs in assembly language. The embedded-C compiler transforms your source code into machine code. The C compiler you use determines the size as well as the execution time of your code. Many ways exist for determining these factors, so running your own test programs is also important. Don't depend on the results from a compiler-software company that runs its own tests. Many times, these companies can consciously or unconsciously skew the results.

2

Concepts of Operating System

OPERATING SYSTEM

INTRODUCTION

The 1960's definition of an operating system is "the software that controls the hardware". However, today, due to microcode we need a better definition. We see an operating system as the programs that make the hardware useable. In brief, an operating system is the set of programs that controls a computer. Some examples of operating systems are UNIX, Mach, MS-DOS, MS-Windows, Windows/NT, Chicago, OS/2, MacOS, VMS, MVS, and VM.

Controlling the computer involves software at several levels. We will differentiate kernel services, library services, and application-level services, all of which are part of the operating system. Processes run Applications, which are linked together with libraries that perform standard services. The kernel supports the processes by providing a path to the peripheral devices.

The kernel responds to service calls from the processes and interrupts from the devices. The core of the operating system is the kernel, a control program that functions in privileged state (an execution context that allows all hardware instructions to be executed), reacting to interrupts from external devices and to service requests and traps from processes. Generally, the kernel is a permanent resident of the computer. It creates and terminates processes and responds to their request for service.

Operating Systems are resource managers. The main resource is computer hardware in the form of processors, storage, input/output devices, communication devices, and data. Some of the operating system functions are: implementing the user interface, sharing hardware among users, allowing users to share data among themselves, preventing users from interfering with one another, scheduling resources among users, facilitating input/output, recovering from errors, accounting for resource usage, facilitating parallel operations, organizing data for secure and rapid access, and handling network communications.

OBJECTIVES OF OPERATING SYSTEMS

Modern Operating systems generally have following three major goals. Operating systems generally accomplish these goals by running processes in low privilege and providing service calls that invoke the operating system kernel in high-privilege state.·

To Hide Details of Hardware by Creating Abstraction

An abstraction is software that hides lower level details and provides a set of higher-level functions. An operating system transforms the physical world of devices, instructions, memory, and time into virtual world that is the result of abstractions built by the operating system.

There are several reasons for abstraction:

- *First,* the code needed to control peripheral devices is not standardized. Operating systems provide subroutines called device drivers that perform operations on behalf of programs for example, input/output operations.
- *Second,* the operating system introduces new functions as it abstracts the hardware. For instance, operating system introduces the file abstraction so that programs do not have to deal with disks.
- *Third,* the operating system transforms the computer hardware into multiple virtual computers, each belonging to a different program. Each program that

is running is called a process. Each process views the hardware through the lens of abstraction. *Fourth,* the operating system can enforce security through abstraction.

To Allocate Resources to Processes (Manage resources)

An operating system controls how processes (the active agents) may access resources (passive entities).

Provide a Pleasant and Effective user Interface

The user interacts with the operating systems through the user interface and usually interested in the "look and feel" of the operating system. The most important components of the user interface are the command interpreter, the file system, on-line help, and application integration. The recent trend has been towards increasingly integrated graphical user interfaces that encompass the activities of multiple processes on networks of computers.

One can view Operating Systems from two points of views: Resource manager and Extended machines. Form Resource manager point of view Operating Systems manage the different parts of the system efficiently and from extended machines point of view Operating Systems provide a virtual machine to users that is more convenient to use. The structurally Operating Systems can be design as a monolithic system, a hierarchy of layers, a virtual machine system, an exokernel, or using the client-server model.

The basic concepts of Operating Systems are processes, memory management, I/O management, the file systems, and security.

CONCEPTS

The CPU (Central Processing Unit) is the heart of any computer, but the operating system is the brain. Unfortunately, understanding exactly how these things really work can be difficult, because it's fairly hard to "play" with the operating system that you are actually using. You can do quite a bit with sophisticated debuggers, but eventually you run into confusion and difficulty. And, as you try more complex tasks, you run the risk of interfering with the real machine's operating system. Finally, modern CPU's are very complex, and that complexity can make it more difficult to understand basic concepts.

I therefore thought it would be interesting to emulate CPU's and other hardware in software. By doing that, we can present simple ideas and build on that understanding. We'll start very simply, and build from there, eventually demonstrating more advanced concepts like virtual memory, disk filesystems, and even multitasking.

A SIMPLE CPU

Our first CPU is very simple. The code to run it is a simple Perl. We have no input and output; we have to preload everything we need into our programs. The earliest computers weren't much different: front panel switches and lights to show register contents.

You don't need to understand this script at all as long as it works on your system. If it doesn't work, it's probably either (Unix/Linux) that the first line needs to be changed to match where Perl is found on your machine ("which perl") or (Windows) that you haven't associated the ".pl" extension with Perl, or you haven't installed Perl at all.

This CPU reads its instructions from a file called "memory1" in your current directory. It only understands three instructions, which are the letters "L" for LOAD, "A" for ADD, and "H" for HALT. You get these instructions into memory simply by editing "memory1" with a text editor. Then just run cpu1.pl to see the results.

For example, we might create memory1 to contain:

- LA1LB2AABABBH

You can do that with "vi". If you are using Windows, it will probably be easier if you modify "cpu1.pl" to read from "memory1.txt" and use Notepad to create the file. Our program doesn't do much: it loads "1" into register A, "2" into register B, adds B to A, and finally adds A to B. Pretty weak, but not so very many years ago a machine that could do just that was pretty amazing stuff.

If you create the file, run "./cpu1.pl", and type "g" after the first display and you will get:

```
REGISTERS A: 0 B: 0 C: D:
IP: 0 CMD: LOAD A 1
==================================
REGISTERS A: 1 B: 0 C: D:
IP: 3 CMD: LOAD B 2
==================================
REGISTERS A: 1 B: 2 C: D:
IP: 6 CMD: ADD A B
==================================
REGISTERS A: 3 B: 2 C: D:
IP: 9 CMD: ADD B B
==================================
REGISTERS A: 3 B: 4 C: D:
IP: 12 CMD: HALT
==================================
```

If you just press ENTER instead of "g" you will "single-step" through the code. Our simple CPU ignores instructions it doesn't understand, and will stop automatically when it reaches the end of its memory (the end of "memory1"). So, you can "run" this CPU on arbitrary text. It won't necessarily do anything useful of course.

So what is this teaching us? First, all CPU's use registers, which are simply storage on the CPU chip itself. The advantage of registers (on real CPU's) is that manipulation of data in registers is very fast-much faster than memory. The "IP" is the Instruction Pointer: the address in memory that it is reading instructions from. This is simply the number of bytes it has read into our "memory1" file: The 6th character of our test file is A followed by AB. Our simple CPU can't handle numbers greater than 9, at least on the LOAD command. And it only shows you four registers: A through D. So, even if it were real hardware, it wouldn't be very useful. Yet, the very first CPU's didn't have much more power than this.

A little More Power

To get more power, we need more instructions, and we

need an easier way to write programs. Our second CPU is a little more powerful you don't need to understand either of these. The "asm2.pl" is an assembler for our cpu2.pl processor; it will create "machine language" instructions in a file called "memory2". Our first program will be very simple.

Put this text into a file called "prog1":

- LOADA 1
- LOADB 2
- LOADC 2
- LOADD 1
- HALT

If you are using a Linux or Unix system, run the commands

- ./asm2.pl prog1 &&./cpu2.pl

If not, run asm2.pl and cpu2.pl separately.

You should get:

```
REGISTERS A: 0 B: 0 C: D:
AB: 0 0 CD: 0 0
ABCD: 0 0
FLAGS:
IP: 0 CMD: LOAD A 1
==================================
REGISTERS A: 1 B: 0 C: D:
AB: 256 1 CD: 0 0
ABCD: 16777216 1
FLAGS:
IP: 3 CMD: LOAD B 2
==================================
REGISTERS A: 1 B: 2 C: D:
AB: 258 513 CD: 0 0
ABCD: 16908288 513
FLAGS:
IP: 6 CMD: LOAD C 2
==================================
REGISTERS A: 1 B: 2 C: 2 D:
AB: 258 513 CD: 512 2
ABCD: 16908800 131585
FLAGS:
```

```
IP: 9 CMD: LOAD D 1
==================================
REGISTERS A: 1 B: 2 C: 2 D: 1
AB: 258 513 CD: 513 258
ABCD: 16908801 16908801
FLAGS:
IP: 12 CMD: ADD A D
==================================
REGISTERS A: 2 B: 2 C: 2 D: 1
AB: 514 514 CD: 513 258
ABCD: 33686017 16908802
FLAGS:
IP: 15 CMD: HALT
==================================
```

Of you like, you can see what the assembler put into memory by examining "memory2". On Linux/Unix, "od -cx memory2" is a good way to see it. Or just enter "D" while the cpu is running. You'll notice that we've tried to use ASCII characters where possible; for example LOAD A will end up in memory as LA. No real cpu would be so wasteful: a single byte would likely encode the instruction and the register it referenced. That is done for efficiency in hardware and assemblers. We have no need of efficiency, and it's helpful to have memory dumps a little easier to decode.

We still have some limitations with this version. First, our registers can't hold any more than 255-an 8 bit number. In this little "prog1" we didn't use anything that large anyway. Fact is, CPU registers are always going to be limited as to how big a number they can hold. On modern CPU's, that's going to be more than 8 bits, and might even be 64 bits on the latest hardware, but it will always be limited. And while 64 bits is a very large number, your programming may need to work with bigger numbers. You'll certainly need to deal with more than 255, so our cpu2.pl is a rather useless processor, right?

Well, maybe.

You may have noticed these lines in the output:

- *AB:* 514 514 CD: 513 258
- *ABCD:* 33686017 16908802

Those are what the registers would represent if you strung them together. This is binary math (I know, your head hurts already), but lets not worry about how that works just now. Just accept that if register A is "1" and register B is "2", then A and B together are either 513 or 258, depending on how your machine looks at numbers. Huh? Which is it? Well, as I said, it depends. If your computer uses "little-endian" numbers (Intel for example), it's 258, but on a Mac (normally big-endian), it's 513. For our purposes here, it really doesn't matter: we could write programs to add up larger numbers either way simply by deciding which way we want to look at the numbers. To write such a program we need some new instructions.

Save this as "prog2" and run "./asm2.pl prog2 &&./cpu2.pl".

- LOAD A 0
- LOAD B 0
- LOAD C 1
- LOAD D 5
- LOAD E 253
- LOAD F 0
- *LOOP:* ADDREGS A E JUMPNOTZERO CHECK:
- ADDREGS B C
- *CHECK:* SUBTRACTREGS D C
- *JUMPNOTZERO LOOP:*
- HALT
- *JUMP LOOP:*

This program will multiply 253 by 5 and the result will be in AB. Note that we have the ability to set labels in our code and to jump to the address represented by the label. We also introduce the concept of "flags", which are simply a special kind of register that will be set when a condition becomes true.

For the moment, we have only two flags: OV, which is set when a register rolls over from its maximamum value of 255, and ZERO, which is set when the result of an add or subtract is zero. We then need a JUMPNOTZERO instruction to make use of the flags (in this simple CPU, "ZERO" is set for the OV condition also). If you step through this (or just hit G), you'll see that the value of A increments. When it overflows at 255, it becomes 0 but we then add 1 to B, and continue. We do that 5 times and stop.

What would happen if we didn't stop after 5? Of course B would keep on incrementing and eventually it would overflow too. That wouldn't take all that long: our emulated CPU is very slow, but it wouldn't take but a very few minutes. On a real Pentium class machine, executing similar instructions would overflow a 32 bit register in a very few seconds, but when we start using 64 bit registers we get an entirely different animal.

For example, Pentium CPU's have a 64 bit register called the TSC (Time Stamp Counter) that counts processor clock cycles since reset (or since it was programmatically zeroed). Consider that a 1 Gigahertz cpu increments that register 1 billion times per second: start it from 0, wait 1 second and its value is 1 billion.

Of course 64 bits can hold values up to 16 billion billion, so it will take 16 billion seconds to overflow (actually it's 4GB * 4GB so it's a bit longer, but 16 billion is a nice round figure) That's 500 years or so; a bit of a wait. That's one of the reasons we designed this fake cpu with arbitrarily small registers: it's easier to see overflows happen.

With very little more effort, we could actually use this to multiply numbers. This multiplies 253 by 5 and the result is in AB. Our simple CPU has a very limited repertoire. We don't have a lot of power in this cpu, yet we can actually (with enough effort) do almost any programming task with just these simple instructions.

A hundred years ago that would have been more than incredible, and even 40 years ago we didn't demand a lot more than that. I'll continue with this series as I have the time; we'll add simulations of virtual memory, a protected memory mode, i/o, primitive task scheduling and more.

FUNDAMENTAL CONCEPT

Fundamental concept of computer operating systemstarts with the structure of the OS. Conceptually, an operating system can be broken down into the kernel, shell and system utilities. The kernel is the core of the operating system, and in some cases, the distinction between the kernel and the shell is clear; in others, the distinction is only conceptuai. A process is a program in execution.

New processes are spawned when needed and terminated to free memory and other resources. Files are a method of organizing the information on disk.

Files are usually organized in an inverted tree-like structure. A system call is a program that requests something from the operating system.

The roles of an operating system vary with the hardware and user programs it was designed to work with. The earliest operating systems were designed to help applications interact with hardware. This has grown to the point that the operating system now defines the machine. The operating system provides an interface to the underlying hardware, the application programs, and the user.

The operating system manages:

- Hardware
- CPU
- Memory
- Device Drivers
- I/O
- Applications

There are four basic types of operating systems:

1. Real time operating system
2. Single user, single task operating system
3. Single user, multi task operating system
4. Multi user operating system

HISTORY OF OPERATING SYSTEM

History of operating system was started with the first generation computers. They operated on a purely mechanical basis. There was no concept of an operating system. The user fed data and the program into the computer using punched cards. The programs were debugged using front panel switches and lights. The second-generation computers were batch systems where the jobs and instructions were put together so that they could be processed without interruptions.

The third generation computers used the concepts of multiprogramming and time-sharing. Spooling batch systems were the first and simplest of multiprogramming systems. The major advantage was that the output from the jobs was available as soon as the job was completed. The fourth generation saw the advent of modern operating systems for PCs, workstations and servers and also includes networking and distributed operating systems.

The early *operating systems* were diverse, with each vendor producing their own operating systems specific to their hardware.

This continued until the 1960s when IBM developed the S/360 series of machines, where all machines ran the same operating system, OS/360. CP/M (Control Program for Microcomputers) was the first generic operating system for microcomputers.

Before CP/M, every brand of computer had its own unique operating system.

Because of this, programs could not be shared between computers and software had to be rewritten for every type of computer.

The nearest to the operating system was the "job control language" (JCL) required to submit a program for execution on the mainframe.

CP/M was a complete software development environment that enabled to write software that was machine-independent, and move CP/M itself to other computers. OS/2 was the first operating system to provide intrinsic multitasking based on hardware support.

It was text-mode only and allowed only one program to be on the screen at a time, even though other programs could be running in the background.

BASIC CONCEPTS OF REAL -TIME OPERATING SYSTEMS

THE FUNDAMENTALS

To most people, embedded systems are not recognizable

as computers. Instead, they are hidden inside everyday objects that surround us and help us in our lives.

Embedded systems typically do not interface with the outside world through familiar personal computer interface devices such as a mouse, keyboard and graphic user interface. Instead, they interface with the outside world through unusual interfaces such as sensors, actuators and specialized communication links.

Real-time and embedded systems operate in constrained environments in which computer memory and processing power are limited.

They often need to provide their services within strict time deadlines to their users and to the surrounding world. It is these memory, speed and timing constraints that dictate the use of real-time operating systems in embedded software.

BASIC KERNEL SERVICES

In the discussion below, we will focus on the "kernel"– the part of an operating system that provides the most basic services to application software running on a processor. The "kernel" of a real-time operating system ("RTOS") provides an "abstraction layer" that hides from application software the hardware details of the processor (or set of processors) upon which the application software will run. This is shown in Figure.

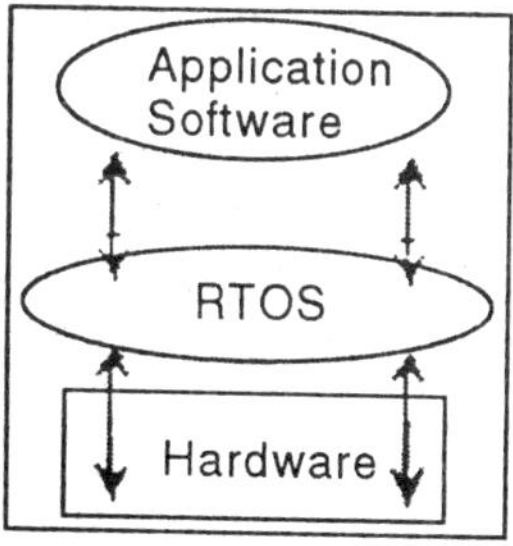

Fig. An RTOS Kernel Provides an Abstraction Layer between Application Software and Embedded Hardware

In providing this "abstraction layer" the RTOS kernel supplies five main categories of basic services to application software, as seen in Figure.

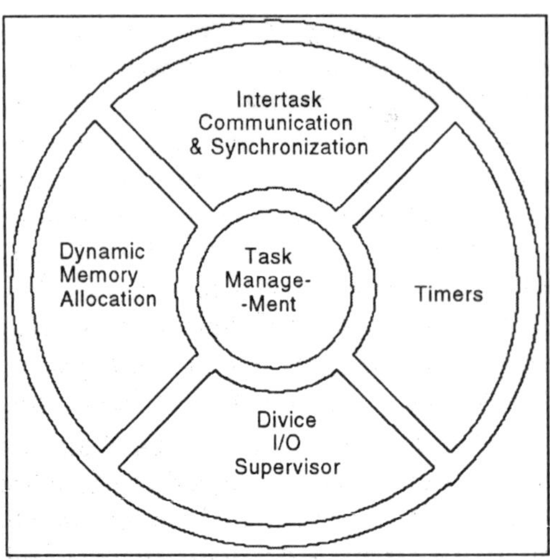

Fig. Basic Services Provided by a Real-Time Operating System Kernel

The most basic category of kernel services, at the very center of Figure, is Task Management. This set of services allows application software developers to design their software as a number of separate "chunks" of software—each handling a distinct topic, a distinct goal, and perhaps its own real-time deadline. Each separate "chunk" of software is called a "task." Services in this category include the ability to launch tasks and assign priorities to them. The main RTOS service in this category is the scheduling of tasks as the embedded system is in operation. The Task Scheduler controls the execution of application software tasks, and can make them run in a very timely and responsive fashion. The second category of kernel services, shown at the top of Figure, is Intertask Communication and Synchronization.

These services make it possible for tasks to pass information from one to another, without danger of that information ever being damaged. They also make it possible for tasks to coordinate, so that they can productively cooperate with one another. Without the help of these RTOS services, tasks might well communicate corrupted information or otherwise interfere with each other.

Since many embedded systems have stringent timing requirements, most RTOS kernels also provide some basic Timer services, such as task delays and time-outs. These are shown on the right side of Figure.

Many (but not all) RTOS kernels provide Dynamic Memory Allocation services. This category of services allows tasks to "borrow" chunks of RAM memory for temporary use in application software.

Often these chunks of memory are then passed from task to task, as a means of quickly communicating large amounts of data between tasks. Some very small RTOS kernels that are intended for tightly memory-limited environments, do not offer Dynamic Memory Allocation services.

Many (but not all) RTOS kernels also provide a "Device I/O Supervisor" category of services. These services, if available, provide a uniform framework for organizing and accessing the many hardware device drivers that are typical of an embedded system.

In addition to kernel services, many RTOSs offer a number of optional add-on operating system components for such high-level services as file system organization, network communication, network management, database management, user-interface graphics, etc.

Although many of these add-on components are much larger and much more complex than the RTOS kernel, they rely on the presence of the RTOS kernel and take advantage of its basic services.

Each of these add-on components is included in an embedded system only if its services are needed for implementing the embedded application, in order to keep program memory consumption to a minimum.

In this paper, we will focus on the basic RTOS kernel services for task management, intertask communication and synchr nization, and dynamic memory allocation.

RTOSS VS. GENERAL-PURPOSE OPERATING SYSTEMS

Many non-real-time operating systems also provide

similar kernel services. The key difference between general-computing operating systems and real-time operating systems is the need for " deterministic " timing behaviour in the real-time operating systems.

Formally, "deterministic" timing means that operating system services consume only known and expected amounts of time.

In theory, these service times could be expressed as mathematical formulas. These formulas must be strictly algebraic and not include any random timing components. Random elements in service times could cause random delays in application software and could then make the application randomly miss real-time deadlines–a scenario clearly unacceptable for a real-time embedded system.

General-computing non-real-time operating systems are often quite non-deterministic. Their services can inject random delays into application software and thus cause slow responsiveness of an application at unexpected times.

If you ask the developer of a non-real-time operating system for the algebraic formula describing the timing behaviour of one of its services (such as sending a message from task to task), you will invariably not get an algebraic formula.

Instead the developer of the non-real-time operating system (such as Windows, Unix or Linux) will just give you a puzzled look. Deterministic timing behaviour was simply not a design goal for these general-computing operating systems.

On the other hand, real-time operating systems often go a step beyond basic determinism. For most kernel services, these operating systems offer constant load-independent timing: In other words, the algebraic formula is as simple as:*T(message_send) = constant,* irrespective of the length of the message to be sent, or other factors such as the numbers of tasks and queues and messages being managed by the RTOS.

TASK SCHEDULING

Most RTOSs do their scheduling of tasks using a scheme called "priority-based preemptive scheduling." Each task in a software application must be assigned a priority, with higher priority values representing the need for quicker responsiveness.

Very quick responsiveness is made possible by the "preemptive" nature of the task scheduling. "Preemptive" means that the scheduler is allowed to stop any task at any point in its execution, if it determines that another task needs to run immediately.

The basic rule that governs priority-based preemptive scheduling is that at every moment in time, "The Highest Priority Task that is Ready to Run, will be the Task that Must be Running." In other words, if both a low-priority task and a higher-priority task are ready to run, the scheduler will allow the higher-priority task to run first. The low-priority task will only get to run after the higher-priority task has finished with its current work.

What if a low-priority task has already begun to run, and then a higher-priority task becomes ready? This might occur because of an external world trigger such as a switch closing. A priority-based preemptive scheduler will behave as follows: It will allow the low-priority task to complete the current assembly-language instruction that it is executing. [But it won't allow it to complete an entire line of high-level language code; nor will it allow it to continue running until the next clock tick.] It will then immediately stop the execution of the low-priority task, and allow the higher-priority task to run. After the higher-priority task has finished its current work, the low-priority task will be allowed to continue running. This is shown in Figure, where the higher-priority task is called "Mid-Priority Task."

Of course, while the mid-priority task is running, an even higher-priority task might become ready. This is represented in Figure by "Trigger_2" causing the "High-Priority Task" to become ready. In that case, the running task ("Mid-Priority Task") would be preempted to allow the high-priority task to run. When the high-priority task has finished its current work, the mid-priority task would be allowed to continue. And after both the high-priority task and the mid-priority task complete their work, the low-priority task would be allowed to continue running. This situation might be called "nested preemption."

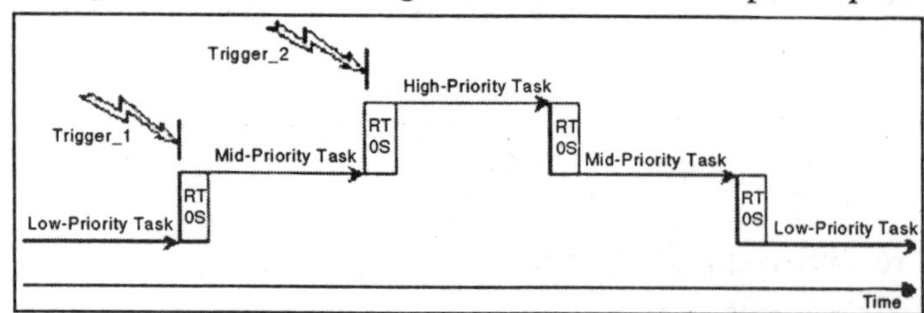

Fig. Timeline for Priority-based Preemptive Scheduling Examples

Each time the priority-based preemptive scheduler is alerted by an external world trigger (such as a switch closing) or a software trigger (such as a message arrival), it must go through the following 5 steps:

1. Determine whether the currently running task should continue to run. If not ...
2. Determine which task should run next.
3. Save the environment of the task that was stopped (so it can continue later).
4. Set up the running environment of the task that will run next.
5. Allow this task to run.

These 5 steps together are called "task switching."

FIXED-TIME TASK SWITCHING

The time it takes to do task switching is of interest when evaluating an operating system. A simple general-computing (non-preemptive) operating system might do task switching only at timer tick times, which might for example be ten milliseconds apart. Then if the need for a task switch arises anywhere within a 10-millisecond timeframe, the actual task switch would occur only at the end of the current 10-millisecond period. Such a delay would be unacceptable in most real-time embedded systems. In more sophisticated preemptive task schedulers, the scheduler may need to search through arrays of tasks to determine which task should be made to run next. If there are more tasks to search through, the search will take longer. Such searches are often done by general-computing operating systems, thus making them non-deterministic. Real-time operating systems, on the other hand, avoid such searches by using incrementally updated tables that allow the task scheduler to identify the task that should run next in a rapid fixed-time fashion.

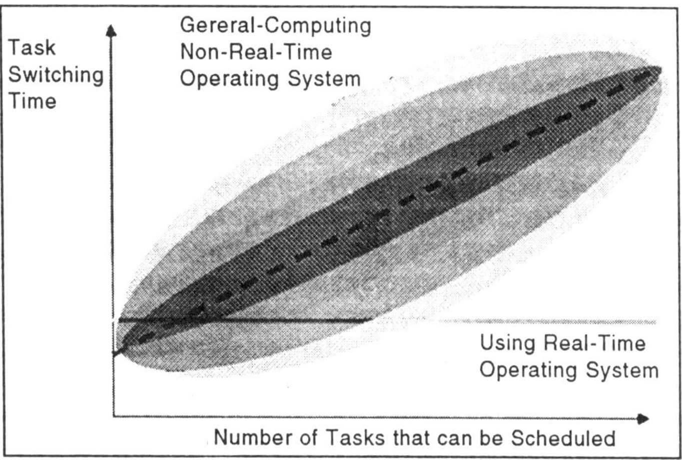

Fig. These Two Types of Timing Behaviour for Task Switching can be Seen in Figure.

Task Switching Timing: In this figure, we see that for a general-computing (non-real-time) operating system, the task switching time generally rises as a software system includes more tasks that can be scheduled. However, the actual time for a task switch is not the time shown by the dashed red line. Instead, in any given task switch instance, it might be well above or well below the time shown by the dashed red line. The shaded regions surrounding the dashed red line simply show the likelihood of the actual task switch time being that far above or below the dashed red line. On the other hand, the horizontal solid green line shows the task switching time characteristic of a real-time operating system. It is constant, independent of any load factor such as the number of tasks in a software system.

Please note that in some instances, such as the leftmost area of the graph, the task switching time might in special cases be quicker for a general-computing non-real-time operating system, than for a real-time operating system. This does not detract from the appropriateness of a real-time operating system for real-time embedded applications. For, in fact, the term "real-time" does not mean "as fast as possible" but rather "real-time" demands consistent, repeatable, known timing performance. Although a non-real-time operating system might do some faster task switching for small numbers of tasks, it might equally well introduce a long time delay the next time it does the same task switch. The strength of a real-time operating system is in its known, repeatable timing performance, which is also typically faster than that of a non-deterministic task scheduler in situations of large numbers of tasks in a software system. Most often, the real-time operating system will exhibit task-switching times much faster than its non-real-time competitor when the number of tasks grows above 5 or 10.

INTERTASK COMMUNICATION AND SYNCHRONIZATION

Most operating systems, including RTOSs, offer a variety of mechanisms for communication and synchronization between tasks. These mechanisms are necessary in a preemptive environment of many tasks, because without them the tasks might well communicate corrupted information or otherwise interfere with each other. For instance, a task might be preempted when it is in the middle of updating a table of data. If a second task that preempts it reads from that table, it will read a combination of some areas of newly-updated data plus some areas of data that have not yet been updated.

[New Yorkers would call this a "mish-mash."] These updated and old data areas together may be incorrect in combination, or may not even make sense. An example is a data table containing temperature measurements that begins with the contents "10 C." A task begins updating this table with the new value "99 F", writing into the table character-by-character. If that task is preempted in the middle of the update, a second task that preempts it could possibly read a value like "90 C" or "99 C." or "99 F", depending on precisely when the preemption took place. The partially updated values are clearly incorrect, and are caused by delicate timing coincidences that are very hard to debug or reproduce consistently.

An RTOS's mechanisms for communication and synchronization between tasks are provided to avoid these kinds of errors. Most RTOSs provide several mechanisms, with each mechanism optimized for reliably passing a different kind of information from task to task. Probably the most popular kind of communication between tasks in embedded systems is the passing of data from one task to another. Most RTOSs offer a message passing mechanism for doing this, as seen in Figure. Each message can contain an array or buffer of data.

Fig. Intertask Message Communication

If messages can be sent more quickly than they can be handled, the RTOS will provide message queues for holding the messages until they can be processed. This is shown in Figure. Another kind of communication between tasks in embedded systems is the passing of what might be called "synchronization information" from one task to another. "Synchronization information" is like a command, where some commands could be positive, and some negative. For example, a negative command to a task would be something like "Please don't print right now, because my task is using the printer." Or more generally, "I want to lock the for my own use only." A positive command would be something like "I've detected a cardiac emergency, and I want you to help me handle it." Or more generally, "Please join me in handling..."

Most RTOSs offer a semaphore or mutex mechanism for handling negative synchronization (sometimes called "mutual exclusion"). These mechanisms allow tasks to lock certain embedded system resources for their use only, and subsequently to unlock the resource when they're done.

For positive synchronization, different RTOSs offer different mechanisms. Some RTOSs offer event-flags, while others offer signals. And yet others rely on message passing for positive synchronization as well as data passing duties.

DETERMINISM AND HIGH-SPEED MESSAGE PASSING

Intertask message communication is another area where different operating systems show different timing characteristics. Most operating systems actually copy messages twice as they transfer them from task to task via a message queue. The first copying is from the message-sender task to an operating system-owned "secret" area of RAM memory (implementing the "message queue"); and the second copying is from the operating system's "secret" RAM area to the message-receiver task. Clearly this is non-deterministic in its timing, as these copying activities take longer as message length increases.

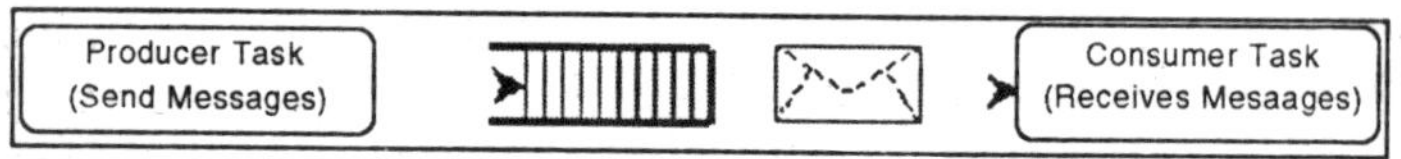

Fig. Message Transfer via Message Queue

An approach that avoids this non-determinism and also accelerates performance, is to have the operating system copy a pointer to the message and deliver that pointer to the message-receiver task without moving the message contents at all. In order to avoid access collisions, the operating system then needs to go back to the message-sender task and obliterate its copy of the pointer to the message. For large messages, this eliminates the need for lengthy copying and eliminates non-determinism.

DYNAMIC MEMORY ALLOCATION

Determinism of service times is also an issue in the area of dynamic allocation of RAM memory. Many general-computing non-real-time operating systems offer memory allocation services from what is termed a "Heap." The famous "malloc" and "free" services known to C-language programmers work from a heap. Tasks can temporarily borrow some memory from the operating system's heap by calling "malloc", and specifying the size of memory buffer needed. When this task (or another task) is finished with this memory buffer it can return the buffer to the operating system by calling "free." The operating system will then return the buffer to the heap, where its memory might be used again, perhaps as part of a larger buffer. Or perhaps it may in the future be broken into several smaller buffers.

Heaps suffer from a phenomenon called "External Memory Fragmentation" that may cause the heap services to degrade. This fragmentation is caused by the fact that when a buffer is returned to the heap, it may in the future be broken into smaller buffers when "malloc" requests for smaller buffer sizes occur. After a heap undergoes many cycles of "malloc"s and "free"s, small slivers of memory may appear between memory buffers that are being used by tasks. These slivers are so small that they are useless to tasks. But they are trapped between buffers that are being used by tasks, so they can't be coagulated ("glued") together into bigger, useful buffer sizes. Over time, a heap will have more and more of these slivers. This will eventually result in situations where tasks will ask for memory buffers ("malloc") of a certain size, and they will be refused by the operating system—even though the operating system has enough available memory in its heap.

The problem: That memory is scattered in small slivers distributed in various separate parts of the heap. In operating system terminology, the slivers are called "fragments", and this problem is called "external memory fragmentation."

This fragmentation problem can be solved by so-called "garbage collection" (defragmentation) software. Unfortunately, "garbage collection" algorithms are often wildly non-deterministic–injecting randomly-appearing random-duration delays into heap services. These are often seen in the memory allocation services of general-computing non-real-time operating systems.

This puts the embedded system developer who wants to use a general-computing non-real-time operating system into a quandry: Should the embedded system be allowed to suffer occasional randomly-appearing random-duration delays if/

when "garbage collection" kicks in?... Or, alternatively, should the embedded system be allowed to fragment its memory until application software "malloc" requests to the heap are refused even though a sufficient total amount of free memory is still available? Neither alternative is acceptable for embedded systems that need to provide service continually for long periods of time.

Real-time operating systems, on the other hand, solve this quandry by altogether avoiding both memory fragmentation and "garbage collection", and their consequences. RTOSs offer non-fragmenting memory allocation techniques instead of heaps. They do this by limiting the variety of memory chunk sizes they make available to application software. While this approach is less flexible than the approach taken by memory heaps, they do avoid external memory fragmentation and avoid the need for defragmentation. For example, the "Pools" memory allocation mechanism allows application software to allocate chunks of memory of perhaps 4 or 8 different buffer sizes per pool. Pools totally avoid external memory fragmentation, by not permitting a buffer that is returned to the pool to be broken into smaller buffers in the future. Instead, when a buffer is returned the pool, it is put onto a "free buffer list" of buffers of its own size that are available for future re-use at their original buffer size. This is shown in Figure.

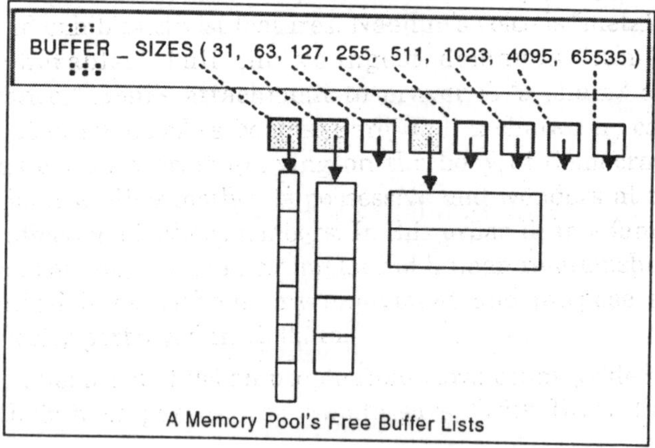

Fig. A Memory Pool's Free Buffer Lists

Memory is allocated and de-allocated from a pool with deterministic, often constant, timing.

SUMMARY

Real-time and embedded systems are used in many applications such as airborne computers, medical instruments and communication systems. Embedded systems are characterized by limited processor memory, limited processing power, and unusual interfaces to the outside world. Real-time requirements impose stringent time deadlines for delivering the results of embedded processing. RTOS kernels hide from application software the low-level details of system hardware, and at the same time provide several categories of services to application software. These include: task management with priority-based preemptive scheduling, reliable intertask communication and synchronization, non-fragmenting dynamic memory allocation, and basic timer services.

The issue of timing determinism is important in differentiating general-computing operating systems from real-time operating systems. This issue crops up in many parts of operating system kernels, such as task schedulers, dynamic memory allocation and intertask message communication. While general-computing operating systems often offer non-deterministic services in these areas, fully deterministic solutions are needed for real-time and embedded systems. A number of real-time operating systems implement these solutions in their compact high-performance kernels.

GOALS AND FUNCTIONS OF OPERATING SYSTEM

GOALS

Developing a single application for multiple platforms is a difficult task. The most significant issue is the need for a clean solution for developing Graphical User Interfaces [GUI's]. FOX aims to address this by providing a single GUI library that can run on different computer hardware and operating system environments. The benefits to application vendors and developers are clear:

Development Effort to Support Multiple Environments is Substantially Reduced

After development, your FOX based application is only a compile away from running on other operating systems. When multiple hardware and software combinations are required by customers operating in a heterogeneous environment, using a single GUI system such as FOX is clearly the most cost-effective method to achieve the goal.

Availability of your Software on Other Platforms will Engender Additional Revenues

Without the necessity of additional development work, the cost of which would have to be amortized over the number of sales, additional revenues can be engendered by having your software be available on multiple hardware and software environments. Software development is a costly undertaking; because of this, software vendors typically limit the number of platforms to a small subset of the platforms being used by *all* customers, effectively leaving certain customers in the dark. FOX allows applications to be developed on one platform, then simply recompile the application on a number of other hardware/software systems. Because the cost of doing so is negligible, this approach will be able to generate positive cashflow even with low sales volumes.

Captive Audience

If the application you're developing is available on all platforms, you may be able to create a captive customer base on hardware/software systems where your competitor is absent; you may in fact even be able to charge premium prices. Using the additional revenues derived from these customers, your product will be able to derive a steady addional revenue stream which will allow you to compete more aggressively against your single-platform competitor.

Higher Quality

For programmers, the benefits of multi-platform development v.s. single platform development are the additional confidence and code quality that compiling under different environments will give. For example, I have compiled FOX on a number of different systems, and different compilers will discover different types of code bugs. By compiling on all these different systems, FOX has gotten quite a bit better in the course of time.

Control Your Destiny

Programmers understand it as a matter of course that they need to continually work to track the changes in a system's API's. But what if the system vendor is also your competitor? In such a case, you *will* loose, sooner or later. The FOX GUI Library provides a platform-independent escape hatch that relies only on core system facilities which can be expected to be present on any modern operating system.

Approach

FOX attains the goal of platform independence by eliminating all system dependencies from its public interfaces. In fact, a typical FOX application may not even need to include any system-specific header files at all! By not including *e.g.* X-Windows header files, applications can not even accidentally slip up and introduce platform dependencies. This strategy is also carried out inside FOX itself. Thus, large parts of FOX are in fact defined entirely in FOX itself. The only dependencies are concentrated in a few select base classes where this couldn't be avoided. The following salient points highlight some fundamental benefits of FOX *vis-a-vis* other purported platform independent toolkits:

Eliminate all platform specific header files.

Applications should only include header files from FOX, and a few header files for such basic system services as opening files etc.

Internal Layering

FOX itself relies largely on FOX base classes, and therefore a large fraction of FOX itself is platform independent as well.

Rely only on low-level system facilities

FOX relies only on core system facilities, and does NOT wrap native GUI libraries or toolkits. This has the following benefits:

Identical Behaviour

The behaviour will be close to identical on all systems, as the behaviour is completely controlled by the FOX implementation, rather than some underlying library.

Identical Looks

FOX applications will look the same no matter what system you're running it on.

Ability to **subclass**

Because FOX is written from the ground up in C++, and is NOT a C++ wrapper around some other legacy toolkit or library, FOX Controls may be subclassed and extended by application programmers. Moreover, if these additions can be done by calling upon FOX built-in facilities, those additions will be platform independent also.

Higher Quality

It is a given in software development that those facilities which are most frequently used are the ones which are most stable. Thus, by using core system facilities instead of higher-level transient API's, the impact of the underlying system's instability is minimized. A chain is as strong as the weakest link, and while I can not control the quality of the links, I can minimize the number of them.

Higher Speed

Eliminating layers between FOX and the underlying system not only increases the application's quality, it will also make it faster, and reduce memory overhead.

Go to the Bedrock

FOX's core facilities needed from the target system are

things like mouse/keyboard event handling, and basic graphics facilities such as drawing of lines and rectangles [and some other system facilities].

In most operating systems, these are fairly mature API's and not subject to much change. If you want to build a big building, you need to go down to the solid bedrock. This is what FOX does.

FOX is Extensible

The FOX library is designed to be open-ended and extensible. What this means is that unlike other libraries which take the approach of wrapping legacy GUI toolkits, FOX may be extended with *Custom Controls* and Widgets which will set your application apart from the others.

Building Custom Controls is extremely easy in FOX, as it is essentially just a matter of C++ subclassing.

FOX is Available under Library GNU Public License

Since FOX is distributed in source form under LGPL, you have the ability to make changes or extensions to FOX to suit your needs. Having FOX inspected by 1000's of programmers all over the world will iron out any bugs it may have very quickly. This process is already under way.

I care a great deal about software quality; I imagine, so do you. In the course of my programming life, I have ran into many situations where the bugs I needed to fix were not in my own code, but in someone else's, and of course I didn't have the source.

Thus, the quality of my own software was limited by the quality of someone else's. Problem is, the developers of the libraries and software I depend on are frequently not motivated to make their software correct.

This has made me a firm believer in the *GPL* or *Open Source* model of software development. FOX was started in part because I didn't want to explain to our customers that the reason X or Y didn't work was because of the broken software or libraries on their machine. The only way one can create high-quality applications is to bring as much of the underlying system under one's control as possible. Hence the *Go to the Bedrock* philosophy.

FOX is not perfect. But as the source code is available under LGPL, it has the advantage that its imperfections can be addressed as soon as they are discovered.

Purpose

The purpose of this HOWTO is to describe a methodology for managing multiple operating systems on a single computer system. It is intended for Linux users who have a basic familiarity with both Linux and LILO installations. Nothing here is terribly complex however, considering the amount of time it takes to install some operating systems it can be relatively time consuming. It is different from other methods in that it doesn't require multiple operating systems on the boot disk. Instead it uses a fixed internal disk containing a single primary operating system and a selection of removable disks with one or more operating systems installed on each of them. If you absolutely have to have two, three, or four different operating systems on a single disk and are trying to get them to behave with each other, this HOWTO is not for you.

Its specific goals are:

- A primary/operational disk that once configured and installed is rarely changed. This includes not having to repartition or otherwise modify the disk it resides on.
- Easy selection of multiple alternative operating systems at boot time without having to go through more than one or two menu selections.
- No need to modify the BIOS, LILO, or any other configuration to access an O/S once it is installed.
- Easy addition/removal of operating systems depending on requirements at the moment.
- Inexpensive and scalable to allow for an increasing number of operating systems and versions as time goes on.

I think I succeeded admirably in the first three of these requirements. You can form your own opinions on the last two.

OPERATING SYSTEM FUNCTIONS

Usually Operating system is there to manage all pieces of a complex system Imagine what will happen if three programs running on a computer all try to print their output simultaneously on the same printer. The first few lines might be from program one and the next few lines might be from program two and so on with the result resulting in chaos. The operating system can bring order to potential chaos by buffering all the output destined for the printer on the disk.

The primary task of operating system is to keep track of who is using which resource, to grant resource request, to account for usage, and to meditate conflicting request from different programs and users.

When a computer has multiple users, the need for managing and protecting the memory, input/output devices and other resources are even more apparent. This need arises because it is usually necessary to share expensive resource such as tapes drives and phototypesetters.

Operating systems perform basic tasks, such as recognizing input from the keyboard, sending output to the display screen, keeping track of files anddirectories on the disk, and controlling peripheral devices such as disk drives and printers.

For large systems, the operating system has even greater responsibilities and powers. It is like a traffic cop—it makes sure that different program and usersrunning at the same time do not interfere with each other. The operating system is also responsible for security, ensuring that unauthorized users do not accessthe system.

The set of software products that jointly controls the system resource using these resources on a computer system is known as operating system. Examples are Unix, Windows.

What is an Operating System

The operating system is the core software component of your computer. It performs many functions and is, in very basic terms, an interface between your computer and the outside world. In the section about hardware, a computer is described as consisting of several component parts including your monitor, keyboard, mouse, and other parts. The operating system provides an interface to these parts using what is referred to as "drivers". This is why sometimes when you install a new printer or other piece of hardware, your system will ask you to install more software called a driver.

What does a Driver do?

A driver is a specially written program which understands the operation of the device it interfaces to, such as a printer, video card, sound card or CD ROM drive. It translates commands from the operating system or user into commands understood by the the component computer part it interfaces with. It also translates responses from the component computer part back to responses that can be understood by the operating system, application program, or user. The below diagram gives a graphical depiction of the interfaces between the operating system and the computer component.

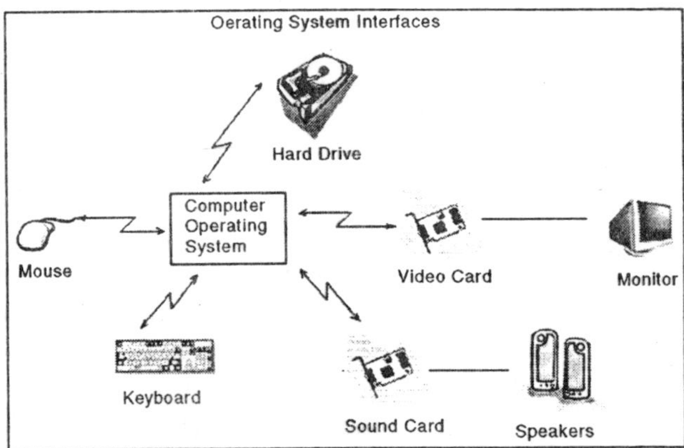

Other Operating System Functions

The operating system provides for several other functions including:

- System tools (programs) used to monitor computer performance, debug problems, or maintain parts of the system.
- A set of libraries or functions which programs may

use to perform specific tasks especially relating to interfacing with computer system components.

The operating system makes these interfacing functions along with its other functions operate smoothly and these functions are mostly transparent to the user.

Operating System Concerns

As mentioned previously, an operating system is a computer program. Operating systems are written by human programmers who make mistakes. Therefore there can be errors in the code even though there may be some testing before the product is released. Some companies have better software quality control and testing than others so you may notice varying levels of quality from operating system to operating system. Errors in operating systems cause three main types of problems:

System crashes and instabilities-These can happen due to a software bug typically in the operating system, although computer programs being run on the operating system can make the system more unstable or may even crash the system by themselves. This varies depending on the type of operating system. A system crash is the act of a system freezing and becoming unresponsive which would cause the user to need to reboot.

Security flaws-Some software errors leave a door open for the system to be broken into by unauthorized intruders. As these flaws are discovered, unauthorized intruders may try to use these to gain illegal access to your system. Patching these flaws often will help keep your computer system secure. Sometimes errors in the operating system will cause the computer not to work correctly with some peripheral devices such as printers.

NECESSITY OF OPERATING SYSTEM

The evolution of software and hardware technology has also determined big changes in current operating systems, therefore constant development of newer versions. The big problems are when users try to install older software apps on the newest operating systems or when the latest software version does not have the same functionalities as the older ones. There are many situations where incompatibilities get in the way of proper functionality and where they cannot be repaired.

The release of a new version of a certain software platform does not necessarily ask for an upgrade, because usually the latest versions of an application may require the presence of the newest operating system and the computer hardware might not support it. On the other hand, it is possible that the latest version of an application does not have the features of the previous version or shows a higher number of bugs than the older editions.

Web developers and generally programmers don't need the complexity of the graphical interface of a new operating system. Instead, what they are interested in is having their development tools functioning at full capacity on a compatible operating system.

Usually, software companies do not provide access to the older releases and if you reinstall the operating system, the software version you are used to work with might not be available anymore. As a consequence, the existence of older software databases is completely justified. These websites allow you to download both current versions of certain software apps, as well as various older versions. If you need to download older software editions, you could find them on existing databases, like OldVersion.com or OldApps.com for example. Even if the trend is to update your applications constantly, chances are that you use a software app that, on a new release, would also require a higher processor speed or came bundled with unnecessary plugins. It is recommended to carefully select the development tools you are working with in order to avoid frequent software updates or changes of the operating system.

NECESSITY WITH WINDOWS XP AND VISTA

Why do we now have to deal with registry problems on the new operating systems, Windows XP and Vista when we didn't have to worry about our registries so much with Windows 98 and 95? Doesn't it seem like a new, improved operating system would give us less problems.

In this article, we're going to discuss these things and see if we can make some sense of the irony that newer operating systems need more attention than older ones!

Hierarchal Structure

A Windows Operating System's registry is organized in a hierarchal structure exactly the same way your documents are arranged in your Word program. There is one major directory in your registry which would be the equivalent of your MyDocuments folder. Under that directory, there are many, many, many directories and each one of these directories may or may not have files contained in them.

Certainly, way down at the bottom in the very lowest directory there are lots of files. Now, multiply this MyDocuments structure by 5 and you have something that looks very much like a Windows Registry.

A Long Trip

Many times, the command you give at your keyboard or mouse spans across many registry directories and needs to travel back and forth through the registry to carry out one command. So, you can see that one little keystroke needs to wend its way through a lot of files before it is executed. When these files become disorganized the trip can become much longer.

Tangible Programs?

When we add a program or anything tangible to the computer, we add entries to the registry. When that tangible program is removed, many of the entries are left behind. These entries that are no longer needed are known as registry corruption. There are other forms of registry corruption, but this is a common one. It is important to note viruses, spyware, adware and malware are all tangible programs and most of us use spyware cleaners daily to remove these things from our computer. Since these parasites are a lot more prevalent now than they were in Windows 98's hay-day, and they are usually, a lot bigger and more complicated than they used to be, removing them leaves much more corruption nowadays than it used to. As time goes on, this registry corruption causes the computer to act up. The computer will probably slow down at first and after the corruption gets more plentiful, the computer is likely to suffer crashes.

So, What Do I Do?

What all this means is in today's world, we have many more tangible programs in the form of viruses/spyware and such that are being added and removed regularly from our operating system; probably thousands times more than 10 years ago. Add to this fact newer Windows operating systems and their tangible programs are way larger than the early Windows operating systems and their tangible programs and you can see how registry corruption has become a much bigger issue than it used to be! It is easy enough to take care of registry corruption. Just install a good registry cleaner on your computer and run it periodically and your computer will be fine! The best time to run a registry cleaner is after spyware and/or viruses have been removed. By the way, you do have a good spyware cleaner installed on your computer.

TYPES OF OPERATING SYSTEM

There are many types of operating systems. The most common is the Microsoft suite of operating systems. They include from most recent to the oldest:

WINDOWS XP PROFESSIONAL EDITION

- A version used by many businesses on workstations. It has the ability to become a member of a corporate domain.

WINDOWS XP HOME EDITION

- A lower cost version of Windows XP which is for home use only and should not be used at a business.

WINDOWS 2000

A better version of the Windows NT operating system which works well both at home and as a workstation at a business. It includes technologies which allow hardware to be automatically detected and other enhancements over Windows NT.

WINDOWS ME

- A upgraded version from windows 98 but it has been historically plagued with programming errors which may be frustrating for home users.

WINDOWS 98

- This was produced in two main versions. The first Windows 98 version was plagued with programming errors but the Windows 98 Second Edition which came out later was much better with many errors resolved.

WINDOWS NT

- A version of Windows made specifically for businesses offering better control over workstation capabilities to help network administrators.

WINDOWS 95

The first version of Windows after the older Windows 3.x versions offering a better interface and better library functions for programs.

There are other worthwhile types of operating systems not made by Microsoft. The greatest problem with these operating systems lies in the fact that not as many application programs are written for them. However if you can get the type of application programs you are looking for, one of the systems listed below may be a good choice.

UNIX

A system that has been around for many years and it is very stable. It is primary used to be a server rather than a workstation and should not be used by anyone who does not understand the system. It can be difficult to learn. Unix must normally run an a computer made by the same company that produces the software.

UNIX is a multi-user and multi-tasking operating system. It is very popular operating system used in microcomputers to Supercomputer. It provides the command line interface. It was developed at AT&T Bell Laboratories of USA. It was specially developed at AT&T for their own minicomputers. Microsoft Company of USA also developed a version of UNIX, which is named as XENIX. It is mainly used in network environment because it has powerful security features

LINUX

Linux is similar to Unix in operation but it is free. It also should not be used by anyone who does not understand the system and can be difficult to learn.

APPLE MACINTOSH

Most recent versions are based on Unix but it has a good graphical interface so it is both stable (does not crash often or have as many software problems as other systems may have) and easy to learn. One drawback to this system is that it can only be run on Apple produced Hardware.

SINGLE USER

Single-user allows one single user to login at a time. There is no user account database which makes the level of security low and so users cannot protect their files from being viewed, copied or deleted. Examples of this type are DOS and Windows 98.

List of single user operating system

- MS-DOS
- Amiga OS
- Classic Mac OS (System 1 through Mac OS 9).
- Windows 1.0
- Windows 2.0
- Windows 3.0

- Windows 3.1x
- Windows 95
- Windows 98
- Windows ME

MULTI-USER

The Multi-user has a user database account which states the right that users have on certain resources. They are more secure than the single user since access is limited. Example of this is UNIX

In computing, an operating system that enables several users to access centrally stored data and programs simultaneously over a network. Each user has a terminal, which may be local (connected directly to the computer) or remote (connected to the computer via a modem and a telephone line). The growth of the internet has given rise to new forms of application level multi-user systems. Multi-user online games and meeting software are examples of a growing range of collaboration and interaction systems.

Multi-access is usually achieved by time-sharing: the computer switches very rapidly between terminals and programs so that each user has sole use of the computer for only a fraction of a second but can work as if she or he had continuous access.

Multi-user systems are becoming increasingly common in the workplace, and have many advantages–such as enabling employees to refer to and update a shared corporate database. The travel industry uses a multi-user system to manage bookings of airline tickets; travel agents around the world using the system can access information on available seats as readily as an airline's own office.

Networked/Work Alone/

Stand alone are usually not connected to a network and thus cannot access networked resources. They are usually more secured than and remote users cannot log into the computer. A network operating System uses a standard communication protocol for UNIX networks and over the internet(we have the

TCP/IP). For Novell Netware internetwork Packet Exchange/ Sequenced Packet Exchange (IPX/SPX). They are less secure than Standalone and should be protected (most times by creating user accounts. More examples are Windows NT 5.0, Windows 98,

Multi-Tasking/single Tasking:

Multitasking allows one or more programs to run, at time. Each process is given a prioritised amount of time on the processor. Single-user allows are programs to run at a time. It is usually faster than multi-tasking Systems +as some time is taken to in switching in multi-user. But multi-user is more efficient as they allow other tasks to run when a task is not performing any operation. Single-users are more robust, as multi-programs are require to communicate with each other which can cause synchronization problems (deadlock).

Multi Processor/Single Processor: Some Operating System allows for more than one processor to use on the system. This allows more than one task to be run, at a time, on different processors. Windows NT/2000 supports multi processors (up to 4). Single Processor, Multitasking involves running each of the processor for a given time slice or a single processor where with multi processor, they can all run at the same.

TIME SHARING OF OPERATING SYSTEM

INTRODUCTION

The last dozen years of computer usage have seen great strides. In the early 1950's, the problems solved were largely in the construction and maintenance of hardware; in the mid-1950's, the usage languages were greatly improved with the advent of compilers; now in the early 1960's, we are in the midst of a third major modification to computer usage: the improvement of man-machine interaction by a process called time-sharing.

Much of the time-sharing philosophy, expressed in this paper, has been developed in conjunction with the work of an MIT preliminary study committee, chaired by H. Teager, which examined the long range computational needs of the Institute, and a subsequent MIT computer working committee, chaired by J. McCarthy. However, the views and conclusions expressed in this paper should be taken as solely those of the present authors.

Before proceeding further, it is best to give a more precise interpretation to time-sharing. One can mean using different parts of the hardware at the same time for different tasks, or one can mean several persons making use of the computer at the same time. The first meaning, often called multi programming, is oriented towards hardware efficiency in the sense of attempting to attain complete utilization of all components. The second meaning of time-sharing, which is meant here, is primarily concerned with the efficiency of persons trying to use a computer. Computer efficiency should still be considered but only in the perspective of the total system utility.

The motivation for time-shared computer usage arises out of the slow man-computer interaction rate presently possible with the bigger, more advanced computers. This rate has changed little (and has become worse in some cases) in the last decade of widespread computer use.

In part, this effect has been due to the fact that as elementary problems become mastered on the computer, more complex problems immediately become of interest.

As a result, larger and more complicated programs are written to take advantage of larger and faster computers. This process inevitably leads to more programming errors and a longer period of time required for debugging. Using current batch monitor techniques, as is done on most large computers, each program bug usually requires several hours to eliminate, if not a complete day. The only alternative presently available is for the programmer to attempt to debug directly at the computer, a process which is grossly wasteful of computer time and hampered seriously by the poor console communication usually available.

Even if a typewriter is the console, there are usually lacking the sophisticated query and response programs which are vitally necessary to allow effective interaction. Thus, what is desired is to drastically increase the rate of interaction between the programmer and the computer without large economic loss and also to make each interaction more meaningful by extensive and complex system programming to assist in the man-computer communication.

To solve these interaction problems we would like to have a computer made simultaneously available to many users in a manner somewhat like a telephone exchange. Each user would be able to use a console at his own pace and with-out concern for the activity of others using the system. This console could as a minimum be merely a typewriter but more ideally would contain an incrementally modifiable self-sustaining display. In any case, data transmission requirements should be such that it would be no major obstacle to have remote installation from the computer proper.

The basic technique for a time-sharing system is to have many persons simultaneously using the computer through typewriter consoles with a time-sharing supervisor program sequentially running each user program in a short burst or quantum of computation. This sequence, which in the most straightforward case is a simple round-robin, should occur often enough so that each user program which is kept in the high-speed memory is run for a quantum at least once during each approximate human reaction time (~.2 seconds). In this way, each user sees a computer fully responsive to even single key strokes each of which may require only trivial computation; in the non-trivial cases, the user sees a gradual reduction of the response time which is proportional to the complexity of the response calculation, the slowness of the computer, and the total number of active users.

It should be clear, however, that if there are n users actively requesting service at one time, each user will only see on the average 1/n of the effective computer speed. During the period of high interaction rates while debugging programs, this should not be a hindrance since ordinarily the required amount of computation needed for each debugging computer response is small compared to the ultimate production need.

Not only would such a time-sharing system improve the ability to program in the conventional manner by one or two orders of magnitude, but there would be opened up several new forms of computer usage.

There would be a gradual reformulation of many scientific and engineering applications so that programs containing decision trees which currently must be specified in advance would be eliminated and instead the particular decision branches would be specified only as needed. Another important area is that of teaching machines which, although frequently trivial computationally, could naturally exploit the consoles of a time-sharing system with the additional bonus that more elaborate and adaptive teaching programs could be used.

Finally, as attested by the many small business computers, there are numerous applications in business and in industry where it would be advantageous to have powerful computing facilities available at isolated locations with only the incremental capital investment of each console. But it is important to realise that even without the above and other new applications, the major advance in programming intimacy available from time-sharing would be of immediate value to computer installations in universities, research laboratories, and engineering firms where program debugging is a major problem.

Implementation Problems

As indicated, a straightforward plan for time-sharing is to execute user programs for small quantums of computation without priority in a simple round-robin; the strategy of time-sharing can be more complex as will be shown later, but the above simple scheme is an adequate solution. There are still many problems, however, some best solved by hardware, others affecting the programming conventions and practices. A few of the more obvious problems are summarized:

Hardware Problems

- Different user programs if simultaneously in core

memory may interfere with each other or the supervisor program so some form of memory protection mode should be available when operating user programs.

- The time-sharing supervisor may need at different times to run a particular program from several locations. (Loading relocation bits are no help since the supervisor does not know how to relocate the accumulator, etc.) Dynamic relocation of all memory accesses that pick up instructions or data words is one effective solution.
- Input-output equipment may be initiated by a user and read words in on another user program. A way to avoid this is to trap all input-output instructions issued by a user's program when operated in the memory protection mode.
- A large random-access back-up storage is desirable for general program storage files for all users. Present large capacity disc units appear to be adequate.
- The time-sharing supervisor must be able to interrupt a user's program after a quantum of computation. A program-initiated one-shot multivibrator which generates an interrupt a fixed time later is adequate.
- Large core memories (*e.g.* a million words) would ease the system programming complications immensely since the different active user programs as well as the frequently used system programs such as compilers, query programs, etc. could remain in core memory at all times.

Programming Problems

- The supervisor program must do automatic user usage charge accounting. In general, the user should be charged on the basis of a system usage formula or algorithm which should include such factors as computation time, amount of high-speed memory required, rent of secondary memory storage, etc.
- The supervisor program should coordinate all user

input-output since it is not desirable to require a user program to remain constantly in memory during input-output limited operations. In addition, the supervisor must coordinate all usage of the central, shared high-speed input-output units serving all users as well as the clocks, disc units, etc.

- The system programs available must be potent enough so that the user can think about his problem and not be hampered by coding details or typographical mistakes. Thus, compilers, query programs, post-mortem programs, loaders, and good editing programs are essential.
- As much as possible, the users should be allowed the maximum programming flexibility both in choices of language and in the absence of restrictions.

Usage Problems:

- Too large a computation or excessive typewriter output may be inadvertently requested so that a special termination signal should be available to the user.
- Since real-time is not computer usage-time, the supervisor must keep each user informed so that he can use his judgment regarding loops, etc.
- Computer processor, memory and tape malfunctions must be expected. Basic operational questions such as "Which program is running?" must be answerable and recovery procedures fully anticipated.

An Experimental Time-sharing System for the IBM 7090

Having briefly stated a desirable time-sharing performance, it is pertinent to ask what level of performance can be achieved with existent equipment. To begin to answer this question and to explore all the programming and operational aspects, an experimental time-sharing system has been developed. This system was originally written for the IBM 709 but has since been converted for use with the 7090 computer. The 7090 of the MIT Computation Center has, in addition to three channels with 19 tape units, a fourth channel with the standard Direct Data Connection. Attached to the Direct Data Connection is a real-time equipment buffer and control rack designed and built under the direction of H. Teager and his group. [This group is presently using another approach (ref.9) in developing a time-sharing system for the MIT 7090.] This rack has a variety of devices attached but the only ones required by the present systems are three flexowriter typewriters. Also installed on the 7090 are two special modifications (*i.e.* RPQ's): a standard 60 cycle accounting and interrupt clock, and a special mode which allows memory protection, dynamic relocation and trapping of all user attempts to initiate input-output instructions.

In the present system the time-sharing occurs between four users, three of whom are on-line each at a typewriter in a foreground system, and a fourth passive user of the background Fap-Mad-Madtran-BSS Monitor system similar to the Fortran-Fap-BSS Monitor System (FMS) used by most of the Center programmers and by many other 7090 installations.

Significant design features of the foreground system are:

- It allows the user to develop programs in languages compatible with the background system,
- Develop a private file of programs,
- Start debugging sessions at the state of the previous session, and
- Set his own pace with little waste of computer time.

Core storage is allocated such that all users operate in the upper 27,000 words with the time-sharing supervisor (TSS) permanently in the lower 5,000 words. To avoid memory allocation clashes, protect users from one another, and simplify the initial 709 system organization, only one user was kept in core memory at a time. However, with the special memory protection and relocation feature of the 7090, more sophisticated storage allocation procedures ar being implemented.

In any case, user swaps are minimized by using 2-channel overlapped magnetic tape reading and writing of the pertinent locations in the two user programs. The foreground system is organized around commands that each user can give on his typewriter and the user's private program files which presently (for want of a disc unit) are kept on a separate magnetic tape for each user.

For convenience the format of the private tape files is such that they are card images, have title cards with name and class designators and can be written or punched using the off-line equipment. (The latter feature also offers a crude form of large-scale input-output.) The magnetic tape requirements of the system are the seven tapes required for the normal functions of the background system, a system tape for the time-sharing supervisor that contains most of the command programs, and a private file tape and dump tape for each of the three foreground users.

The commands are typed by the user to the time-sharing supervisor (not to his own program) and thus can be initiated at any time regardless of the particular user program in memory. For similar coordination reasons, the supervisor handles all input-output of the foreground system typewriters. Commands are composed of segments separated by vertical strokes; the first segment is the command name and the remaining segments are parameters pertinent to the command. Each segment consists of the last 6 characters typed (starting with an implicit 6 blanks) so that spacing is an easy way to correct a typing mistake. A carriage return is the signal which initiates action on the command. Whenever a command is received by the supervisor, "WAIT", is typed back followed by "READY." when the command is completed. (The computer responses are always in the opposite colour from the user's typing.) While typing, an incomplete command line may be ignored by the "quit" sequence of a code delete signal followed by a carriage return. Similarly after a command is initiated, it may be abandoned if a "quit" sequence is given. In addition, during unwanted command typeouts, the command and output may be terminated by pushing a special "stop output" button.

The use of the foreground system is initiated whenever a typewriter user completes a command line and is placed in a waiting command queue. Upon completion of each quantum, the time-sharing supervisor gives top priority to initiating any waiting commands.

The system programs corresponding to most of the commands are kept on the special supervisor command system tape so that to avoid waste of computer time, the supervisor continues to operate the last user program until the desired command program on tape is positioned for reading. At this point, the last user is read out on his dump tape, the command program read in, placed in a working status and initiated as a new user program.

However, before starting the new user for a quantum of computation, the supervisor again checks for any waiting command of another user and if necessary begins the look-ahead positioning of the command system tape while operating the new user.

Whenever the waiting command queue is empty, the supervisor proceeds to execute a simple round-robin of those foreground user programs in the working status queue. Finally, if both these queues are empty, the background user program is brought in and run a quantum at a time until further foreground system actively develops.

Foreground user programs leave the working status queue by two means. If the program proceeds to completion, it can reenter the supervisor in a way which eliminates itself and places the user in dead status; alternatively, by a different entry the program can be placed in a dormant status (or be manually placed by the user executing a quit sequence). The dormant status differs from the dead status in that the user may still restart or examine his program.

User input-output is through each typewriter, and even though the supervisor has a few lines of buffer space available, it is possible to become input-output limited. Consequently, there is an additional input-output wait status, similar to the dormant, which the user is automatically placed in by the supervisor program whenever input-output delays develop. When buffers become near empty on output or near full on input, the user program is automatically returned to the working status; thus waste of computer time is avoided.

Commands

To clarify the scope of the foreground system and to indicate the basic tools avail-able to the user, a list of the important commands follows along with brief summaries of their operations:

- I Alpha
  - Alpha = arbitrary text treated as a comment.
- Login I alpha Ibeta
  - Alpha = user problem number
  - Beta = user programmer number
  - Should be given at beginning of each user's
  - session. Rewinds user's private file tape; clears time accounting records.
- Logout
  - Should be given at end of each user's session. Rewinds user's private file tape; punches on-line time accounting cards.
- Input
  - Sets user in input mode and initiates automatic generation of line numbers. The user types a card image per line according to a format appropriate for the programming language. (The supervisor collects these card images at the end of the user's private file tape.) When in the automatic input mode, the manual mode may be entered by giving an initial carriage return and typing the appropriate line number followed by I and line for as many lines as desired. To reenter the automatic mode, an initial carriage return is given.
- The manual mode allows the user to overwrite previous lines and to insert lines. (cf. File Command.)
  - Edit I alpha I beta
  - Alpha = title of file
  - Beta = class of file

The user is set in the automatic input mode with the designated file treated as initial input lines. The same conventions apply as to the input command.

- File | alpha | beta
  - Alpha = title to be given to file
  - Beta = class of language used during input

The created file will consist of the numbered input lines (*i.e.* those at the end of the user's private file tape) in sequence; in the case of duplicate line numbers, the last version will be used. The line numbers will be written as sequence numbers in the corresponding card images of the file.

For convenience the following editing conventions apply to input lines:

- An underline signifies the deletion of the previous characters of the line.
- A backspace signifies the deletion of the previous character in the field.

The following formats apply:

- *FAP:* Symbol, tab, operation, tab, variable field and comment.
- *MAD, MADTRAN, FORTRAN:* statement label, tab, statement. To place a character in the continuation column: statement label, tab, backspace, character, statement.
- *DATA:* Cols. 1-72.
- fap | alpha
  - Causes the file designated as alpha,fap to be translated by the FAP translator (assembler). Files alpha,symtb and alpha,bss are added to the user's private file tape giving the symbol table and the relocatable binary BSS form of the file.
- mad | alpha
  - Causes file alpha,mad to be translated by the MAD translator (compiler). File alpha,bss is created.
- madtrn | alpha
  - Causes file alpha,madtrn (*i.e.* a pseudo-Fortran language file) to be edited into an equivalent file alpha,mad (added to the user's file) and translation occurs as if the command mad|alpha had been given.

- load | alpha-1 | alpha-2 |... | alpha-n
  - Causes the consecutive loading of files alpha,bss (i=l,2...,n). An exception occurs if alpha-i = (libe), in which case file alpha-i+1,bss is searched as a library file for all subprograms still missing. (There can be further library files.)
- Use | alpha-1 | alpha-2 |... | alpha-n
  - This command is used whenever a load or previous use command notifies the user of an incomplete set of subprograms. Same alpha-i conventions as for load.
- Start | alpha | beta
  - Starts the program setup by the load and use commands (or a dormant program) after first positioning the user private file tape in front of the title card for file alpha,beta. (If beta is not given, a class of data is assumed; if both alpha and beta are not given, no tape movement occurs and the program is started.)
- pm | alpha
  - Alpha = "lights", "stomap", or the usual format of the standard Center post-mortem (F2PM) request: subprogram name | loc-1 | loc-2 | mode | direction where mode and direction are optional.

Produces post-mortem of user's dormant program according to request specified by alpha. (*E.g.* matrix | 5 | 209 | flo | rev will cause to be printed on the user's typewriter the contents of subprogram "matrix" from relative locations 5 to 209 in floating point form and in reverse sequence.)

- Skippm
  - Used if a pm command is "quit" during output and the previous program interruption is to be restarted.
- listf
  - Types out list of all file titles on user's private file tape.
- Printf | alpha | beta | gamma

- Types out file alpha,beta starting at line number gamma. If gamma is omitted, the initial line is assumed. Whenever the user's output buffer fills, the command program goes into an I/O wait status allowing other users to time-share until the buffer needs refilling.

- xdump I alpha Ibeta
  - Creates file alpha,beta (if beta omitted, xdump assumed) on user's private file tape consisting of the complete state of the user's last dormant program.
- Xundump I alpha I beta
  - Inverse of xdump command in that it resets file alpha,beta as the user's program, starting it where it last left off.

Although experience with the system to date is quite limited, first indications are that programmers would readily use such a system if it were generally available, It is useful to ask, now that there is some operating experience with the system, what observations can be made. [Note: Operating experience was initially gained using the system on the 709 computer; due to equipment conversion difficulties, it was not possible to use the system on the logically equivalent 7090 computer by May 3.] An immediate comment is that once a user gets accustomed to computer response, delays of even a fraction of a minute are exasperatingly long, an effect analogous to conversing with a slow-speaking person. Similarly, the requirement that a complete typewritten line rather than each character be the minimum unit of man-computer communication is an inhibiting factor in the sense that a press-to-talk radio-telephone conversation is more stilted than that of an ordinary telephone.

Since maintaining a rapid computer response on a character by character basis requires at least a vestigial response program in core memory at all times, the straightforward solution within the present system is to have more core memory available. At the very least, an extra bank of memory for the time-sharing supervisor would ease compatibility problems with programs already written for 32,000 word 7090's.

For reasons of expediency, the weakest portions of the present system are the conventions for input, editing of user files, and the degree of rapid interaction and intimacy possible while debugging. Since to a large extent these areas involve the taste, habits, and psychology of the users, it is felt that proper solutions will require considerable experimentation and pragmatic evaluation; it is also clear that these areas cannot be treated in the abstract for the programming languages used will influence greatly the appropriate techniques. A greater use of symbolic referencing for locations, program names and variables is certainly desired; symbolic post-mortem programs, trace programs, and before-and-after differential dump programs should play useful roles in the debugging procedures.

In the design of the present system, great care went into making each user independent of the other users. However, it would be a useful extension of the system if this were not always the case. In particular, when several consoles are used in a computer controlled group such as in management or war games, in group behaviour studies, or possibly in teaching machines, it would be desirable to have all the consoles communicating with a single program.

Another area for further improvement within the present system is that of file maintenance, since the presently used tape units are a hindrance to the easy deletion of user program files. Disc units will be of help in this area as well as with the problem of consolidating and scheduling large-scale central input-output generated by the many console users.

Finally, it is felt that it would be desirable to have the distinction between the foreground and background systems eliminated. The present-day computer operator would assume the role of a stand-in for the background users, using an operator console much like the other user consoles in the system, mounting and demounting magnetic tapes as requested by the supervisor, receiving instructions to read card decks into the central disc unit, etc.

Similarly the foreground user, when satisfied with his program, would by means of his console and the supervisor program enter his program into the queue of production background work to be performed. With these procedures implemented the distinction of whether one is time-sharing or not would vanish and the computer user would be free to choose in an interchangeable way that mode of operation which he found more suitable at a particular time.

A Multi-Level Scheduling Algorithm

Regardless of whether one has a million word core memory or a 32,000 word memory as currently exists on the 7090, one is inevitably faced with the problem of system saturation where the total size of active user programs exceeds that of the high-speed memory or there are too many active user programs to maintain an adequate response at each user console.

These conditions can easily arise with even a few users if some of the user programs are excessive in size or in time requirements. The predicament can be alleviated if it is assumed that a good design for the system is to have a saturation procedure which gives graceful degradation of the response time and effective real-time computation speed of the large and long-running users.

To show the general problem, Figure qualitatively gives the user service as a function of n, the number of active users. This service parameter might be either of the two key factors: computer response time or n times the real-time computation speed. In either case there is some critical number of active users, N, representing the effective user capacity, which causes saturation.

If the strategy near saturation is to execute the simple round-robin of all users, then there is an abrupt collapse of service due to the sudden onset of the large amount of time required to swap programs in-and-out of the secondary memory such as a disc or drum unit. Of course, Figure is quite qualitative since it depends critically on the spectrum of user program sizes as well as the spectrum of user operating times.

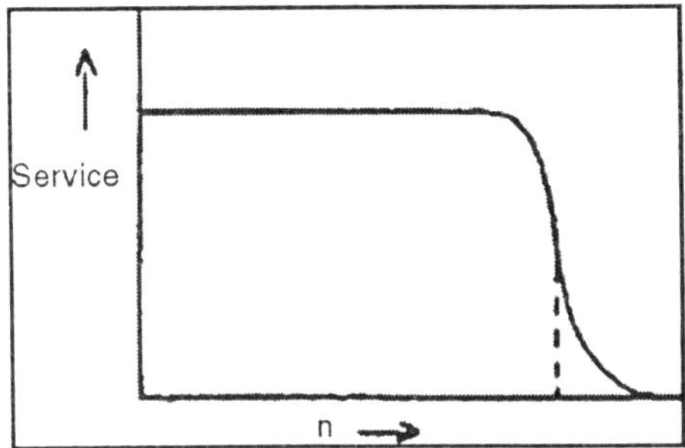

Fig. Service vs. Number of Active Users

To illustrate the strategy that can be employed to improve the saturation performance of a time-sharing system, a multi-level scheduling algorithm is presented. This algorithm also can be analysed to give broad bounds on the system performance.

The basis of the multi-level scheduling algorithm is to assign each user program as it enters the system to be run (or completes a response to a user) to an ell-th level priority queue. Programs are initially entered into a level ell-sub-0, corresponding to their size such that

$$\ell_o = \left[\log_2 \left(\left[\frac{w_p}{w_q} \right] + 1 \right) \right]$$

where w-sub-p is the number of words in the program, w-sub-q is the number of words which can be transmitted in and out of the high-speed memory from the secondary memory in the time of one quantum, q, and the bracket indicates "the integral part of".

Ordinarily the time of a quantum, being the basic time unit, should be as small as possible without excessive overhead losses when the supervisor switches from one program in high-speed memory to another.

The process starts with the time-sharing supervisor operating the program at the head of the lowest level occupied queue, ell, for up to 2**ell quanta of time and then if the program is not completed (*i.e.* has not made a response to the user) placing it at the end of the ell+1 level queue. If there are no programs entering the system at levels lower than ell, this process proceeds until the queue at level ell is exhausted; the process is then iteratively begun again at level ell+1, where now each program is run for 2**(ell+1) quanta of time.

If during the execution of the 2**ell quanta of a program at level ell, a lower level, ell-prime, becomes occupied, the current user is replaced at the head of the ell-th queue and the process is reinitiated at level ell-prime.

Similarly, if a program of size w-sub-p at level ell, during operation requests a change in memory size from the time-sharing supervisor, then the enlarged (or reduced) version of the program should be placed at the end of the ell-double-prime queue where

$$\ell'' = \ell + \left[\log_2 \left(\left[\frac{w_p''}{w_p} \right] \right) \right]$$

Again the process is re-initiated with the head-of-the-queue user at the lowest occupied level of ell-prime.

Several important conclusions can be drawn from the above algorithm which allow the performance of the system to be bounded.

Computational Efficiency

- Because a program is always operated for a time greater than or equal to the swap time (*i.e.* the time required to move the program in and out of secondary memory), it follows that the computational efficiency never falls below one-half. (Clearly, this fraction is adjustable in the formula for the initial level, ell-0.) An alternative way of viewing this bound is to say that the real-time computing speed available to one out of n active users is no worse than if there were 2n active users all of whose programs were in the high-speed memory.

Response Time

- If the maximum number of active users is N, then

an individual user of a given program size can be guaranteed a response time,

$$t_r \le 2Nq\left(\left[\frac{w_p{}''}{w_p}\right]+1\right)$$

since the worst case occurs when all competing user programs are at the same level. Conversely, if t-sub-r is a guaranteed response of arbitrary value and the largest size of program is assumed, then the maximum permissible number of active users is bounded.

Long Runs

- The relative swap time on long runs can be made vanishingly small. This conclusion follows since the longer a program is run, the higher the level number it cascades to with a correspondingly smaller relative swap time. It is an important feature of the algorithm that long runs must in effect prove they are long so that programs which have an unexpected demise are detected quickly. In order that there be a finite number of levels, a maximum level number, L, can be established such that the asymptotic swap overhead is some arbitrarily small percentage, p:

$$L = \left[\log_2\left(\frac{\left\lfloor w_{p\max}\right\rfloor}{pw_q}\right)+1\right]$$

where w-sub-pmax is the size of the largest possible program.

Multi-level vs. Single-level Response Times

- The response time for programs of equal size, entering the system at the same time, and being run for multiple quanta, is no worse than approximately twice the response-time occurring in a single quanta round-robin procedure. If there are n equal sized programs started in a queue at level 1, then the worst case is that of the end-of-the-queue program which is ready to respond at the very first quantum run at the ell+j level. Using the multi-level algorithm, the total delay for the end-of-the-queue program is by virtue of the geometric series of quanta:

$$T_m \sim q2^{\ell}\left\{n(2^J - 1) + (n-1)2^J\right\}$$

Since the end-of-the-queue user has computed for a time of (2**ell)*((2**j)-1) quanta, the equivalent single-level round-robin delay before a response is:

$$T_s \sim q2^{\ell}\left\{n(2^J - 1)\right\}.$$

Hence,

$$\frac{T_m}{T_s} \sim 1 + \left(\frac{n-1}{n}\right)\left(\frac{2^J}{2^J - 1}\right) \sim 2$$

and the assertion is shown. It should be noted that the above conditions, where program swap times are omitted, which are pertinent when all programs remain in high-speed memory, are the least favourable for the multi-level algorithm; if swap times are included in the above analysis, the ratio of (T-sub-m/T-sub-s) can only become smaller and may become much less than unity. By a similar analysis it is easy to show that even in the unfavourable case where there are no program swaps, head-of-the-queue programs that terminate just as the quanta are completed receive under the multi-level algorithm a response which is twice as fast as that under the single-level round-robin (*i.e.* (T-sub-m/T-sub-s) = 1/2).

Highest Serviced Level

- In the multi-level algorithm the level classification procedure for programs is entirely automatic, depending on performance and program size rather than on the declarations (or hopes) of each user. As a user taxes the system, the degradation of service occurs progressively starting with the higher level users of either large or long-running programs; however, at some level no user programs may be run because of too many active users at lower levels. To determine a bound on this cut-off point we consider N active users at level ell each running 2**ell quanta, terminating, and reentering the system again at level ell at a user response time, t-sub-u, later. If there is to be no service at level ell+1, then the computing time, Nq(2**ell), must be greater than or equal to t-sub-u. Thus the guaranteed active levels, are given by the relation:

$$\ell_a \leq \left[\log_2 \left(\frac{t_u}{Nq} \right) \right]$$

In the limit, t-sub-u could be as small as a minimum user reaction time (~.2 sec.), but the expected value would be several orders of magnitude greater as a result of the statistics of a large number of users.

The multi-level algorithm as formulated above makes no explicit consideration of the seek or latency time required before transmission of programs to and from disc or drum units when they are used as the secondary memory, (although formally the factor w-sub-q could contain an average figure for these times).

One simple modification to the algorithm which usually avoids wasting the seek or latency time is to continue to operate the last user program for as many quanta as are required to ready the swap of the new user with the least priority user; since ordinarily only the higher level number programs would be forced out into the secondary memory, the extended quanta of operation of the old user while seeking the new user should be but a minor distortion of the basic algorithm.

Further complexities are possible when the hardware is appropriate. In computers with input-output channels and low transmission rates to and from secondary memory, it is possible to overlap the reading and writing of the new and old users in and out of high-speed memory while operating the current user. The effect is equivalent to using a drum giving 100% multiplexor usage but there are two liabilities, namely, no individual user can utilize all the available user memory space and the look-ahead procedure breaks down whenever am unanticipated scheduling change occurs (*e.g.* a program terminates or a higher-priority user program is initiated).

Complexity is also possible in storage allocation but certainly an elementary procedure and a desirable one with a low-transmission rate secondary memory is to consolidate in a single block all high-priority user programs whenever sufficient fragmentary unused memory space is available to read in a new user program. Such a procedure is indicated in the flow diagram of the multi-level scheduling algorithm which is given as Figure.

It should also be noted that Figure only accounts for the scheduling of programs in a working status and still does not take into account the storage allocation of programs which are in a dormant (or input-output wait status). One systematic method of handling this case is to modify the scheduling algorithm so that programs which become dormant at level ell are entered into the queue at level ell+1.

The scheduling algorithm proceeds as before with the dormant programs continuing to cascade but not operating when they reached the head of a queue. Whenever a program must be removed from high-speed memory, a program is selected from the end-of-the-queue of the highest occupied level number.

Finally, it is illuminating to apply the multi-level scheduling algorithm bounds to the contemporary IBM 7090.

The following approximate values are obtained:

```
q = 16 m.s. (Based on 1% Switching Overhead)
wq= 120 Words (Based on One IBM 1301 Model
    2 Disc Unit Without Sock or Latency
    Times Included
tr <  8Nfsec. Based on Programs of (32k) f Words)
la <  Log2 (1000/N) (Based on  tu = 16 Sec.)
lo <  8 (Based on a maximum Program Size of
      32k Words)
```

Using the arbitrary criteria that programs up to the

maximum size of 32,000 words should always get some service, which is to say that max ell-sub-a = max ell-sub-0, we deduce as a conservative estimate that N can be 4 and that at worst the response time for a trivial reply will be 32 seconds.

The small value of N arrived at is a direct consequence of the small value of w-sub-q that results from the slow disc word transmission rate.

This rate is only 3.3% of the maximum core memory multiplexor rate. It is of interest that using high-capacity high-speed drums of current design such as in the Sage System or in the IBM Sabre System it would be possible to attain nearly 100% multiplexor utilization and thus multiply w-sub-q by a factor of 30.

It immediately follows that user response times equivalent to those given above with the disc unit would be given to 30 tines as many persons or to 120 users; the total computational capacity, however, would not change. In any case, considerable caution should be used with capacity and computer response time estimates since they are critically dependent upon the distribution functions for the user response time, t-sub-u, and the user program size, and the computational capacity requested by each user.

Past experience using conventional programming systems is of little assistance because these distribution functions will depend very strongly upon the programming systems made available to the time-sharing users as well as upon the user habit patterns which will gradually evolve.

In conclusion, it is clear that contemporary computers and hardware are sufficient to allow moderate performance time-sharing for a limited number of users. There are several problems which can be solved by careful hardware design, but there are also a large number of intricate system programs which must be written before one has an adequate time-sharing system. An import-ant aspect of any future time-shared computer is that until the system programming is completed, especially the critical time-sharing supervisor, the computer is completely worthless. Thus, it is essential for future system design and imple-mentation that all aspects of time-sharing system problems be explored and understood in prototype form on present computers so that major advances in computer organization and usage can be made.

REMINISCENCES ON THE HISTORY OF TIME SHARING

Remember thinking about time-sharing about the time of my first contact with computers and being surprised that this wasn't the goal of IBM and all the other manufacturers and users of computers. This might have been around 1955.

By time-sharing, I meant an operating system that permits each user of a computer to behave as though he were in sole control of a computer, not necessarily identical with the machine on which the operating system is running. Christopher Strachey may well have been correct in saying in his letter to Donald Knuth that the term was already in use for time-sharing among programs written to run together. This idea had already been used in the SAGE system. I don't know how this kind of time-sharing was implemented in SAGE. Did each program have to be sure to return to an input polling program or were there interrupts? Who invented interrupts anyway? I thought of them, but I don't believe I mentioned the idea to anyone before I heard of them from other sources.

My first attempts to do something about time-sharing was in the Fall of 1957 when I came to the M.I.T. Computation Center on a Sloan Foundation fellowship from Dartmouth College. It was immediately clear to me that the time-sharing the IBM 704 would require some kind of interrupt system. I was very shy of proposing hardware modifications, especially as I didn't understand electronics well enough to read the logic diagrams. Therefore, I proposed the minimal hardware modification I could think of. This involved installing a relay so that the 704 could be put into trapping mode by an external signal. It was also proposed to connect the sense switches on the ccnsole in parallel with relays that could be operated by a Flexowriter (a kind of teletype based on an IBM typewriter).

When the machine went into trapping mode, an interrupt to a fixed location would occur the next time the machine attempted to execute a jump instruction (then called a transfer). The interrupt would occur when the Flexowriter had set up a character in a relay buffer. The interrupt program would then read the character from the sense switches into a buffer, test whether the buffer was full, and if not return to the interrupted program. If the buffer was full, the program would store the current program on the drum and read in a program to deal with the buffer. It was agreed (I think I talked to Dean Arden only.) to install the equipment, and I believe that permission was obtained from IBM to modify the computer. The connector to be installed in the computer was obtained.

However, at this time we heard about the "real time package" for the IBM 704. This RPQ (request for price quotation was IBM jargon for a modification to the computer whose price wasn't guaranteed), which rented for $2,500 per month had been developed at the request of Boeing for the purpose of allowing the 704 to accept information from a wind tunnel. Some element of ordinary time-sharing would have been involved, but we did not seek contact with Boeing. Anyway it was agreed that the real time package, which involved the possibility of interrupting after any instruction, would be much better than merely putting the machine in trapping mode. Therefore we undertook to beg IBM for the real time package. IBM's initial reaction was favourable, but nevertheless it took a long time to get the real time package-perhaps a year, perhaps two.

It was then agreed that someone, perhaps Arnold Siegel, would design the hardware to connect one Flexowriter to the computer, and later an installation with three would be designed. Siegel designed and build the equipment, the operating system was suitably modified (I don't remember by whom), and demonstration of on-line LISP was held for a meeting of the M.I.T. Industrial Affiliates. This demonstration, which I planned and carried out, had the audience in a fourth floor lecture room and me in the computer room and a rented closed circuit TV system.

Steve Russell, who worked for me, organized the practical details including a rehearsal. This demonstration was called time-stealing, and was regarded as a mere prelude to proper time-sharing. It involved a fixed program in the bottom of memory that collected characters from the Flexowriter in a buffer while an ordinary batch job was running. It was only after each job was run that a job that would deal with the characters typed in would be read in from the drum. This job would do what it could until more input was wanted and would then let the operating system go back to the batch stream. This worked for the demonstration, because at certain hours, the M.I.T. Computation Center operated at certain hours a batch stream with a time limit of one minute on any job.

Around the time of this demonstration, Herbert Teager came to M.I.T. as an assistant professor of Electrical Engineering and expressed interest in the time-sharing project. Some of the ideas of time-sharing overlapped some ideas he had had while on his previous job, but I don't remember what they were. Philip Morse, the Director of the Computation Center, asked me if I was agreeable to turning over the time-sharing project to Teager, since artificial intelligence was my main interest. I agreed to this, and Teager undertook to design the three Flexowriter system. I'm not sure it was ever completed. There was a proposal for support for time-sharing submitted to NSF and money was obtained. I don't remember whether this preceded Teager, and I don't remember what part I had in preparing it or whether he did it after he came. This should be an important document, because it will contain that year's conception of and rationale for time-sharing.

Besides that, IBM was persuaded to make substantial modifications to the IBM 7090 to be installed at the M.I.T. Computation Center. These included memory protection and relocation and an additional 32,768 words of memory for the time-sharing system. Teager was the main specifier of these modifications. I remember my surprise when IBM agreed to his proposals. I had supposed that relocation and memory protection would greatly slow the addressing of the computer, but this turned out not to be the case.

Teager's plans for time-sharing were ambitious and, it seemed to many of us, vague. Therefore, Corbato undertook an "interim" solution using some of the support that had been obtained from NSF for time-sharing work. This system was demonstrated some time in 1962, but it wasn't put into regular operation. That wasn't really possible until ARPA support for Project MAC permitted buying a separate IBM 7090.

Around 1960 I began to consult at BBN on artificial intelligence and explained my ideas about time-sharing to Ed Fredkin and J. C. R. Licklider. Fredkin, to my surprise, proposed that time-sharing was feasible on the PDP-1 computer. This was D.E.C.'s first computer, and BBN had the prototype. Fredkin designed the architecture of an interrupt system and designed a control system for the drum to permit it to be used in a very efficient swapping mode.

He convinced Ben Gurley, the chief engineer for D.E.C. to build this equipment. It was planned to ask NIH for support, because of potential medical applications of time-sharing computers, but before the proposal could even be written, Fredkin left BBN. I took technical charge of the project as a one-day-a-week consultant, and Sheldon Boilen was hired to do the programming. I redesigned the memory extension system proposed by D.E.C. and persuaded them to build the modified system instead of the two systems they were offering, but fortunately hadn't built. I also supervised Boilen.

Shortly after this project was undertaken, D.E.C. decided to give a PDP-1 to the M.I.T. Electrical Engineering Department. Under the leadership of Jack Dennis, this computer was installed in the same room as the TX-0 experimental transistorized computer that had been retired from Lincoln Laboratory when TX-2 was built. Dennis and his students undertook to make a time-sharing system for it. The equipment was similar, but they were given less memory than the BBN project had. There wasn't much collaboration.

My recollection is that the BBN project was finished first in the summer of 1962, but perhaps Corbato remembers earlier demonstrations of CTSS. I left for Stanford in the Fall of 1962, and I hadn't seen CTSS, and I believe I hadn't seen Dennis's system operate either. BBN didn't operate the first system and didn't even fix the bugs. They had few computer users and were content to continue the system whereby users signed up for the whole computer. They did undertake a much larger follow-on project involving a time-shared PDP-1 that was installed in Massachusetts General Hospital, where it was not a success. The computer was inadequate, there were hardware and software bugs, and there was a lack of application programs, but mainly the project was premature.

At the same time that CTSS, the BBN system, and the EE Department systems were being developed, M.I.T. had started to plan for a next generation computer system. The management of M.I.T. evidently started this as an ordinary university planning exercise and appointed a high level committee consisting of Philip Morse, Albert Hill and Robert Fano to supervise the effort. However, the actual computer scientists were persuaded that a revolution in the way computers were used-to time-sharing-was called for. The lower level committee was chaired by Teager, but after his ideas clashed with those of everyone else, the committee was reconstituted with me as chairman.

The disagreement centered around how ambitious to be and whether to go for an interim solution. Teager wanted to be very ambitious, but the rest of us thought his ideas were vague, and he wanted M.I.T. to acquire an IBM 7030 (Stretch) computer as an interim solution. As it turned out, acquiring a Stretch would have been a good idea.

Our second report to M.I.T. proposed that M.I.T. send out a request for proposals to computer manufacturers. On the basis of the responses, we would then ask the Government for the money. The RFP was written, but M.I.T. stalled perhaps for two reasons. The first reason was that our initial cost estimates were very large for reasons of conservatism. Secondly, IBM asked M.I.T. to wait saying that they would make a proposal to meet M.I.T.'s needs at little or no cost. Unfortunately, the 360 design took longer than IBM management expected, and along about that time, relations between M.I.T. and IBM became very strained because of the patent lawsuit about the invention of magnetic core memory. As part of the stall, President Stratton proposed a new study with a more thorough market survey to establish the demand for time-sharing among M.I.T. computer users. I regarded this as analogous to trying to establish the need for steam shovels by market surveys among ditch diggers and didn't want to do it. About this time George Forsythe invited me to come back to Stanford with the intention of building a Computer Science Department, and I was happy to return to California.

In all this, there wasn't much publication. I wrote a memo to Morse dated January 1, 1959 proposing that we time-share our expected "transistorized IBM 709". It has been suggested that the date was in error and should have been 1960. I don't remember now, but I believe that if the memo had been written at the end of 1959, it would have referred to the 7090, because that name was by then current. Most of my argumentation for time-sharing was oral, and when I complained about Fano and Corbato crediting Strachey with time-sharing in their 1966 Scientific American article, Corbato was surprised to find my 1959 memo in the files.

Teager and I prepared a joint abstract for an ACM meeting shortly after he arrived, and I gave a lecture in an M.I.T series called Management and the Computer of the Future. In this lecture I referred to Strachey's paper "Time-sharing of large fast computers" given at the 1959 IFIP Congress in Paris. I had read the paper carelessly, and supposed he meant the same thing as I did. As he subsequently pointed out, he meant something quite different that did not involve a large number of users, each behaving as though he had a machine to himself.

As I recall, he mainly referred to fixed programs, some of which were compute bound and some input-output bound. He did mention debugging as one of the time-shared activities, but I believe his concept involved one person debugging while the other jobs were of the conventional sort.

My 1959 memo advertised that users generally would get the advantage of on-line debugging. However, it said nothing about how many terminals would be required and where they would be located. I believe I imagined them to be numerous and in the users' offices, but I cannot be sure. Referring to an "exchange" suggests that I had in mind many terminals. I cannot now imagine what the effect was on the reader of my failure to be explicit about this point. I'm afraid I was trying to minimize the difficulty of the project. The major technical error of my 1959 ideas was an underestimation of the computer capacity required for time-sharing. I still don't understand where all the computer time goes in time-sharing installations, and neither does anyone else.

Besides M.I.T.'s NSF proposal, there ought to be some letters to IBM and perhaps some IBM internal documents about the proposal, since they put more than a million dollars worth of equipment into it. Gordon Bell discusses D.E.C.'s taking up time-sharing in Bell and Newell book, but I don't recall that they discuss Ben Gurley's role. Fredkin and perhaps Alan Kotok would know about that.

After I came to Stanford in 1962, I organized another PDP-1 time-sharing project. This was the first time-sharing system based on display terminals. It was used until 1969 or 1970 for Suppes's work on computer aided instruction.

DISTRIBUTED REAL-TIME

Abstract. Modern parallel and distributed computing solutions are often built onto a "middleware" software layer providing a higher and common level of service between computational nodes. Harness is an adaptable, plugin-based middleware framework for parallel and distributed computing. This paper reports recent research and development results of using Harness for real-time distributed computing applications in the context of an industrial environment with the needs to perform several safety critical tasks.

The presented work exploits the modular architecture of Harness in conjunction with a lightweight threaded implementation to resolve several real-time issues by adding three new Harness plug-ins to provide a prioritized lightweight execution environment, low latency communication facilities, and local timestamped event logging.Key words: Distributed Computing, Middleware, Real-Time, Harness, Plugin

INTDRODUCTION

Parallel and distributed computing solutions provide the means for computational performance for High-End Computing (HEC) applications beyond the limits of single processor technology. The actual implementation of complex parallel and distributed software systems can be enormously eased by the adoption of an intermediate software layer, a "middleware". A middleware is defined as a connectivity software that consists of a set of enabling services that allow multiple processes running on one or more machines to interact across a network."

A very specific topic of HEC applications is real-time computation. The term real-time pertains to computer applications whose correctness depends not only on results, but also on the time at which results are delivered. A real-time system (RTS) is a computer system that is able to run real-time applications and fulfill their requirements in a deterministic fashion. Thus, when defining a real-time system, we actually define requirements about its response time, meaning with this average value or the tail distribution of it. Distributed real-time systems development requires a well suited real-time oriented middleware as a supporting layer.

PREVIOUS WORK

Traditional solutions in distributed real-time environments refer to Parallel Virtual Machine (PVM) and Message Passing Interface (MPI) libraries. Although PVM is a solid and simple solution, its process-based architecture is a little outdated, and the service set does not fit well into an industrial context. MPI is not well suited when compared to modern middlewares because it provides just a communication abstraction. More recent and rich products include Real-Time Innovations Data Distribution Service (RTI DDS, formerly NDDS) and the Adaptive Communication Environment (ACE) Object Request Broker (ORB) in conjunction with TAO [5].

RTI DDS provides a communication abstraction data-centric layer that realises a publish-subscribe semantic. It is a performing and well-featured product, which offers real-time oriented features, like a fine tunable QoS performance level, and an efficient low-latency implementation based on an open standard from OMG group [6]. However, it is especially suited for dynamically changing network topologies and to cover reliability issues. Moreover, it is a commercial (and thus closed) product, while in the industrial context being able to lower costs and customise the product at will is of key importance.

The ACE ORB, on the other hand, is an open source project that implements the Object Request Broker semantic. TAO is a very complex and complete middleware, but it is designed around the ORB specification and is meant to be used with the existing plethora of CORBA services. This means that the internal architecture of TAO involves many different components. Moreover, its service-oriented nature makes it not easily tailorable for embedded applications. The approach described in this paper is more simple and streamlined, it avoids the role of the broker node, and it integrates nicely with the Harness framework.

MODERN MIDDLEWARE

Our effort focuses on an emerging technology in this field, the Harness project, a joint development effort between the Oak Ridge National Laboratory (ORNL), the University of Tennessee, and Emory University. Harness is a distributed, reconfigurable and heterogeneous computing environment that supports dynamically adaptable parallel and distributed applications. The unique feature of Harness relies on its almost total level of pluggability.

The aim is to build a virtual environment that can dynamically change (almost) anything at runtime. In this highly adaptable framework, several parallel and distributed user applications can reside, all executed on top of its distributed virtual machine (DVM) and runtime environment (RTE) concepts, a PVM successor. Harness runs a RTE on every computational unit as the "shell" in which it hosts the user applications and the resource management routines that belong to the distributed environment. Every RTE is realised by a Harness kernel, the core of the unit, which is capable of loading and unloading plugin modules and consists of a communication module, a module dedicated to process control, and a module dedicated to resource management, plus possibly a number of other plugins. Several Harness prototypes have been developed, in Java and C. The work presented in this paper focuses on the C variant developed at ORNL, which runs on GNU/Linux.

Its design focuses on a lightweight and pluggable middleware layer with a Harness kernel running as a Linux daemon process. The kernel performs process management, thread pool management, and dynamic plugin loading/ unloading. The process management module can fork and execute a user application, and provides means for passing arguments, sending input, and retrieving output for these external processes. The thread pool is the heart of the lightweight execution environment provided by Harness. It creates a set of working threads that keep trying to empty a job queue data structure. It provides interfaces for adding a new job to the queue with proper arguments and cleanup function in case of thread cancellation. The plugin loader builds on top of the Linux dynamic library loader, and provides interfaces for loading/unloading modules and publishing their functionalities to the whole runtime environment.

The communication facilities are effectively provided through RMIX (Remote Method Interface eXtensible). RMIX is a dynamic, heterogeneous, reconfigurable communication framework that allows software components to communicate using various RMI/RPC protocols by employing provider plugins in order to support different protocol stacks. RMIX emulates the Java RMI structure, allowing components to remotely call methods, retrieve the output, and export locally available methods.

EXISTING REAL-TIME ISSUES

Within the middleware definition we can outline a set of requirements expected from such a software. The first assumption we make Is that the services on top of which the middleware is built retain themselves realtime capabilities. We cannot avoid this assumption because the aim is to work on a middleware that is a relatively high-level software, thus built on top of a set of services, and the performances of the resulting system are bound to those of that services. Secondly, remote services have to be designed without concurrency issues. In this context, the meaning of concurrency is twofold:

Call Concurrency: Simultaneous access of the same service offered by the same computational resource Service concurrency: simultaneous access of different services offered by the same computational resource A real-time middleware has to guarantee both kinds of concurrency support in order to be seamlessly scalable with the growth of the execution flows. Finally, services have to be locally executed without scheduling issues by providing a proper priority-aware execution environment. The hosted application should be able to run a number of real-time tasks that are expected to be scheduled in a deterministic manner.

In order to address all these issues, three Harness plugins have been developed:

- A plugin to provide a prioritized lightweight execution environment
- A plugin for low latency communication facilities
- A plugin to support local timestamped event logging

DEVELOPED PLUGINS

The aim of our work is exploiting the pluggable nature of Harness in order to implement a set of services enabling the development and execution of successful real-time applications.

Real-Time Thread Pools

The lightweight execution environment provided by Harness is designed for great efficiency, but lacks in direct support for operating system scheduler directives. The thread pool solution is indeed a lightweight solution for job processing, but lacks the ability to exploit the preemptability of the latest Linux kernels. POSIX threads, like processes, can control their scheduling priority and contention scope, which can be set to either process or system scope.

By using the latter it is possible to grant absolute schedule priority to the thread. Therefore, the first developed plugin focuses on providing a greater level of control on thread pools to user applications. It allows to define an arbitrary number of job classes, and for each level to specify the scheduler policy and priority of the related thread pool. Each pool tries to empty a different job queue.

If not otherwise specified, the plugin is configured by default to create three pools of threads, in addition to the original one, it adds two pools entirely made of threads with real-time scheduling properties. The first additional thread pool adopts a round-robin scheduling algorithm with priority p1. The second additional thread pool uses a first-in/first-out scheduling algorithm with priority p2, where p1 < p2 and global contention scope hold. This way we scaled the priority of the executing threads from one to three levels, allowing the application executing on top of Harness to have control over the scheduling of its tasks. The default configuration should provide more than enough means for executing real-time applications without worries for scheduling issues. If a more fine-grained solution is needed, it is still possible to explicitly specify the pool parameters.

Real-Time Remote Procedure Calls

The second plugin faces a problem of the RMIX framework in its actual form. The standard provider plugin builds on top of the TCP transport layer. This solution, while providing a reliable and stream oriented communication, is not well suited for distributed real-time applications. In order to address this issue, an RMIX provider plugin was built to implement the RMIX primitives over UDP, while keeping a real-time job (as explained in the previous subsection) serving the incoming and outgoing communications.

This way we bring into the Harness middleware layer a more efficient implementation of the Remote Procedure Call communication scheme built onto a connectionless transport level. While losing the reliability and the complex acknowledgment system of TCP, we gain performance in response time metric, both in its absolute value and in variance of its distribution. This solution exploits the pluggable nature of the RMIX Framework, that itself is seen as a plugin by the Harness Framework. This double-layered pluggability has the added benefit of not requiring modifications to applications already using the RMIX Communication Framework.

Real-Time Event Logging

A common source of unpredictable latency is the access to file or screen I/O devices, as a plain printf() function call is a very time consuming task. While this effect can easily be ignored in standard distributed applications, it cannot be tolerated in a distributed real-time system. The third developed plugin implements a simple event logging system. Loading this module enables the application to push the event to be logged in a temporary shared buffer, while storing information about the source of the event, the timestamp, and the description of the event itself. This operation is a low overhead one, while the buffer will be emptied by a regular Harness thread waiting on the event queue, and optionally formatting the output in a simple XML or plain text file. This way an application can effectively maintain logs of events with accurate timestamps in a lightweight fashion, that is, without perturbating the execution environment as seen by real-time threads.

EXPERIMENTAL TESTS AND EVALUATION

The development process in industrial, high performance, and time-critical environments includes an extensive and thorough performance testing. It is important to build a test environment that resembles the operational environment as closely as possible, both in hardware and software, and to perform tests in adequately set up stress conditions.

Test Environment

The Operational Environment of an industrial time-critical

application is mainly composed by "Command and Control" (C2) applications. We model a C2 distributed application as constituted by components of one of three types: A sensor type component that receives the data from the environment, an elaborator component that computes the actions to be taken in response to data received from sensor, and an actuator component that finally executes these actions in order to modify one or more entities of the environment to be controlled.

Following this scheme, a distributed application was developed in order to realistically mimic this behaviour. The application testing utilizes a fictional remote control of a vector in a 2D space along the two coordinates and speed. Such an application is computationally very similar to real-world C2 applications used in industrial, aerospace, and military contexts, because it involves geometric algorithms on 2D polygons as well as trigonometric and floating-point operations. Moreover, to perform stress tests, benchmark programs are used to synthetically generate the load that simulates extreme operational conditions. Stress tests are necessary for an industrial and mission-critical real-time system to check if the software retains its performance level even in presence of high or spike load. The Ubench and Hackbench benchmarks were used in order to study the behaviour of the application under varying load circumstances.

Test Results

The test were performed with unloaded systems, with Ubench load (CPU and memory), and with different Hackbench load parameters. The goal was to determine how the performance of the distributed application as a whole was affected in scenarios of high load. Figure shows the round trip time (RTT) of the distributed application in the Ubench-loaded configuration, *i.e.*, the time that occurs between the data capture from the sensor component and the action taken by the actuator component. The total RTT of the application roughly doubles under loaded conditions, due to the number of context switches needed between the benchmark program and the application, but never exceeds the value of 2.2 milliseconds, as reported in Table.

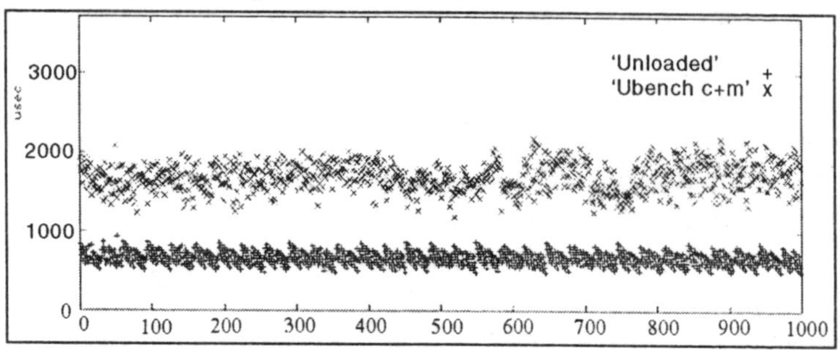

Fig. Computational and Memory Load Sensitivity–Ubench

Table. Round Trip Time Latency Comparison-Ubench

Average	Standard	Deviation	Maximum
Unloaded	669.67μs	81.62μs	932μs
Loaded	1694.39μs	178.45μs	2182μs

In the Hackbench tests we measured mean, maximum, and standard deviation values of the application RTT while varying the coefficient of load (passed as parameter to the benchmark). The results do not show a significant relation between the rise of the load parameter and the RTT either in its maximum value or in mean and variance. It is worth noting that both load Configurations were tested thoroughly with increasing loads until reaching instability of the host systems. Yet the performance of the distributed application was predictable and reliable, and retained real-time class performance.

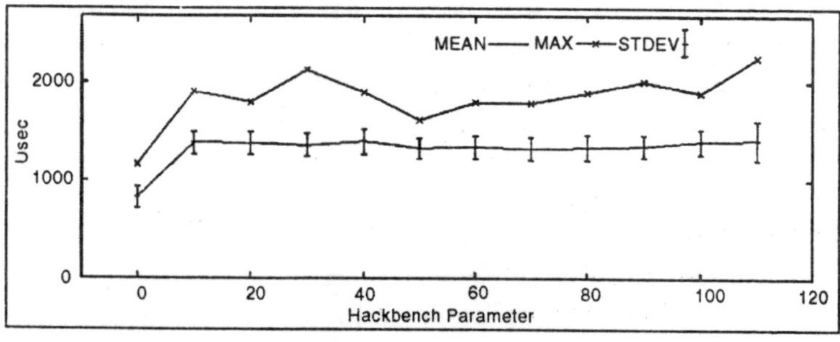

Fig. Task Scheduling Load Sensitivity

REAL-TIME CONTENT DISTRIBUTION

There dso not exist any versatile unpatented unencumbered open real-time audio-video distribution standards, nor in fact any algorithms. There are plenty of compression algorithms (some of which are patent free), and there are a few proprietary real-time video standards (such as Adobe Flash Media Server). However, having video and audio compression isn't enough, in the face of massive changes in the bandwidth capabilities of the clients.

So a radical rethink is needed about how the content should be distributed. Perhaps unsurprisingly, cooperative distribution (also known as peer-to-peer distribution) immediately springs to mind. Fortunately, given that DRM is not an issue (because it cannot be made to work), peer-to-peer cooperative distribution techniques can be considered. In place of DRM, Digital Signatures can be utilised to great effect, thus unequivocably marking the content as belonging to the Copyright Holders, and thus ensuring a legal basis for blatant and widespread copyright violations, if they occur. Key to the success of a massively-distributed video distribution algorithm will be "layered prioritisation" of incremental differences to frames at increasing quality-all simultaneously distributed.

All packets must be subdivided into UDP requests using Peer-to-Peer Query Technology (such as Kademlia), the basic principle of which is to make an MD5 or SHA hash of a unique key (such as the programme name, the type of information required plus the Time Signature on the A/V Frame) and then "broadcast" that out to all the nearest neighbour nodes. If the neighbours do not have the information cached, they forward the query on to their neighbours, and so on. At each level of prioritisation a *separate* network of peer-to-peer nodes must be maintained, with queries *only* being made and distributed for data at the specific "priority" level. The absolute top priority will be the audio component, with a mono soundtrack being the first priority and, like FM radio, a stereo soundtrack which is a "diff" of the Left and Right channels being the second priority. Additional tracks, providing ambient sound (or Dolby Surround), can also be considered.

The second priority will be a 5fps 180x120 picture, with "full-frame" sent every second (or two), and "update" frames sent thereafter. This will providing the absolute basic minimum viewing experience that would work even over utterly unreliable connections and very slow ones. As little as 10k per second should be enough to get audio and video. The third priority will be the alternate frames on the 180x120 picture, thus requiring double the bandwidth, and also providing 10fps. The fourth priority will be to expand the picture size up by approximately 40% (square root of 2), thus requiring-again-approximately double the bandwidth.

This will be done by a mathematically exact and precise transformation of the 180x120 picture data, which need not be absolutely accurate because it will be corrected by the application of the "diff" at the 240x160 level. The transformation/expansion process should be easily performed using integer arithmetic, assembly level instructions or SIMD/ MMX instructions: as might be surmised already, there are going to be quite a few of these transformations.

Each layer of prioritisation should be targetted to increase the required bandwidth by between 50 an 100%, with 50% being preferred. In this way, the "upload" link of ADSL subscribers can be utilised to exponentially distribute at least the minimum acceptable quality picture WITHOUT overloading or burdening ISPs with an ill-adviseable cost. If, however, an ISP makes a decision to put in "cacheing", all that is needed is a computer which participates in the "watching" of a particular programme, and, given that every single node in the network is also a "cache", automatically the computer on the ISP's premises also becomes part of the cache. The Peer-to-peer infrastructure will make an effort to detect its nearest neighbours by analysing the IP address range, use of broadcast UDP traffic, traceroute ICMP traffic and analysis of packet response times. Priority must be given to making queries to the nearest neighbours. Additionally, participants in the distribution of the channel should add UDP broadcast-not just UDP point-to-point and TCP point-to-point-as the method of distribution, at all levels.

Participants should be prepared to receive-and cache-UDP broadcasted channel fragments. In this way, where ISPs and/or Network Administrators do not block UDP broadcasts, the distribution of channel content will be much less network-intensive. Content distributors will need to do the most amount of processing. The creation of so many diffs of picture frames and frame sizes will be *enormously* CPU intensive. Fortunately, however, there is only one location where that work need be done: at the source! All other participants will be purely "ferrying" that traffic, and the only location where it is actually reconstructed is for display on the end-user's screen.

The whole system will be self-adjusting to suit the network, in real time. As the underlying infrastructure improves, with Fibre-Optic cables being added and brought to people's homes, the whole system will "uprate" automatically. The addition of "cacheing" technology at ISP sites is also a "nice improvement" rather than an absolute prerequisite. And users will be able to specify the bandwidth allocation that they are prepared to tolerate, with an immediately obvious trade-off in picture quality that they can decide whether to accept, or pay for additional bandwidth.

What is particularly nice is that the slower speed connections will still be helped by the faster speed ones, as the slower end-user connections will simply drop out of the sharing process without being adversely affected by neither sending nor receiving of data that the connection simply cannot cope with.

OFFLINE CONTENT AND DELAYED VIEWING

Offline content (downloading of higher quality) and delayed viewing-pausing-is an automatic feature provided by the design of this system. The viewers' station simply begins participating in the "higher rate" peer-to-peer networks. They will begin to receive data, at a much slower rate than they would otherwise be able to see in real-time, but they will receive it nonetheless. Nodes which have already viewed the higher-rate channel data will be able to participate in the peer-to-peer distribution to these slower off-line systems, thus reducing the burden on the distribution infrastructure. All in all, the entire system fits to the maximum capacity of the overall network and still provides viewers with what they want, in the format that they want it, for an amount that they are prepared to pay.

OPERATING SYSTEM RESOURCES MANAGER

SIMPLE RULES TO HELP GET IT RIGHT!

When programming in a GUI operating system, you allocate operating system resources for widgets, images, fonts, and other graphical objects. Since there is a platform limit on the amount of resources you can allocate, you must be careful to free any objects that you allocate in your application. If you allocate a resource and do not free it when you are done with it, your application is "leaking" resources. An application that repeatedly leaks resources will eventually consume all of the available resources, forcing the user to reboot the operating system. Fortunately, SWT makes resource allocation and disposal a straightforward process. There are only two rules that you need to remember when allocating and freeing SWT resource-based objects:

Rule 1

This is a simple rule. SWT makes it easy for you to remember when operating system resources are allocated: all SWT resource-based objects (like Colour, Cursor,Display, Font, GC, Image, Printer, Region, Widget and subclasses) allocate any needed operating system resources in their constructor. There are no exceptions to this rule. There are no methods in SWT (other than constructors) that allocate operating system resources that the programmer must manage. If you didn't call the constructor, then you don't need to free the resources, so don't call dispose on the object. For example, in the following line of code, an operating system font is allocated:

```
Font font = new Font (display, "Courier", 10,
SWT.NORMAL);
```

Since you called the Font constructor to create the resource, you must dispose the font when you are finished with it, as follows:

```
font.dispose();
```

In the following line of code, however, a constructor is not called:

```
Font font = control.getFont ();
```

Therefore, you must not call dispose. The font variable does contain an operating system font resource, but you did not allocate it. If you were to dispose of this font, you would be leaving the control without a font! The results are undefined. So, if you are using any getter that returns an SWT resource-based object that you did not allocate, do not dispose the object.

This rule occasionally leads to API that seems artificial. For example, GC.getClipping (Region) forces the programmer to create a Region in order to get the clipping region from a GC. Although it might have been a bit "prettier" to provide GC.getClipping () that returned a Region, this would break the rule because it would have to allocate an operating system resource outside of a constructor. While it could be documented that the programmer needs to free the Region returned by GC.getClipping (), programmers don't always read the documentation. Making the programmer call the constructor for the Region makes it clear that it is theprogrammer's responsibility to free the resource.

Rule 2

When you dispose a Shell, its children are disposed. In fact, disposing any Composite will dispose all of the Composite's children. Disposing a Menu disposes all menu items. Disposing a Tree or TreeItem disposes all child items. Why does this make sense? Apart from the obvious burden of having to dispose each child if this were not the case, the fact that a widget cannot exist in the operating system without a parent implies that when the parent is disposed, the child *must* also be disposed. What about the fonts and colours that you created and set into a *Widget*? Since they are not children of the widget, they are not disposed when the parent is disposed. A widget will never dispose a resource that you allocated. To do so would mean that the widget was breaking rule 1. Because fonts and colours can be shared by different widgets, disposing a resource in one widget would dispose it in another, leading to unpredictable results.

Extensions to Rule 2

There are two extensions to rule 2. These are places where a relationship exists that is not strictly a parent-child relationship, but where it still makes sense for rule 2 to apply.

MenuItem.setMenu

Disposing a cascade *MenuItem* that has a submenu set with setMenu (Menu) disposes the submenu. This is a natural extension of rule 2. It would be a burden to the programmer to dispose each individual submenu. It's also common behaviour in most operating systems to do this automatically. Both Windows® and X dispose submenus when a cascade menu item is disposed.

Control.setMenu

Disposing a *Control* that has a pop-up menu set with setMenu (Menu) disposes the pop-up menu. Many application programmers expected this behaviour, even though many operating systems don't do this automatically. Leaving the application programmer responsible for disposing a pop-up menu when disposing the *Control* led to temporary leaks. (The leak was only temporary because the pop-up menu is eventually disposed when the shell is disposed).

WHY FREE AT ALL?

The operating system frees all of a program's resources when the program exits. Why not just rely on this? Operating system resources are not infinite. If your program doesn't free up resources as they are no longer needed, it can run out of resources.

It can also cause other programs to run out of resources.

So waiting until the program exits to free up resources is generally a bad idea. Leak tools exist to help detect resource leaks. You can use the *Sleak* tool to look for leaks in your SWT application.

JAVA LANGUAGE A GARBAGE COLLECTION

The Java language successfully uses a garbage collector to manage the memory used by Java objects. Why doesn't SWT use the Java garbage collector to manage operating system resources too? Many Java programmers ask this question. We will answer it with the following discussion on finalization.

FINALIZATION

Most attempts to use the Java garbage collector to manage operating system resources involve finalization. When an object is about to become garbage, the garbage collector sends it the finalize message. This seems like a logical place to free the resource, right?

One of the main reasons that this statement is true is that there is no guarantee how soon after an object becomes garbage that the finalize method for the object will run. Even if you could predict this time interval for a particular VM, you certainly couldn't guarantee it for new versions of the VM. Worse still, if there is plenty of memory or if an exception occurs in an object's finalize method, there is no guarantee that the object will be finalized at all! All of this is stated right in

The Java Language Specification: "The Java programming language does not specify how soon a finalizer will be invoked, except to say that it will happen before the storage for the object is reused.... If an uncaught exception is thrown during the finalization, the exception is ignored and finalization of that object terminates." Releasing operating system resources is critical to correct program execution. Freeing resources at some unknown time in the future (or not at all) typically leads to program failure.

Here are some examples of typical problems encountered when using finalization:

- If a non-garbage object references another object, that

object is not garbage and won't be collected. If the object has operating system resources that it frees in its finalize method, those resources will never be freed because finalize will never be called. This is a classic programming error because it's easy to hang on to objects accidentally in an inner class or a static variable.

- It is possible to starve other operating system processes by creating lots of "garbage resources" that have not yet been finalized. When another program attempts to acquire a resource, it fails because it cannot run the Java finalizer. SWT could run the finalizer if it couldn't get a resource, but other programs (*i.e.* non-Java programs or even Java programs running in a different VM)-and operating system calls that allocate and free resources internally-can't run the Java finalizer.
- Some resources are very limited. For example, only a small number of cached HDCs are available on Windows 98. It is essential to free these up right away, instead of waiting for finalization.
- Different types of resource are shared on the same operating system heap, so a failure to acquire one resource may be caused by failure to free another. For example, on Windows 98, HBRUSH and HFONT are both allocated from the GDI heap, so failure to create an HBRUSH can happen if too many HFONTs are awaiting finalization. This can cause applications to have some strange dependencies on the timing of finalizer runs.

The non-deterministic nature of finalization is sufficient reason to avoid using it to free resources, but even if we decided to go against conventional wisdom and implement a resource management scheme using finalization, we would still face many other problems.

The implementation would require the addition of some very complex, platform-specific code that would be difficult to get right, and tough to debug. Here are a few examples of some of the tricky issues that would need to be carefully coded around in each object's finalize method:

- Operating system objects can have subtle limitations on when particular objects can be disposed. For example in the X Window System, a GC can contain a Font. If you dispose the Font before the GC, you leave the operating system in an indeterminate state. The following quote from *The Java Language Specification* hints at the complexity of the code that would be required to handle such limitations for each object finalizer:

"The Java programming language imposes no ordering on finalize method calls. Finalizers m*ay be called in any order, or even concurrently.*"

Add to this that for some operating systems, subtle platform behaviour in this area may be undocumented and can change in future versions of the operating system.

- On some platforms, operating system resources need to be disposed in the UI thread. According to *The Java Language Specification*:

"... the language does not specify which thread will invoke the finalizer for any given object." This means that SWT finalize methods would need to synchronize with the UI thread, which would mean that there would be a significant cost overhead for each dispose. In addition, given the previous point that disposal order is important for some resources, we think it is possible to get into a deadlock situation if we are trying to reorder multiple concurrent threads that are trying to synchronize with the UI thread.

- The Java objects that model operating system objects need to capture all of the subtle relationships between the operating system objects. For example, on Windows, an HBRUSH can be referenced in the operating system by an HDC, but not referenced in Java code. When the Java object representing the HBRUSH becomes garbage, freeing it will cause unexpected results. In fact, it's necessary to break the reference from the HDC first before attempting to free the HBRUSH. If these relationships are not captured and managed, it is possible for a resource to be finalized when there are still references to it in the operating system.

- Freeing some resources automatically frees others. For example, on Windows, destroying a parent HWND automatically destroys the children HWNDs. On some operating systems, freeing a top level window also frees the icon associated with the window. Different rules for freeing resources need to be custom coded on a per platform basis.
- Freeing resources can be time consuming, so a critical memory allocation may need to wait until finalization is complete.
- Long waits in finalizers can also make it difficult to get good benchmarks when you are trying to performance tune your code.

Our Final Point Against Finalization is This: SWT keeps as much state in the operating system as possible to simplify the implementation (less code, smaller objects). If we were to use finalization, we could not store resources only in the operating system. We would have to hold on to them in Java code so that they would not get garbage collected. For example, when you set a *Font* into a *Button,* SWT sets the font resource in the OS button. The *Button* doesn't keep a reference to the font resource, because it doesn't need to. The state is in the operating system. In order to determine the *Button*'s font, we query the OS. There is no point caching the font resource in Java code, because it just takes up space and complicates the *Button* code, which now has to make sure there are no stale cache problems.

Given that there are many problems when trying to use finalization to free resources, we think it's dangerous to offer it as a solution in SWT, which is designed to expose operating system functionality. We believe it is reasonable to expect programs to explicitly free operating system resources. We see this as simply a fact of life because the current generation of operating systems do not support garbage collection.

WHEN SHOULD YOU FREE?

You have created an SWT resource, so when do you free it? First of all, for many of the reasons mentioned above, we do not recommend that you use finalization to manage your SWT resources either. If you feel you absolutely must implement a finalize method in your classes, do so only as a "safety net" or "backup", and dispose your resource as usual. *Remember to synchronize with the UI thread, as follows:*

```
protected void finalize() {//NOT recommended
super.finalize();
             display.asyncExec(new Runnable() {
public void run() {
                  if !myResource.isDisposed()){
                         myResource.dispose();
}
}
});
}
```

Even this minimal "safety net" use of finalizers is not recommended, because if memory is limited, your application could end up having to wait for a bunch of your finalize methods to run before the memory from those objects can be reclaimed. The best way to manage SWT resources is to dispose them as soon as you are through with them. In the case of certain resource types, such as GC and Printer, you almost always create them and dispose them within the scope of the same method. This makes it easy to verify that the resource is being disposed properly, because you only have to go to one place to see the code to create the resource and the code to dispose it.

For example:

```
GC gc = new GC(canvas);
gc.draw...//do some drawing on    the  canvas
using the GC
gc.dispose();
```

In the case of resources that are set into a GC for drawing, you need to be careful not to dispose them while they are still set into the GC. Dispose the GC before the resource.

For example:

```
Font font = new Font (display, "Courier", 10,
SWT.NORMAL);
GC gc = new GC(canvas);
gc.setFont(font);
gc.drawText...//do some text drawing on the
canvas using the GC
gc.dispose();
font.dispose();
```

Remember that you do not dispose the GC that is passed to you in a paint listener, because you did not allocate it!

```
public void paintControl(PaintEvent event) {
event.gc.draw...
//do NOT call event.gc.dispose();
}
```

If you are using graphics resources in a widget-for example, widget.setFont(font)-it is often best to clean these up when the widget they are used in is disposed, so you can hook a dispose listener on the widget as follows:

```
widget.addDisposeListener(new DisposeListener() {
public void widgetDisposed(DisposeEvent e) {
font.dispose()
}
}
```

If resources are shared by multiple widgets (or other objects) in your application, then you may want to implement a reference-counting scheme in a "resource manager" class, which would keep track of the number of references to a resource, and dispose the resource when the reference count reaches 0.

In this case, you would ask your resource manager for each resource you need, perhaps something like this:

```
Image image = myResource Manager.getName dRe
source("imageName");
and the dispose listener on your widget(s) might
look something like this:
widget.addDisposeListener(new DisposeListener() {
   public void widgetDisposed(DisposeEvent e) {
```

```
   myResource Manager.dispose(image);
}
});
```

Whether or not to use a reference-counting scheme, and how to implement it, are design decisions that must be made on a per-application basis. Widgets themselves do not usually need to be disposed programmatically. A shell and its children are disposed when the user closes its window. There are a couple of places where shells are typically disposed programmatically: when the user selects File->Exit in an application window, or OK in a dialog. Here is an example of disposing a shell when File->Exit is selected:

```
//Create menu bar
Menu menuBar = new Menu(shell, SWT.BAR);
//Create File menu
MenuItem item = new MenuItem(menuBar,
SWT.CASCADE);
item.setText("File");
Menu fileMenu = new Menu(shell, SWT.DROP_DOWN);
item.setMenu(fileMenu);
//Create File -> Exit menu item and add selection
listener
item = new MenuItem(fileMenu, SWT.NULL);
item.setText("Exit");
item.addSelectionListener(new SelectionAdapter()
{
    public void widgetSelected(SelectionEvent
event) {
        shell.close();//calls dispose()-see note
below
        }
  });
```

Note that we actually call close() instead of dispose(). This gives the application a chance to cancel the close operation if necessary (for example, if something was not saved) inside of a shell listener. We could call dispose(), which would simply destroy the shell without invoking the shell listener, but it's better style to callclose().

OS PROCESS

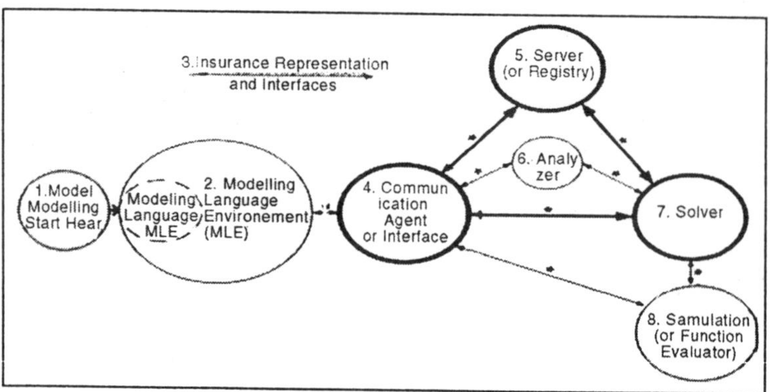

The process of the optimization system in the above figure is self-explanatory. Typically the process starts from a modeler who has a model (1) to be solved. He constructs the model in an MLE (2). The MLE in turn compiles the model and generates an instance representation (3). The MLE then delegates a communication agent (4) to send the instance to a solver (7). In a local environment, where there is no agent, the link between 4 and 7 is an interface through which the MLE instantiates the solver in memory. In a distributed environment, the MLE may first discover a registered solver through registry (5), therefore the respective discovery link between 4 and 5 and registration link between 5 and 7.

The communication with the analyser (6) is similar to that with a solver (7). The link between communication agent (4) and simulation (8) means that the agent may call the simulation to get a function value, although in an optimization scenario, it is usually the solver (7) that calls the simulation (8) iteratively. The triangle between communication agent (4), registry (5) and solver (7) is called a Service-oriented Architecture (SOA). The design philosophy of SOA serves as the basis of our Optimization Services framework. A "service" is intended to serve customers.

For our optimization system, there are mainly three categories of "human" customers:

1. Application developers create and build system

components such as modeling language environments and solvers as part of a larger optimization system. The components together take care of such generic functions as managing data, solving optimization problems, and presenting solutions nicely.

2. Modelers work in a modeling language environment or GUI to build optimization models and get acceptable solutions.
3. Users run application packages that perform optimization at some stage through the optimization system. Users are usually the ultimate customers of any optimization system.

Modelers and application developers may see optimization in different ways. For modelers, a mathematical program is an abstract representation to be analysed and understood; for application developers, a mathematical program is a concrete instance to be represented, communicated and solved. Modelers benefit most immediately from innovations that help people to choose and experiment with optimization software. Some application developers are also modelers, while others deal mainly with the inputs and outputs of optimization models set up by modelers. Users may not even realise that they are running optimization system components such as solvers, although they are often aware of optimization goals, such as minimizing costs or maximizing profits. The decentralized architecture of Optimization Services makes it similar to the Internet. Internet

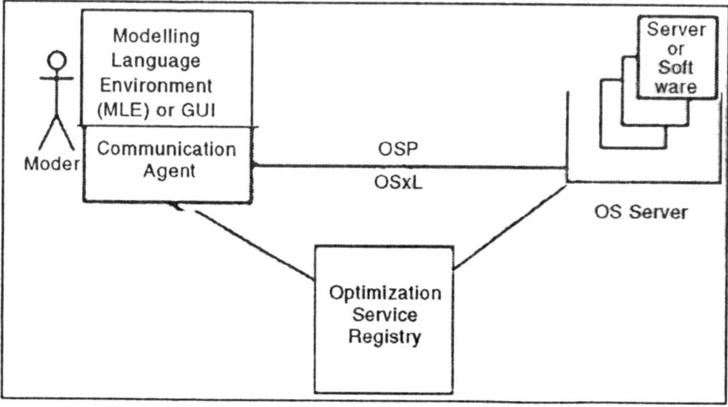

In order to "surf the Internet" (above figure, top), a user uses an Internet browser to view the Web pages, which usually contain interactive links and forms.

Clicking the links and filling in forms are what we call the user inputs. In the scenario of Optimization Services (above figure, bottom), the user is a modeler and his inputs are a model and the model's data.

Instead of the browser, the modeler constructs the model in a Modeling Language Environment or in a Graphical User Interface (GUI) environment and instead of sending the model inputs to a web server, the MLE or GUI sends the inputs to an OS server.

The OS server hosts solvers rather than Web pages. Although the Internet existed long before it became popular, the entertaining Web pages were what made the Internet successful.

The same can be said about Optimization Services. Without the actual "contents" provided by the solvers, OS is just an empty skeleton that can never be widely used no matter how well the skeleton is designed. o further apply the analogy, it is never the browser that contacts a web server. Rather the browser opens a socket, and through the socket, the browser sends the request and waits for the response.

These all happen without the user's knowledge. The exact equivalent of the socket in Optimization Services is the communication agent.

The MLE or GUI delegates the agent to send an optimization instance to the remote OS server that hosts the solver. Like the socket, the agent understands all the communication protocols in order to establish the connection. But instead of using the HTTP protocol and sending/receiving HTML instances, the agent uses the OSP communication protocol and sends/receives OS instances.

Nowadays people heavily rely on search engines to find Web pages. The Optimization Services registry serves the function of a search engine. But unlike the Internet search engines, there has to be a unique registry in the whole Optimization Services system to ensure Quality of Service

(QoS). Communication agents always know where the registry is, as there is only one. This registry has complete information of available services, as this is the only place that the services can register.

The OS registry will not be overburdened as no software is connected through it. When a certain query is sent to the OS registry, usually from an MLE or GUI, the OS registry returns the locations of the found software and the MLE or GUI makes a peer-to-peer contact with the software at the provided location.

This discovery process is similar to the search engine process, with the exception that everything in the OS system happens automatically between the software components, without user interaction. On the opposite side of the discovery process is the registration process. In the case of the Internet, it is usually the search engine "crawlers" that automatically collect the contents of all the Web pages.

In the Optimization Services case, it is the OR software developer's responsibility to send the required information to, and get approved by, the OS registry, possibly through a mixture of automatic and manual procedures. This is primarily due to two reasons. One is that the quantity of OR software packages is not nearly large enough to be crawled efficiently.

A second, and more important reason, is that the requirement of QoS on the OS registry is much stricter in order to ensure smooth functioning between OS components. The mechanism of "wantonly" crawling and storing "unwarranted" things found on the hyperlink paths degrades the Optimization Services. In the following figure, we show that most of the components in the Optimization Services system have a corresponding similar part in the Internet architecture. The similarity is not the initial intention of the OS project; rather it is the result that both are good designs based on a decentralized architecture.

DEVICE

Any device connected internally or externally to a computer and used in the transfer of data. A personal computer or workstation processes information and, strictly speaking, that is all the computer does. Data (unprocessed information) must get into the computer, and the processed information must get out. Entering and displaying information is carried out on a wide variety of accessory devices called peripherals, also known as input/output (I/O) devices. Some peripherals, such as keyboards, are only input devices; other peripherals, such as printers, are only output devices; and some are both. See also Digital computer; Microcomputer.

The monitor is the device on which images produced by the computer operator or generated by the program are displayed on a cathode-ray tube (CRT). Electron guns-one in a monochromemonitor, three in a colour monitor-irradiate phosphors on the inside of the vacuum tube, causing them to glow. The flat-panel displays on most portable computers, known as liquid-crystal displays (LCDs), use two polarizing filters with liquid crystals between them to produce the image.

The computer keyboard, based on the typewriter keyboard, contains keys for entering letters, numbers, and punctuation marks, as well as keys to change the meaning of other keys. The function keys perform tasks that vary from program to program. See also Typewriter. The mouse is a device that is rolled on the desktop to move the cursor on the screen. A ball on the bottom of the mouse translates the device's movements to sensors within the mouse and then through the connecting port to the computer. There are also mice that substitute optical devices for mechanical balls, and mice that use infrared rather than physical connections.

The trackball is essentially an upside-down mouse, with the ball that is used to move the cursor located on the top rather than on the bottom. joystick is a pointing device used principally for games. The light pen performs the same functions as a mouse or trackball, but it is held up to the screen, where its sensors detect the presence of pixels and send a signal through a cable to the computer.

The graphics, or digitizing, tablet is a pad with electronics beneath the surface which is drawn upon with a pointed device, called a stylus. The shapes drawn appear on the monitor's screen. The most common input, or storage, device in personal computers or workstations is a hard disk drive, a stack of magnetized platters on which information is stored by heads generating an electrical current to represent either 1 or 0 in the binary number system. The device is called hard because the platters are inflexible, and is called a drive because it spins at 3600 revolutions or more a minute, within a sealed case. Diskettes, made of flexible film like that used in recording tape, are usually stored within a hard shell and are spun by their drives at about 360 revolutions per minute. Data can also be stored and retrieved with light, the light of a laser beam reading a pattern of pits on an optical disk. The most familiar type of optical disk is the CD-ROM (compact disk-read only memory). Another kind of optical disk is the WORM (write once read many times).

As a consequence of their greater efficiency and speed, disk drives have quickly replaced tape drives as the primary means of data and program storage. Tape drives are still in use for backup storage, copying the contents of a hard disk as insurance against mechanical failure or human error.

The scanner converts an image of something outside the computer, such as text, a drawing, or a photograph, into a digital image that it sends into the computer for display or further processing. The image is viewed as a graphics image, not a text image, so it can be altered with a graphics program but cannot be edited with a word-processing program, unless the scanner is part of a character-recognition system.

To digitize photographs, a scanner may dither the image (put the dots a varying amount of space apart), or use the tagged image file format (TIFF), storing the image in 16 gray values. Some scanners can use standard video cameras to capture images for the computer. The printer puts text or other images produced with a computer onto paper or other surfaces. Printers are either impact or nonimpact devices.

Daisy-wheel or thimble printers are so called from the shape of the elements bearing raised images of the characters. Their speed, perhaps 30 characters per second, is now considered unacceptably slow. Dot-matrix printers produce their images by striking a series of wire pins, typically, 9, 18, or 24, through the ribbon in the pattern necessary to form the letter, number, line, or other character. Ink-jet printers carry their ink in a well, where it is turned into a mist by heat or vibration andsprayed through tiny holes to form the pattern of the character on paper.

Laser printers are similar to photocopying machines. The quality of laser-printer output is the highest generally available. The modem connects one computer to another, ordinarily through the telephone lines, to exchange information.

TYPES OF COMPUTER STORAGE DEVICES

Computer storage devices can be classified into either primary storage, secondary storage, or tertiary storage. Each of these storage devices are used to store certain files and data and are accessed in different ways by the computer's CPU. Here's a brief explanation of the differences.

Primary Computer Storage Devices

Primary storage refers to the computer's memory, which connects directly to the computer's CPU. The computer's memory evolved into what is now known as random access memory (RAM) which is a volatile form of storage. Volatile storage means that you totally lose data when you switch the system off. Aside from the RAM, two other primary storage areas can be found; these are on the CPU itself; the Processor registers and the Processor cache. The Processor register is some form of small storage which resides on the CPU and can contain data which can be accessed quickly. The processor registers are measured by the amount of data the can hold, that is either, 8 bit, 32 bit or 64 bit.

Processor cache on the other hand is used by the CPU for reducing the time it takes to access the main memory. It stores data coming from the most frequently used applications of the CPU. During normal operations, the CPU checks the processor cache before checking the main memory, making the processing time faster.

Secondary Computer Storage Devices

These storage devices are external in nature and non-volatile as compared to primary storage devices. Secondary storage devices do not lose data even when they are turned off. Hence, they are the ideal back-upand data storage devices.

Examples of secondary storage devices include; CD and DVD; flash memory; floppy disks; paper and magnetic tape; RAM disks, also called SSDs; ZIP drives; and punch cards. Since secondary storage devices are not attached to the computer's CPU, it takes a longer time for the CPU to access them. Secondary storage devices need to be formated before they can store data. Secondary storage devices are formated based on a filesystem format data are organized into files and directories. It also includes other pertinent information about the data, which is described in what is called the metadata.

Tertiary Computer Storage Devices

This type of computer storage device is not as popular as the other two storage device types. Its main use is for storing data at a very large-scale. This includes optical jukeboxes and tape libraries.

Tertiary storage devices require a database to organize the data that are stored in them, and the computer needs to go through the database to access those data.

Offline Storage

Aside from these three types of computer storage devices, there is also another type-offline or disconnected storage. It is not directly connected to the computer and is used as a transfer medium only. Offline storage devices are remotely located and accessed as per need only. This storage device also needs human intervention to be read properly by the main computer system.

Offline storage aside, from its use as a data transmission medium, can also serve as a good back-up device since it is remotely located, hence it will not be affected by any disaster that might hit the direct source of data. Offline storage also provides good security for data since you ca

COMPUTER STORAGE DEVICES

Awhile back, we covered the different types of hardware used with computers. You know, basic hardware and the extra hardware you can buy separately, etc. (You can read here for that article). So, I thought it would be nice to cover the different kinds of computer storage devices that are available as well. And that's exactly what I'm going to do today!

Knowing what kinds of storage devices are available can keep you from using up too much space on your computer's hard drive. They can also help keep your computer's hard drive from crashing, along with keeping it running at top speed.

Floppy Disk

- They are plastic square disks, usually with a silver or black sliding piece going across the top. These disks come in a variety of colours and they hold about 144 million bytes. (Bytes are characters, symbols and letters).

Zip Disk

- They look like a floppy disk, but they are a little thicker. This disk also comes in a variety of colours and holds about 200 MB of data.

CD + RW Disc (Compact Disc Rewriteable)

- This disc looks like a regular CD. The only difference is that you can write on this disc and erase it as many times as you want. It works just like a floppy disk or a zip disk. A CD + RW disc holds about 650 MB.

CD + R Disc (Compact Disc Recordable)

- This one is a CD that you can record on. It's mostly used to record audio and once it's been written on, you cannot rewrite or erase anything off of it. This compact disc comes in different sizes, but they are usually silver in colour. (Some CDs are black in colour and they actually don't get as many scratches on them as the silver ones do. They are also a lot less fragile).

A DVD–R Disc (Digital Video Recordable)

- These discs hold the space of about 4.7 GB and are used to record movies on.

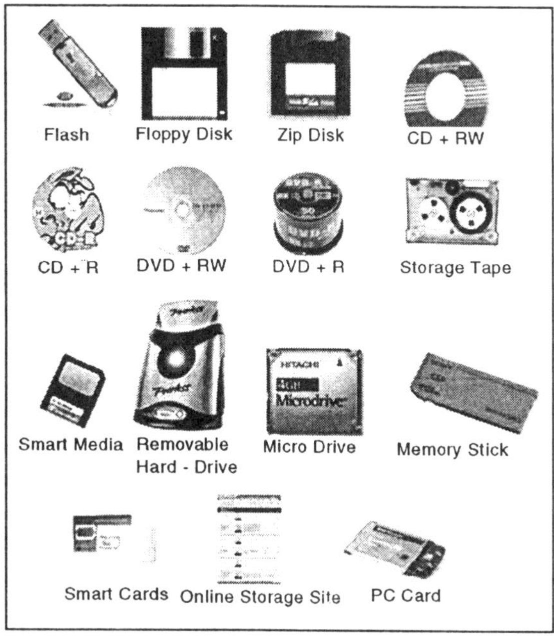

The more uncommon storage devices are:

Removable Hard Drive

- This is a disk drive in which a plastic or metal case surrounds the hard drive. It can be inserted and removed just like a floppy disk. It holds about 2 GB of data.

Internet Hard Drive

- This one is a service on the Internet that provides storage space to computer users. This service offers about 25 MB of space, but it could be more, depending on the service type.

Flash Drive

- This a storage device that comes in many colours and has a stick shape to it. They are very small in size, but they can hold anywhere between 256 MB and 3 GB of material on them.

PC Card

- This is a thin credit card size device that fits into a PC card slot, usually on a notebook computer. This card simply adds storage to most notebooks.

Smart Cards

- These are the size of an ATM card. When inserted into a smart card reader, they can read and update data for you.

Storage Tape

- This one is a magnetically coated ribbon of plastic, capable of storing large amounts of data at a very low cost. Usually, storage tapes are a little bigger than audio tapes. Older computers used tape and tape drives, but even today, some people still back their systems up with storage tape. These tapes hold between 20 GB to about 110 GB of data. An external tape drive can be purchased separately as well, but those are even harder to find.

Miniature Mobile Storage Media

- This is used mostly with handheld computers and digital cameras.

Memory Stick

- This is a rectangular shaped disk that is used mostly with digital cameras and notebook computers. They hold approximately 128 MB as well.

Micro Drive

- This is a square disk that has 1 GB of space and is used with digital cameras and handheld computers.

Smart Media Disc

This is a square disk that has 2 MB to about 128 MB of space on it. It's used with digital cameras, handheld computers and photo printers. There you go! These are just some of the storage devices that are available today. So, the next time you want to save something that takes up a large amount of space on your hard drive, think twice about it and consider using one of these storage devices instead. One of these devices could save you a lot of space on your hard drive and keep your system running at its best!

MEMORY AND FILE MANAGEMENT

MEMORY

Memory is the electronic holding place for instructions and data that the computer's microprocessor can reach quickly. When the computer is in normal operation, its memory usually contains the main parts of the operating system and some or all of the application programs and related data that are being used. Memory is often used as a shorter synonym for random access memory (RAM). This kind of memory is located on one or more microchips that are physically close to the microprocessor in the computer. Most desktop and notebook computers sold today include at least 16 megabytes of RAM, and are upgradeable to include more. The more RAM you have, the less frequently the computer has to access instructions and data from the more slowly accessed hard disk form of storage.

Memory is sometimes distinguished from storage, or the physical medium that holds the much larger amounts of data that won't fit into RAM and may not be immediately needed there. Storage devices include hard disks, floppy disks, CD-ROM, and tape backup systems. The terms auxiliary storage, auxiliary memory, and secondary memory have also been used for this kind of data repository.

Additional kinds of integrated and quickly accessible memory are read-only memory (ROM), programmable ROM (PROMO), erasable programmable ROM (EPROM). These are used to keep special programs and data, such as the basic input/output system, that need to be in the computer all the time.

The memory is a resource that needs to be managed carefully. Most computers have a memory hierarchy, with a small amount of very fast, expensive, volatile cache memory, some number of megabytes of medium-speed, medium-price, volatile main memory (RAM), and hundreds of thousands of megabytes of slow, cheap, non-volatile disk storage. It is the job of the operating system to coordinate how these memories are used.

The part of the operating system that manages the memory hierarchy is the memory manager. It keeps track of parts of memory that are in use and those that are not in use, to allocate memory to processes when they need it and de-allocate it when they are done, and to manage swapping between main memory and disk when main memory is too small to hold all the processes.

Systems for managing memory can be divided into two categories: the system of moving processes back and forth between main memory and disk during execution (known as swapping and paging) and the process that does not do so (that is, no swapping and ping).

Mono Programming Without Swapping or Paging

The most simple memory management scheme is to run one program at a time, sharing the memory between that program and the operating system. As shown in the diagram bellow, there are three variations of this type. The operating system may be at the bottom of the memory in TAM (random access memory), as shown in the diagram 1, or it may be in ROM (read-only memory) at the top of the memory, as shown in diagram 2, or the device drivers may be at the top of the memory in a ROM and the rest of the system in RAM down bellow

With the system organised in this way, only one process at a time can be running. As soon as the user types a command, the operating system copies the request program from a disk to memory and executes it. When the process finishes, the operating system displays a prompt character and waits for a new command. When it receives the command, it loads a new program into memory overwriting the first one.

Mono Programming with fixed Partitions

It is often desirable to allow multiple processes to run at the same time, even on simple operating systems in which multiprogramming is sometimes used. On time-sharing systems, having multiple processes in memory at once means that when one process is blocked waiting for the I/O to finish, another one can use the CPU. This way, multiprogramming increases the CPU utilisation. It is however preferable to be able to run two or more programs at once even on personal computers.

Swapping

The process of organising memory into fixed partitions on batch system is simple compared to time sharing systems or graphically oriented personal computers. On batch systems, each job is loaded into a partition when it gets to the head of the queue. It stays in memory until it has finished. As long as enough jobs can be kept in memory to keep the CPU busy all the time, there is no reason to use anything more complicated. On time-sharing machines, sometimes there is not enough main memory to hold all the currently active processes, therefore excess processes must be kept on disk and brought in to run dynamically. Swapping as an approach to memory management consists of bringing each process in its entirety, running it for a while, then putting it back on the disk.

THE SCENARIO

The problem we are trying to overcome is simply this: You want to develop some kind of file or text editor, and you want your program to be able to load, edit and save files of any size. In fact, you want your program to load and edit the largest sized file possible. Under 32bit Windows this is a 4Gb file. (Actually, Windows NT supports 18 exabyte files with its 64bit

NTFS file system, but I will talk about this type of file later in the series.

Your file editor needs be able to load a 4Gb file in a fraction of a second. In addition, insertions and deletions to and from the file must be as fast for a 4Gb file as they are for a 1Kb file. This series of articles (I haven't decided exactly how many articles there will be yet) will take you through the design decisions and algorithms necessary to accomplish these goals. At the end of the series you will have enough information to develop your own file-handling functions, which will be as powerful and flexible as those used in my HexEdit application.

MEMORY MANAGEMENT

Let's forget about actually editing a large file for the moment, and concentrate just on loading a file into your application. So, your have a 4Gb file saved on your hard disk, and you want to load this file so you can preview any portion of it. Let's assume that our first application will be a simple hex file viewer, with no editing capabilities.

The first decision to take is what memory facilities we will use to gain access to the file's contents. To make this decision, we need to know what memory facilities are available to our program, and base our decision on that. Because our file viewer will be a 32bit Windows program capable of running under Windows 9x and NT/2000, we have the following facilities at our disposal.

I will make a note here for you to go and read "Advanced Windows" by Jeffrey Richter. This book covers the entire memory architecture and memory management in Windows, and will be much more detailed than what I will be describing here.

VIRTUAL MEMORY

Another strategy for managing memory is the virtual memory, which allows programs to run even when they are only partially in main memory. The basic idea behind this strategy is that the combine size of the program, data, and stack may exceed the amount of physical memory available for it.

The operating system keeps those parts of the program currently in use in main memory, and the rest on the disk.

Virtual memory can also work in a multiprogramming system, with bits and pieces pf many programs in memory at once. While a program is waiting for a part of itself to be brought in, it is waiting for I/O and cannot run, so the CPU can be given to another process, the same way as for any other multiprogramming system. Most virtual memory systems use a technique called paging.

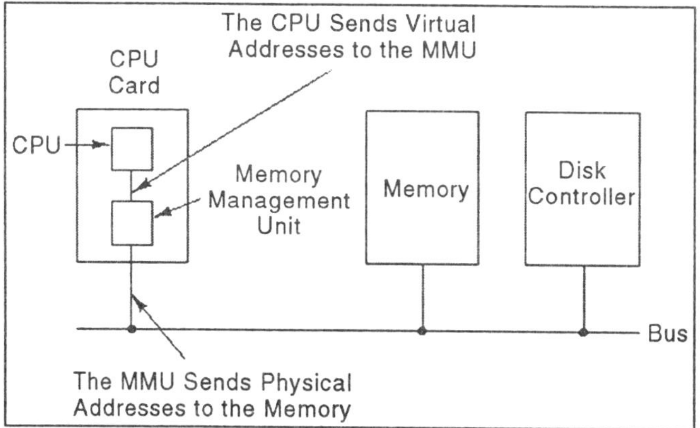

Every 32bit process in Windows has a 4Gb virtual address space, regardless of the amount of physical RAM you have installed. Of this total virtual space, only 2Gb is available for an application's private use. Actually, the available space slightly less than this-128Kb less in WinNT and 4Mb less in Win9x). There are a variety of methods to allocate memory from this 2Gb region of space. All depend on how much memory needs to be allocated, and what its intended use is.

Malloc and New

The simplest is to use the standard C or C++ memory allocation routines (malloc and new[], respectively). Both of these methods use the memory allocation facilities provided by the operating system. In Visual C++ 6.0, malloc and new[] use VirtualAlloc internally. Anyway, malloc and new[] are only really meant for allocating lots of small objects, not one gigantic memory region.

HeapAlloc

The second method to allocate memory in Windows is to use the Heap function–HeapAlloc (or the older LocalAlloc and GlocalAlloc). These functions are also meant for allocating many small objects though-just like malloc and new[]-and are also implemented by calls to VirtualAlloc.

VirtualAlloc

The third way to allocate memory in Windows is to use VirtualAlloc directly. This method is much more flexible because it allows you to specify where you want the memory to be in your address space, and allows you to reserve a region of memory without actually allocating any space from it.

Memory-Mapped-Files

The forth way to allocate memory is by using Memory Mapped Files. Rather than allocating memory, a memory-mapped file is a reserved region of the 2Gb address space, which has mapped into it a region a file stored on disk. The great thing about memory-mapped-files is that they free the programmer from having to do any direct file reading or writing.

Simply reading and writing to the memory-mapped view causes the file's contents to be accessed. The operating system provides clever page caching to make memory-mapped files a very quick way to read/write to a file.

The picture below should help to describe the relationship between the various memory-allocation facilities. The important thing to remember is that all four types of memory allocation provide access to an application's virtual address space in one way or another.

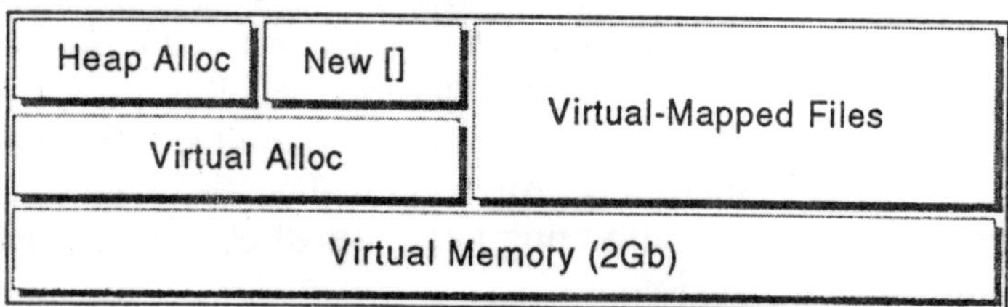

I won't go into any more detail because there is a problem, which is this. With a maximum of 2Gb available, how are we going to allocate enough memory to access our 4Gb file? The answer is simple. It is impossible to allocate more than 2Gb. At this point, you might decide to lower your sights a little, and say that the biggest file we will load in our file viewer will be 2Gb in size. Whilst this is what many hex-editor programs do, this is not good enough for us, is it?

The only solution will be to access the file in sections, as we need them. This has one big disadvantage, which is that, our algorithms to access/search a file become more complicated because we no longer have one contiguous memory region to operate with.

There are three major advantages to balance this one disadvantage though:

1. Because we have decided to access a file in sections, we don't need to allocate very much memory any more. If we access our file in blocks of 64kb for example, we only need one 64kb block of memory in use at any one time. This leaves a vast proportion of our 2Gb address space for other interesting things.
2. Reading and writing a file from disk becomes extremely fast. We now only read what we want, when we want it. If we had tried to load the whole file at one go, this could have taken a long time if the file was very large. Because the block size is so small in comparison, file load time becomes so fast that you will probably never notice it happening.
3. Because we are using such a small amount of memory to access the file, all of the memory facilities that we discarded as being inadequate can be revisited. In fact, any one of the four memory facilities is suitable for our purposes.

AN EXAMPLE FILE VIEWER

Now it's time to present an example. We will use memory-mapped-files as the technique to access the file's contents, simply because they are so flexible. Because of this decision, we must also use API calls to open and close the file. I'll take you through the steps to create the backbone of the file viewer.

A file viewer will typically display a tiny portion of a file in its main window. Whenever the main window needs to redrawn, the file viewer needs to retrieve the portion of the file which is currently being viewed. Most of the memory reads will be to one local area in the file. As long as our memory-mapped view of the file is big enough, then we will very rarely need to re-map the view to another area of the file. 64Kb will certainly be big enough in our case.

Only when the file-viewer scrolls up and down through the file will we potentially need to re-map our view of the file.

The diagram below should help to explain how a 64kb window is used to access a large file's contents. A user of the view (such as our hex-viewer application) is free to access any part of the file within the view. Any accesses outside the range of the view require the view to be re-mapped to that part of the file. Failure to do so would result in a fatal application error.

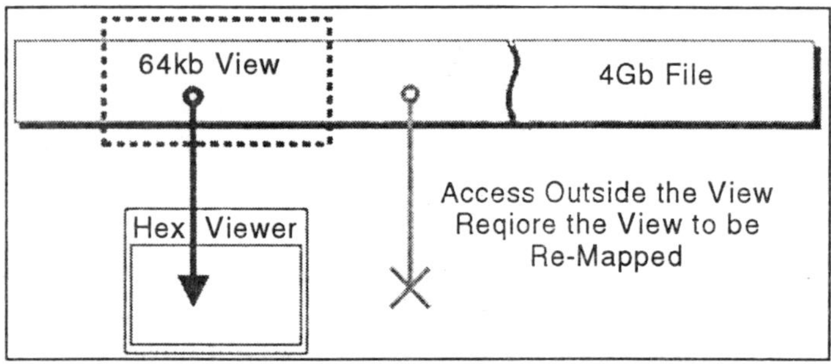

The fact that the file is accessed through a small window should be irrelevant to the display portion of the hex file viewer. All the drawing code requires is a small amount of memory every time the visible window needs to be re-drawn. The diagram above clearly illustrates a division between the window that displays the file, and the memory-mapped window that exposes the file's contents.

This relationship is basically the same as the standard MFC Document/View design, and it is this design that we will use for our file viewer. This means that our underlying implementation of the "Document" can change at any time. The "View" (the visible window) doesn't ever need to know how the Document works–it just requests small amounts of data at a time to satisfy its drawing requirements.

DOCUMENT DESIGN

The "Document" portion of our hex-viewer will be implemented as a C++ class. I chose C++ because it is much easier to perform object encapsulation than just using plain C. I don't intend to use any advanced features of C++ such as templates or inheritance, so feel free to convert the class into a C structure if you really can't stand C++.

The first thing to draw your attention to is the data-type I use to represent the size of files and sequences. I created a new typedef called size_w, which is currently an unsigned integer. This type has to be unsigned, so that the full 4Gb range can be represented. At some time in the future this type could be changed to an unsigned 64-bit integer. With a simple recompile, the sequence would be capable of handling huge 18 exabyte files (18 thousand thousand megabytes!).

This is what the class interface will look like:

```
class sequence
{
public:
sequence();
~sequence();
BOOL init(char *filename);
BOOL close();
    size_w                                size();
    BOOL render(BYTE *buffer, size_w offset,
size_w length);
private:
    BYTE *get_adjusted_ptr(size_w offset);
//private implementation details
HANDLE hMemMap;//memory mapped object
HANDLE hFile;//handle to current file
size_w length;//logical size of this sequence
size_w filebufferlength;//size in bytes of the
```

```
entire file
BYTE *filebuffer;//base of the view of the file
   BYTE *adjustedptr;//an adjusted version of the
filebuffer pointer size_w mappedoffset;//offset
of the current view within the memmap object
size_w mappedlength;//length of the view
   }                                             ;
```

As you can see, the design is very simple. The constructor and destructor don't really do an awful lot apart from setting everything to zero and cleaning up, so I'll start by describing the init() member function.

INITIALISING THE SEQUENCE WITH A FILE

The init() member function simply opens a file, and creating the file mapping which spans the length of the whole file. The rest of the work is resetting all the member variables to their default values. Note that no view of the file has been created at this stage.

```
BOOL sequence::init(char *filename)
{
HANDLE hTemp;
//try to open the specified file for read-only
acces
hTemp = CreateFile(filename, GENERIC_READ,
FILE_SHARE_READ, 0,
OPEN_EXISTING, 0, 0);
//if we failed to open the file, then exit now
class sequenceand keep the current file open
if(hTemp    ==    INVALID_HANDLE_VALUE)
return FALSE;
//now close the CURRENT file, and let the new
file become the current one
close();
hFile = hTemp;
//create a file mapping which spans the entire
file.
//This works even for the 4Gb file sizes
hMemMap = CreateFileMapping(hFile, 0,
```

```
PAGE_READONLY, 0, 0, 0);
length = GetFileSize(hFile, 0);
filebufferlength = length;
return TRUE;
}
```

REQUESTING A POINTER TO THE FILE'S CONTENTS

The "brains" behind the sequence object is the get_adjusted_ptr member function. This function is a private member, so it can't (and doesn't need to) be called from outside the sequence class.

```
BYTE *sequence::get_adjusted_ptr(size_w offset)
{
size_w baseoff = calc_index_base(offset);
//if we already have the right range of memory
mapped in
if(adjustedptr != 0 && mappedoffset == baseoff)
return adjustedptr;
//otherwise, map in the new area
else
{
if(filebuffer)
   UnmapViewOfFile(filebuffer);
mappedlength = min(filebufferlength-baseoff,
MEM_BLOCK_SIZE);
filebuffer = (BYTE *)MapViewOfFile(hMemMap,
FILE_MAP_READ, 0, baseoff, mappedlength);
mappedoffset = baseoff;
adjustedptr = filebuffer-mappedoffset;
return adjustedptr;
  }
}
```

The idea behind get_adjusted_ptr is to hide the details of the memory-mapped file from the rest of the class. As far as the rest of the class is concerned, all get_adjusted_ptr does is to return a pointer to the contents of the current file. This pointer can then be used to access the file using simple array subscripting.

There is one very important detail to mention. The pointer that is returned is ADJUSTED, so that it ALWAYS points to the first byte in the file, regardless of what portion of the file is mapped into memory. Think about this carefully and re-read the previous sentence if you didn't understand it. This may seem a little confusing at first, but read on anyway.

When a 64Kb view of the file is mapped in (aligned to a 64Kb boundary of course), the pointer to the view would be relative to the start of the view, and not the start of the file. This presents a problem, because ideally we want to access the file in as normal a way as possible. By subtracting the current view-offset (the position of the memory-mapped view within the file) from the pointer we get from MapViewOfFile, we get an adjusted pointer to the start of the file. Let's use a very small example. We want to access a region of the file at offset 0x56789.

We request a pointer to the file's contents like this:

- BYTE *filestart = get_adjusted_ptr(0x56789)

Now we have a 64Kb window which encompasses offset 0x56789, through which we can access the file's contents. Note that we are allowed to read at most 64Kb past this pointer.

Let's read some memory from this region of the file.

- BYTE buffer[200];
- Memcpy(buffer, &filestart[0x56789], 200);

Now comes the magic part (bear with me here!). We are adding 0x56789 back onto the adjusted pointer. The result of this is a pointer to the start of the current view, so we are back where we started. The memory is read from the mapped region, instead of from the start of the file, and we now have a nice intuitive way to access the file's contents as if it were one contiguous block of memory. Ok, it doesn't seem like much, and you may even be wondering why I've made such alot of work for myself. The simple fact of the matter is that the pointer arithimetic has to be performed at some stage, simply because we are accessing the file in sections. It just makes sense to hide the arithmetic in one single place, at an early stage, and let the rest of the class design be blissfully un-aware that any pointer arithmetic has to be done at all.

WHAT SECTION DO WE MAP IN?

A view of a memory-mapped file MUST be aligned to a 64Kb boundary, otherwise MapViewOfFile will fail. So, we can't simply map a view of the file at any old offset (such as 0x56789). We need some method to determine the closest 64Kb boundary to the desired access offset, and create a view at this offset instead. This is what the calc_base_index function does. calc_base_index takes one parameter (an offset or index), and returns a new offset which is on a 64Kb boundary. *i.e.* the number returned is a multiple of 65536 (0x1000).

Now, you might just think that the following formula works pretty well:

- offset = offset & 0xffff0000;

What this does is round offset down to the nearest 64Kb boundary, which is exactly what we want. It's not perfect though, for the following reason. Assume that the input offset ranges from 0 to 0xFFFFFFFF. The simple formula above provides us with consequetive 64Kb offsets, one after the other. This problem with this approach is this: What happens when we scroll down the file in our hex-view window? We reach a point when we come to the end of one mapped view, and the next view needs to be mapped in.

No problems so far. The formula above provides us with the next offset to map in. The problem occurs when we want to scroll back. We need to re-map the previous section in, just after we mapped the new one! And what happens if we scroll forwards again? What we really need is a formula which instead of rounding down to the nearest allocation unit, rounds to the middle of the nearest unit. So, if we request a some memory at an offset which is exactly on a 64Kb boundary, we don't get a memory-region starting at this offset-instead, the memory region starts half-way back to the previous 64Kb boundary.

This gives us freedom to move backwards and forwards from the requested memory address, safe in the knowledge that we have half a block-size either side to play with. This has an effect-now we are calculating offsets every 32Kb. All this means is we need to increase our window size to 128Kb to make sure we still get offsets 64Kb-aligned, but that's no problem.

```
size_w inline calc_index_base(size_w index)
{
 if(index < MEM_BLOCK_SIZE/2)
{
return 0;
}
else
{
return ((index + MEM_BLOCK_SIZE/4) &
(~(MEM_BLOCK_SIZE/2-1)))-MEM_BLOCK_SIZE/2;
}
}
```

The formula is especially nasty (it took me a while to come up with it I can tell you!). But, not only does it give us 64Kb aligned offsets, but the sections that we get from it are rounded to the centre of our input offset, not the beginning. This means that our adjusted pointer can move backwards and forwards by 32Kb without causing any views to be remapped.

If you really don't like the function above then just use "return index & 0xffff0000". The work's been done for you though, so you might as well take advantage of it. Feel free to sit down with a pen and paper and figure out how it works!

RENDERING THE SEQUENCE

The rest pf the work is collected in the render() member function. This function will be called whenever the hex-view window wants some data to draw on the screen. Other uses for this function would be copying data to the clipboard, or saving a file to disk in blocks (by repeatedly calling it).

Because we only have access to a "small". section of the file at any one time, we have to be careful when we copy the file's contents into the destination buffer. The copy has to be split into sections if the requested amount of data would overflow our view of the file. The render function handles this with a simple while-loop, as seen below.

```
BOOL sequence::render(BYTE *buffer, size_w offset,
```

```
size_w length)
{
   while(length != 0)
{
   size_w len = min(length, MEM_BLOCK_SIZE/4);
BYTE *source = get_adjusted_ptr(offset);
if(source == 0)
   return FALSE;
memcpy(buffer, source + offset, len);
offset += len;//advance the source position
buffer += len;//advance the destination offset
length -= len;//decrement the length of the copy
}return TRUE; }
```

That really sums up the whole design of the sequence document object. It may seem complicated at first, but there isn't any other way to do this sort of thing. We decided early on that we wanted access to 4Gb of file contents, so we just have to live with the consequences.

HEXVIEW WINDOW DESIGN

The design of the actual window that displays the hex-dump of a file is fairly straightforward. The only time the hex-view needs to access any of the file's contents is when it needs to update its display. When it does this, it calls the sequence::render() method to obtain 1 line (16 bytes) worth of data to display. I'm not going to describe how the hex-view window works because it would take another article to cover just that. The design is very straight-forward, and if you have a little Win32 knowledge then you shouldn't have any difficulty in understanding how the gui part works.

Don't forget I've included the full source-code to the hex-view application, and its pretty well commented. You've now have a good spring-board to develop this file viewer into a full-blown file editing application.

FILE MANAGEMENT

File Management in Windows XP

File management is a necessary evil associated with

computers. It's really not all that much different than rummaging through a heap of papers on your desk except you don't get paper cuts. In either situation, a bit of organization and using the tools available can make the task easier.

Use Full Screen View and Auto Hide

Since the majority of file management takes place in Windows Explorer, why not minimize the amount of scrolling that is inevitable by increasing the viewable area in which you have to work? Simply pressing the F11 key will substantially increase the visible area. By default, the Explorer toolbar at the top with the standard buttons will remain visible. If you want to reclaim that area as well, right click the toolbar and select Auto-Hide. Click anywhere in the main window and the toolbar will disappear. To make it reappear, move the mouse to the top of the window. Pressing F11 again will return Windows Explorer to normal view.

Use Show In Groups

Most users are familiar with the ability to display folders and files using Tile, Icon, List, Thumbnail, and Detail views. They can be easily changed using the View menu or the Views toolbar button. Many users are not aware there is another view called Show in Groups. Right click in the main Explorer pane, select Arrange Icons By and one of the options will be Show In Groups. (Note: The Show in Groups option will not be available if List View is selected. Some say this is by design, others say it's an XP bug) Once Show in Groups has been selected the files will be sorted by alphabetical headings.

Add Sort Options to Details View

When Explorer is set to use Details view the right pane contains a series of details listed across the top of the right pane. The default details are Name, Size, Type, and Date Modified. Any one of the columns may be clicked to set it as the default to be used in the sort order. The small arrowhead following the detail name indicates whether the sort is in ascending or descending order.

For most users the four default columns are more than sufficient, but if you want additional or different options they are available.

Click View > Choose Details... and the Choose Details Property Sheet will open. In addition to the four (4) defaults there are twenty-eight (28) other details that can be added or substituted. Add whatever you want, but if you go for all of them it may take you a month of horizontal scrolling to see them all.

Rename Multiple Files

One of the most tedious tasks imaginable is renaming a series of files one by one. I'm not proud to admit it, but before I discovered file renaming utilities I used to sit and perform this task on digital photo files. XP makes the task a lot easier with a built-in group file rename function. Simply select the files you want to rename and right click on the first file in the group then click Rename. Type the new filename in the following format; filename (1).ext

- Let's say you had a group of related text files you wanted to sequentially name based on creation date. Order the files by creation date then select the group of files using Click+Shift+Click. Right click the first file in the group and click Rename. Enter a filename (Ex: My New Novel (1).doc). Each file would be sequentially renamed in the order My New Novel (1).doc, My New Novel (2).doc, etc.
- The files you select to rename do not have to be contiguous. They can be selected using Click+Ctrl+Click rather than Click+Shift+Click, but they will be renamed in sequential order, not the order you selected the files. The only caveat is to be sure you right click the first file in the series before right clicking and selecting Rename.
- When entering the filename for the series, the character entered in the parenthesis for the first file does not have to be a number and the filename will appear using whatever character you entered—but

the rest of the files will have numbers in the parenthesis starting with (1).

Force My Computer Desktop Icon To Open In Windows Explorer Mode

Many users find My Computer on the desktop to be a convenient starting point for file operations. Clicking My Computer opens to a Task Pane view, which while gaining wider acceptance, has yet to come close to overtaking the more widely accepted and preferred Explorer view. To set the default so My Computer opens in Explorer view:

Launch My Computer > Tools > Folder Options... > File Types tab Select the icon for (NONE) Folder and click the Advanced button In the Actions List, select Explorer and click Set Default Click OK and Close.

"Move This Folder" and "Copy This Folder" Commands

In the previous section I mentioned Task Pane view and that it hasn't achieved wide spread acceptance, but it does have some very nice benefits. Two of them are the "Move this Folder" and the "Copy this Folder" commands. Open Explorer and look at the left pane. If you see a hierarchical tree listing of the system drives, you aren't in Task Pane view. Click the Folders button to change to Task Pane view. It's easily recognizable by the brightly coloured background and three windows labeled File and Folder Tasks, Other Places, and Details. Depending on what is selected in the right pane there may be a fourth window labeled System Tasks.

We as users have been using drag and drop for so long that old habits are hard to break, especially when shuffling folders and files around the system. These two commands and the task pane have become so convenient I hardly use drag and drop anymore for file organization. They are especially useful on a system with multiple drives where expanded file trees can stretch over quite a distance. Granted, there are many file manager shells that can be purchased that give you split screen capabilities, but I actually find this method more convenient.

The commands in the Task Pane are dynamic and change based on what is selected in the right pane. If you find the Task Pane so annoying you can't tolerate its presence (in spite of being able to toggle it on and quickly with the Folders button), you can add the "Move this Folder" and the "Copy this Folder" commands to the toolbar via the Customise Toolbar dialog box.

Creating New Folders from the Quick Launch Toolbar

Anal retentive? Well, that was more of a personal statement than a question, but if it fits you also you're probably constantly creating folders to organize items on the computer. I get tired of right clicking this and that to create new folders, but there is a quick way around the clicks. In Explorer, navigate to C:\Documents and Settings*Username*\Application Data\Microsoft\Internet Explorer\Quick Launch and create a new folder. Leave the name New Folder. Look on the Quick Launch toolbar and you'll see the folder just created.

From now on when you need a new folder, hold down Ctrl and drag and drop the New Folder icon wherever you want to place the new folder. The original New Folder icon will remain in Quick Launch, ready to create as many new folders as your hard drive will hold.

Create Quick Launch Icons to Switch Between Basic Search and Search Companion

The new XP Search Companion has some interesting features, but I grew up on the old, reliable Basic Search tool and I still prefer it in some instances, 'some' being the operative word. If you prefer to do away with the XP Search Companion totally, see this tweak, but I've found switching between the two styles has some benefit as well. Unfortunately, there is no quick, easy way to make the switch without editing the registry.

You can make the switch into a quick, three click process that allows you to switch between the two choices as often as you like. Open regedit.exe using the Run (WinKey+R) dialog box. Navigate to HKEY_CURRENT_USER\ Software\

Microsoft\ Windows\Current Version\Explorer\CabinetState Right click in the right pane and select New > String Value Name the new string Use Search Asst and press enter Double click the string name and enter no (lower case) in the Value Data: line. Click OK

In the left window pane, right click on the key Cabinet State and select Export The Export Registry dialog box will open. Name the file Disable Search Companion. Ensure the radio button in the Export Range section is set to Selected Branch and click Save Close the Registry Editor

Navigate to where you saved the file Disable Search Companion.reg Open the file using Notepad (Do Not Double Click the File) To open the file in Notepad, right click the file, select Open With and then select Notepad Find the line "Use Search Asst"="no" and replace the word no with yes Save the file using the name Enable Search Companion

Technically, that's all you have to do. Double click on the appropriate file to Enable or Disable as desired. I mentioned earlier it takes three (3) clicks. When you click either file it will present two verification boxes you have to accept for the change to be finalized. I prefer to take this tweak one step farther and dress it up a bit. I move the two.reg files into a folder named Search Selection and move it to the C:\Windows directory. Right click each file, drag to the Quick Launch bar and select Create Shortcut.

Arrange the Windows Explorer Toolbar to Your Liking

I don't believe anyone will argue with the fact the Explorer Toolbar (at the top of the screen) is useful, but I think having it stretch over three rows is overkill. With some judicious pruning, moving, and resizing of components you can fit all the essentials on a single row.

Select View > Toolbars > Customise and prune down the buttons to what is essential to the way you work. While you're there, change the size of the icons to small, and as often as we see those icons I imagine you can do without the text labels identifying them. I don't know about you, but I count XP icons when I can't sleep rather than Serta sheep. You can also move the Address Bar onto the same row to save more screen real estate.

While no single idea listed here will revolutionize file management, exploring some of them just might make things a bit easier or at least give you a new perspective on how to accomplish some pretty mundane tasks.

Also Referred to as Simply a *file System* or *file System.*

The systemthat an operating system or program uses to organize and keep track of files. For example, a *hierarchical file system* is one that uses directories to organize files into a tree structure. Although the operating system provides its own file management system, you can buy separate file management systems. These systems interact smoothly with the operating system but provide more features, such as improved backup procedures and stricter file protection.

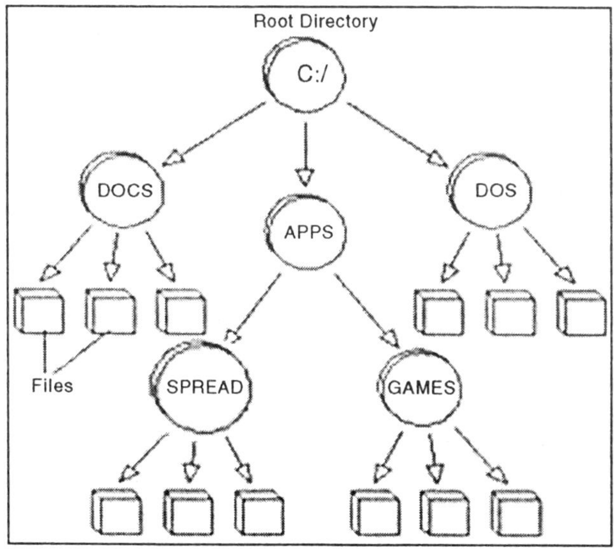

3

DOS

DEFINITION

DOS (Disk Operating System) was the first widely-installedo perating system for personal computers. (Earlier, the same name had been used for an IBM operating system for a line of business computers.)

The first personal computer version of DOS, called PC-DOS, was developed for IBM by Bill Gates and his new Microsoft Corporation. He retained the rights to market a Microsoft version, called MS-DOS. PC-DOS and MS-DOS are almost identical and most users have referred to either of them as just "DOS." DOS was (and still is) a non-graphical line-oriented command- or menu-driven operating system, with a relatively simple interface but not overly "friendly" user interface. Its prompt to enter a command looks like this:

```
C:>
```

The first Microsoft Windows operating system was really an application that ran on top of the MS-DOS operating system. Today, Windows operating systems continue to support DOS (or a DOS-like user interface) for special purposes by emulating the operating system.

In the 1970s before the personal computer was invented, IBM had a different and unrelated DOS (Disk Operating System) that ran on smaller business computers. It was replaced by IBM's VSE operating system.

DOS stands for Disk Operating System. DOS controls the computer's hardware and provides an environment for programs to run. Everything you can do with a GUI can be done at the DOS prompt. There are many flavours of DOS operating systemlike MS-DOS, PC DOS, DR DOS, FreeDOS, etc. There are two types of commands in DOS, internal and external. Internal commands are part of the command processor, whereas external commands exist as executable files. The entire operating system is small enough to fit on a floppy disk.

What is Booting?

To run DOS on a computer, it should be the first program to be executed when the computer is switched on. This led to a problem for the designers: "How can DOS be loaded and executed when there is no DOS program running to load and execute *it*??!!". Well, just as the fictional Baron Munchausen managed to pull himself up by his own bootstraps, the computer manages this seemingly impossible trick, and the term "bootstrapping", or "booting up" is applied to this process.

How do you Communicate with DOS?

DOS is an entirely text based system. All it provides for the user is a prompt: "C:>" or "A:>", where the user can type in commands from the keyboard. The system is entirely case insensitive: so either "ForMAt C:" or "format c:" would erase your hard disk. The latter example is of course a small warning: with DOS comes power, you can very easily mess up your system if you use powerful commands in the wrong way. The commands you should be careful of are: "Format", "Recover", and "Del". All of these perform useful functions, when used correctly, and all the others are pretty much safe to use.

How does DOS Organise Disks?

DOS works within a file, directory and disk drive structure. This means that all program and data files are named, and grouped together in named directories on disks. 'Directories' are just lists of files.

How are Files Named?

While newer versions of DOS support longer filenames,

the standard DOS filename format remains: 1-8 letter name, period, 3 letter extension eg:

PROGRAM.EXE DATA.DAT LETTER.DOC

The extension to a file's name is there to allow files of a similar type to be grouped together. Ie. all wordprocessor files might have the extension.DOC, while all picture files might have the extension.PIC While these extensions can be specified by the user, many programs have used them to differentiate between formats, and so they have gradually become standardised. For example you would expect a ".TXT" file to be a file containing unformatted text, or a ".BMP" file to be in a bit mapped graphics file format.

To completely specify a file on your computer you must specify its drive and directory path, and its filename. However a file does not always have to be specified in this complete form: If it is in the current directory, then you can just enter its filename.

How are Directories Named?

Every disk drive has a root directory which can have subdirectories which are named in the same format as filenames, (though generally without any extension). The subdirectories can have subdirectories and so on. Eg: a floppy disk might contain the following directory structure:

- Pictures
- Holiday
- Italy
- France
- Family
- Pets
- Text
- Letters
- E-mail

A directory path name includes the disk drive and all subdirectories needed to specify a directory on a disk. The disk drive is specified by a single letter. Eg: The floppy disk drive is A and the hard disk drive is C. The drive letter, is followed by a colon, the directory path names are separated by backward slashes (\), (*Not* forward slashes like internet addresses). Eg. In the above example "A:\ PICTURES\ HOLIDAY\FRANCE" would be more than likely to contain pictures of a few baguettes and onions.

How is DOS used?

When you type anything at the DOS prompt, and press enter, you are telling DOS to run a program. It will first look to see if there is an internal command program which has that name, and if it does not find one, then it will look to see if there is a file on disk with that name. If it finds an external file with the extension.COM (command), or.EXE (executable), then the program is loaded and run. At this point DOS looses control of the computer until the program has ended. However parts of it are still used by the programs as they are running, eg to load and save files etc.

Some very useful internal DOS commands:

- *A:*-Change current directory path to the floppy disk drive
- *C:*-Change current directory path to the hard disk drive
- *DIR:*-Display current directory (show all files and sub directories).
- *MD:*-Make a new directory, eg: MD C:\E-MAIL
- *CD:*-Change current directory, eg. CD C:\E-MAIL
- *COPY:*-Copy file(s) from one place to another.
- *Del:*-Delete/erase a file

Any other text on the input line after the file name, is passed to the program. This means that in the command "Copy help.txt help.bak", the text, "help.txt and help.bak" is passed to the copy program which will in this case use it to specify source and destination files for a copy.

DOS Usage Examples

```
DIR [enter]
   Displays the current directory listing. DIR
*.txt [enter]
   Displays any files in the current directory
```

with.TXT as their extension

DIR A:\PICTURES[enter]

Displays a directory listing for the path, A:\PICTURES

A: [enter] CD PICTURES [enter

DIR

Change to the floppy disk drive, change the current directory, and then list the files.

COPY letter.txt letter.bak [enter]

Copy the file "letter.txt" to a file called "letter.bak". (Creates "letter.bak" if it does not exist, and overwrites it if it does).

COPY A:\pictures*.pic C:\ [enter]

Copy any file with an extension PIC, in the PICTURES directory on the floppy disk drive to the root directory of the hard disk. Other useful things to learn about DOS: DOS commands can be listed and automatically executed in predefined sequence in a batch file.

(File extension.BAT), this is an extremely powerful and useful feature. Batch files are run in the same way as COM or EXE files, by simply entering the batch filename at the DOS prompt.

SET PATH=directorypath;directorypath will force DOS to look in these directories every time it is told to run a file. PROMPT $_$p$_What now? will tell DOS to display the current directory together with a more friendly prompt for input. ?-in a filename stands for any digit or letter. *-in a filename is a wildcard which stands for any combination of digits or letters Eg "Del *.txt" would erase any the files with extension txt in a directory. in a directory path stands for the current directory. in a directory path stands for the directory above the current directory, Eg: C:\PICTURES when the current directory is: C:\PICTURES\HOLIDAY.

SUBST X: C:\ Drive letters can also be used to stand for directories on the hard disk, this allows long pathnames, eg: "c:\dos\packages\wordpro\data" to be written as short drive letters, eg: "x:". These can then be used in all subsequent commands. C>

DOS COMMAND PROCESSER

THE COMMAND PROMPT

When you first turn on your computer, you will see some cryptic information flash by. MS-DOS displays this information to let you know how it is configuring your computer. You can ignore it for now.

When the information stops scrolling past, you'll see the following:

- C:\>
  - This is called the command prompt or DOS prompt. The flashing underscore next to the command prompt is called the cursor. The cursor shows where the command you type will appear.
  - If your command prompt looks like the sample command prompt above, skip to the following section, "Typing a Command."
  - If your command prompt does not look like the example, type the following at the command prompt, and then press ENTER:
- cd \
  - Note that the slash leans backward, not forward. You will learn more about the cd command later in the tutorial. If your command prompt still doesn't look like the example, type the following at the command prompt, and then press ENTER:
- prompt pg
  - Your command prompt should now look like the example.

CHANGING DIRECTORIES

Look at the list on your screen. All the names that have <DIR> beside them are directories. You can see a list of the files in another directory by changing to that directory, and then using the dir command again. In this case, you will change to the DOS directory. Before you begin this section, make sure you have a directory named DOS by carrying out the following procedure.

To make sure you have a directory named DOS:

1. Look through the directory list on your screen for a line that looks similar to the following:
   DOS <DIR> 09-02-92 4:23p
2. If you see a line like this, you have a directory named DOS. Skip to the next procedure, "To change from the root directory to the DOS directory."

If you do not see a line in the directory list indicating that you have a directory named DOS,

Type the following at the command prompt:

- dir/s memmaker.exe

You will see a message that includes a line such as the following:

- Directory of C:\DIRNAME

If the name that appears in place of DIRNAME is DOS, you have a DOS directory. Skip to the next procedure.

If the name that appears in place of DIRNAME is not DOS, substitute the name that appears for DOS throughout this tutorial. For example, if the name that appears in place of DIRNAME is MSDOS, type msdos whenever you are instructed to type dos. To change from the root directory to the DOS directory

To change directories, you will use the cd command.

The cd command stands for "change directory."

- Type the following at the command prompt.
  - cd dos
- The command prompt changes. It should now look like the following.
  - C:\DOS>

The command prompt shows which directory you are in. In this case, you know you successfully changed to the DOS directory because the command prompt displays the directory's name. Now the *current directory* is DOS. Next, you will use the dir command to view a list of the files in the DOS directory.

To view a list of the files in the DOS directory

- Type the following at the command prompt.
  - dir

A list of the files in the DOS directory appears, but scrolls by too quickly to read. You can modify the dir command so that it displays only one screen of information at a time.

To view the contents of a directory one screen at a time

- Type the following at the command prompt.
  - dir/p
- One screen of information appears. At the bottom of the screen, you will see the following message:
  - Press any key to continue...
- To view the next screen of information, press any key on your keyboard. Repeat this step until the command prompt appears at the bottom of your screen.

When you typed the dir command this time, you included the/p switch after the command. A *switch* modifies the way MS-DOS carries out a command. Generally, a switch consists of a forward slash (/) that is followed by one or more letters or numbers. When you used the/p switch with the dir command, you specified that MS-DOS should pause after it displays each screen of directory list information. The p actually stands for "page"

Another helpful switch you can use with the dir command is the/w switch. The/w switch indicates that MS-DOS should show a wide version of the directory list.

To view the contents of a directory in wide format

- Type the following at the command prompt.
  - dir/w

The directory list appears, with the filenames listed in wide format. Note that only filenames are listed. No information about the files' size or date and time of creation appears.

- If the directory contains more files than will fit on one screen, you can combine the/p and/w switches as follows.
  - dir/w/p

CHANGING BACK TO THE ROOT DIRECTORY

Next, you will change from the DOS directory to the root directory. The root directory is the directory you were in before you changed to the DOS directory.

Before you begin this section, make sure your command prompt looks like the following:

- C:\DOS>

To change to the root directory:

- Type the following at the command prompt.
  - cd \

Note that the slash you type in this command is a backslash (\), not a forward slash (/). No matter which directory you are in, this command always returns you to the root directory of a drive. The root directory does not have a name. It is simply referred to by a backslash (\).

- The command prompt should now look like the following.
  - C:\>

When your command prompt appears similar to this—that is, when it does not contain the name of a directory—you are in the root directory.

CREATING A DIRECTORY

In this section, you will create two directories. Creating a directory is helpful if you want to organize related files into groups to make them easy to find.

Before you begin this section, make sure the command prompt looks like the following:

- C:\>

To create a directory, you will use the md command. The md command stands for "make directory."

To create and change to a directory named FRUIT

- Type the following at the command prompt.
  - md fruit

You have now created a directory named FRUIT. You won't see the new FRUIT directory until you carry out the dir command in the next step.

- To confirm that you successfully created the FRUIT directory, type the following at the command prompt.
  - dir

  or

  - dir/p

Look through the directory list.

A new entry somewhere in the list should look similar to the following:

- FRUIT <DIR> 09-25-93 12:09p
- To change to the new FRUIT directory, type the following at the command prompt.
  - cd fruit
- The command prompt should now look like the following.
  - C:\FRUIT>

You will now create a directory within the FRUIT directory, named GRAPES.

To create and work with a directory named GRAPES

1 Type the following at the command prompt.
  - md grapes
    - You will not see the new GRAPES directory until you carry out the dir command in the next step.

2. To confirm that you successfully created the GRAPES directory, type the following at the command prompt.
  - dir
  - A list similar to the following appears.
    - Volume in drive C is MS-DOS-6
    - Volume Serial Number is lE49-15E2
    - Directory of C:\FRUIT
    - <DIR> 09-25-93 12:08p
    - <DIR> 09-25-93 12:08p
    - GRAPES <DIR> 09-25-93 12:10p
  3. file(s) 0 bytes 11534336 bytes free

Note that there are three entries in the FRUIT directory. One is the GRAPES directory that you just created. There are two other entries—one looks like a single period (.) and the other looks like a double period (..). These directory entries are important to MS-DOS, but you can ignore them. They appear in every directory and contain information relation to the directory structure.

The GRAPES directory is a *subdirectory* of the FRUIT directory. A subdirectory is a directory within another directory. Subdirectories are useful if you want to further subdivide information.

3. To change to the GRAPES directory, type the following at the command prompt:
   - cd grapes

   The command prompt should now look like the following:
   - C:\FRUIT\GRAPES>
4. To switch back to the FRUIT directory, type the following.
   - cd..

   The command prompt should now look like the following:
   - C:\FRUIT>

When the cd command is followed by two periods (..), MS-DOS moves up one level in the directory structure. In this case, you moved up one level from the GRAPES directory to the FRUIT directory.

DELETING A DIRECTORY

If you no longer use a particular directory, you may want to delete it to simplify your directory structure. Deleting a directory is also useful if you type the wrong name when you are creating a directory and you want to delete the incorrect directory before creating a new one. In this section, you will delete the GRAPES directory.

Before you begin this section, make sure the command prompt looks like the following:

- C:\FRUIT>

To delete a directory, use the rd command. The rd command stands for *"remove directory."*

To delete the GRAPES directory:

1. Type the following at the command prompt.
   - rd grapes
2. To confirm that you successfully deleted the GRAPES directory, type the following at the command prompt.
   - dir

The GRAPES directory should no longer appear in the directory list. Note You cannot delete a directory if you are in it. Before you can delete a directory, you must make the directory that is one level higher the current directory. To do this, type cd.. at the command prompt.

CHANGING DRIVES

This section describes how to change drives. Changing drives is useful if you want to work with files that are on a different drive.

So far, you have been working with drive C. You have other drives you can use to store information. For example, drive A is your first floppy disk drive. The files and directories on drive A are located on the floppy disk in the drive. (You might also have a drive B, which contains the files and directories stored on the floppy disk in that drive.)

Before you begin this section, make sure your command prompt looks like the following:

- C:\FRUIT>

To change to and view files on a different drive:

1. Insert a 3.5" floppy disk in drive A label- side up. Make sure the disk clicks into the drive.

   Type the following at the command prompt:

   - a:

   Note that the command prompt changed to the following:

   - A:\>

   This message may appear:

   - Not ready reading drive A
   - Abort, Retry, Fail?

   If you see this message, the disk may not be inserted properly. Place the disk label-side up in the disk drive, and make sure the disk clicks into the disk drive. Then, type r for Retry. If this message appears again, press F for Fail, and then type b: at the command prompt. If you no longer see this message, type b: instead of a: throughout the rest of the tutorial.

   There must be a floppy disk in the drive that you want to change to.

2. To view a list of the files on the floppy disk in drive A, type the following at the command prompt:
   - dir: A list of the files on the disk appears.
3. Change back to drive C by typing the following at the command prompt:
   - c:

   Your command prompt should return to the following:
   - C:\FRUIT>

When you type a drive letter followed by a colon, you change to that drive. The drive letter that appears in the command prompt shows which drive is the *current drive.* Unless you specify otherwise, any commands you type are carried out on the current drive and in the current directory.

So far, all the commands you typed were carried out on the current drive and in the current directory. You can also carry out a command on a drive that isn't current. For example, you can view the files on a disk in drive A without switching to drive A by following this procedure.

To view files on drive A when drive C is current

1. *Type the following at the command prompt*:
   - dir a:

A list of the files on the floppy disk in drive A appears, even though your command prompt indicates that drive C is current.

By specifying a: After the dir command, you are giving MS-DOS additional information. You are indicating that you want the dir command to show the list of files and directories on drive A instead of drive C. The a: you typed after the dir command is called a *parameter*. A parameter specifies what a command should act on. In the previous example, the parameter you used indicated which directory list you want to view.

The following procedure presents another example of using a parameter.

To view the contents of the DOS directory on drive C

1. Type the following at the command prompt.
   - dir c:\dos

A list of the files in the DOS directory on drive C should

scroll past on your screen. The c:\dos parameter specifies that you want MS-DOS to display the contents of the DOS directory on drive C, e

COPYING FILES

This section describes how to copy a single file and a group of files. Copying files creates a duplicate of the original file and does not remove the original file. This is useful for many reasons. For example, if you want to work on a document at home, you can copy it from your computer at work to a floppy disk and then take the floppy disk home.

To copy a file, you will use the copy command. When you use the copy command, you must include two parameters. The first is the location and name of the file you want to copy, or the source. The second is the location to which you want to copy the file, or the destination. You separate the source and destination with a space.

The copy command follows this pattern:

- Copy source destination
- Copying a Single File

In this section, you will copy the EDIT.HLP and EDIT.COM files from the DOS directory to the FRUIT directory. You will specify the source and destination of these files in two different ways. The difference between the two methods is explained at the end of this section.

Before you begin this section, make sure the command prompt looks like the following:

- C:\FRUIT>

To copy the EDIT.HLP and EDIT.COM files from the DOS directory to the FRUIT directory

Return to the root directory by typing the following at the command prompt:

- cd\

The command prompt should now look like the following:

- C:\>

Change to the DOS directory by typing the following at the command prompt:

- cd dos

The command prompt should now look like the following:

- C:\DOS>
- Make sure the file you are going to copy, EDIT.COM, is located in the DOS directory by using the dir command followed by a filename.

To see if the EDIT.COM file is in the DOS directory, type the following at the command prompt:

- dir edit.com

A list similar to the following appears:

- Volume in drive C is MS-DOS-6
- Volume Serial Number is lE49-15E2
- Directory of C:\DOS
- EDIT Com 413 03-25-93 5:00a
- 1 file(s) 413 bytes 11999232 bytes free

This shows that the EDIT.COM file is located in the DOS directory. You just specified another parameter with the dir command, one that directs MS-DOS to list only the files that match the filename you specified in the command. Since only one file in the DOS directory can be named EDIT.COM, the directory list includes only that file.

To copy the EDIT.COM file from the DOS directory to the FRUIT directory, type the following at the command prompt:

- Copy c:\dos\edit.com c:\fruit

The following message appears:

- 1 file(s) copied

The command you just typed copied the file from its source to its destination. By specifying C:\DOS\EDIT.COM as the source, you indicated that MS-DOS would find the source file EDIT.COM on drive C in the DOS directory. By specifying C:\FRUIT as the destination, you indicated that MS-DOS should place the copy of EDIT.COM on drive C in the FRUIT directory. Next, you will copy the EDIT.HLP file to the FRUIT directory.

To confirm that the EDIT.HLP file is in the DOS directory, type the following at the command prompt:

- dir edit.hlp

To copy the EDIT.HLP file from the DOS directory to the FRUIT directory, type the following at the command prompt:

- copy edit.hlp \fruit

The following message appears:

- 1 file(s) copied

If you forgot to leave a space before typing fruit, the following message will appear:

- Access denied

If this message appears, type the command again and leave a space before fruit. To confirm that you copied the files successfully, view the contents of the FRUIT directory by typing the following at the command prompt:

- dir \fruit

You should see the two files listed in the FRUIT directory. Note that you specified the source and destination in the two copy commands differently. In the command you typed in step 4, you specified the source file as C:\DOS\EDIT.COM and the destination directory as C:\FRUIT. Both C:\DOS\EDIT.COM and C:\FRUIT are called full paths because you specified the drive and directory where these files are located. Specifying the full path is the safest way to copy files, because you provide all the information about which file you want to copy and which directory you want to copy it to.

In the copy command you typed in step 6, you specified EDIT.HLP for the source file and FRUIT for the destination directory. These are relative paths. A relative path specifies only the difference between the current drive and directory and the destination of the files you are copying. The following illustration shows how the DOS directory and the FRUIT directory are related:

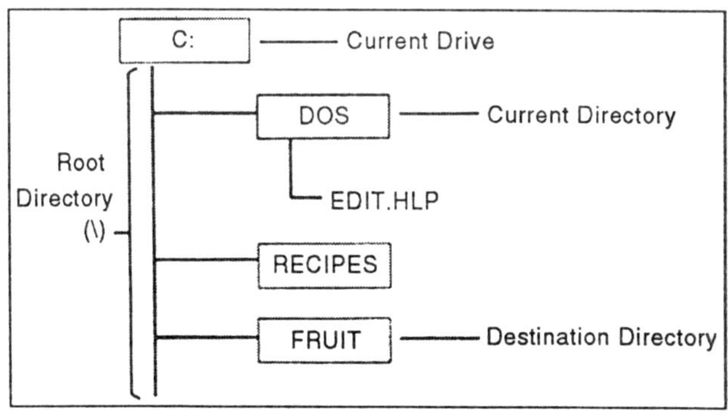

When you typed the second copy command, you specified the source filename as EDIT.HLP instead of C:\DOS\EDIT.HLP. This is because drive C is the current drive, so you did not have to repeat C: in the path. The DOS directory is the current directory, so you did not have to repeat DOS in the path. You had to specify only the filename.

For the destination directory, you specified the relative path as FRUIT instead of C:\FRUIT. Again, you did not need to specify drive C, because drive C is current. However, the FRUIT directory is not current. To access the FRUIT directory from the current directory, DOS, MS-DOS must first return to the root directory (), and then switch to the FRUIT directory, before copying the file to its new location. Therefore, you typed the path MS-DOS must take to switch between the current directory and the FRUIT directory, or \FRUIT.

COPYING A GROUP OF FILES

In this section, you will use wildcards to copy a group of files from the DOS directory to the FRUIT directory. In a card game, a wildcard matches any card in the deck. In MS-DOS, the asterisk (*) wildcard matches any character in that position and all the other positions that follow it. If you want to copy a group of files with similar names, using wildcards is easier than copying each file individually.

In this section, you will first view a group of files by using wildcards, and then copy the files using wildcards.

Before you begin this section, make sure your command prompt looks like the following:

- C:\DOS>

To list all files ending with the extension TXT and copy them from the DOS directory to the FRUIT directory by using wildcards. *View all the files in the DOS directory that end with the extension TXT by typing the following at the command prompt:*

- dir *.txt

Note that there is a space before the asterisk (*), but not after it. This command directs MS-DOS to list all files and subdirectories in the current directory that end with the extension JXT. The asterisk matches the first character of the filename and all other characters that follow it, up to the period () that separates the name from the TXT extension.

A list similar to the following appears:

- Volume in drive C is MS-DOS_6
- Volume Serial Number is lE49-15E2 Directory of C:\DOS
- NETWORKS TXT 8369 11-11-93 5:00a
- OS2 TXT 4587 11-11-93 5:00a
- README TXT 10858 11-11-93 5:00a
- 3 file(s) 23814 bytes

MS-DOS lists all the files that end with a TXT extension. The wildcard in your command specified that MS-DOS should ignore the very different beginnings of the files and focus only on the extensions. Next, you will copy all the files with a TXT extension to the FRUIT directory by using wildcards.

To copy the files with a TXT extension to the FRUIT directory, type the following at the command prompt:

- copy *.txt \fruit

This command copies all the files that have the TXT extension from the current directory (DOS) to the FRUIT directory. To confirm that you copied the files successfully, change to the FRUIT directory by typing the following at the command prompt:

- cd \fruit

To view a list of all the files in the FRUIT directory, type the following at the command prompt:

- dir

A list similar to the following appears:

- Volume in drive C is MS-DOS_6
- Volume Serial Number is lE49-15E2 Directory of C:\FRUIT
- . <DIR> 09-27-93 11:11p
- .. <DIR> 09-27-93 11:11p
- EDIT COM 413 11-11-93 5:00a
- EDIT HLP 17898 11-11-93 5:00a
- NETWORKS TXT 8369 11-11-93 5:00a
- OS2 TXT 4587 11-11-93 5:00a
- README TXT 10858 11-11-93 5:00a

- 7 file(s) 42125 bytes
- 40652800 bytes free

The EDIT.COM and EDIT.HLP files are the files you copied by following the procedure in the previous section. The files with TXT extensions are the ones you just copied by using wildcards.

RENAMING FILES

This section explains how to rename files. You may want to rename a file if the information in it changes or if you decide you prefer another name. To rename a file, you will use the ren command. The ren command stands for "rename." When you use the ren command, you must include two parameters. The first is the file you want to rename, and the second is the new name for the file. You separate the two names with a space.

The ren command follows this pattern:

- Ren oldname newname
- Renaming a File

In this section, you will rename the README.TXT file.

Before you begin this section, make sure your command prompt looks like the following:

- C:\FRUIT>

To rename the README.TXT file to PEACH.TXT, type the following at the command prompt:

- Rsen readme.txt peach.txt

To confirm that you renamed the file successfully, type the following at the command prompt:

- dir

The name PEACH.TXT should appear instead of the name README.TXT. It is the same file, but now has a different name.

RENAMING A GROUP OF FILES

You also can use wildcards to rename a group of files. If you want to rename a group of files that have similar names, using wildcards is easier than renaming the files individually. In this section, you will rename a group of files by using wildcards.

Before beginning this section, make sure your command prompt looks like the following:

- C:\FRUIT>

To rename the files whose names begin with EDIT by using wildcards

List the files in the FRUIT directory that begin with EDIT by typing the following at the command prompt:

- Dir edit.*

A list of the files in the FRUIT directory that begin with EDIT appears.

To rename the files that begin with EDIT to the new name PEAR, type the following command:

- Ren edit.* pear.*

This command specifies that all the files that begin with EDIT should be renamed PEAR, but should keep their original extensions.

To confirm that you renamed the files successfully, type the following at the command prompt:

- Dir pear.*

When the files were renamed, their extensions remained the same. For example, EDIT.COM became PEAR.COM, and EDIT.HLP became PEAR.HLP.

You can also rename extensions this way. For example, suppose you want to indicate that a group of files ending with a TXT extension are old. You can use wildcards to rename the files so they have the extension OLD.

To rename all the files in the current directory whose names end with the extension.TXT

View a list of all the files in the current directory with the extension TXT by typing the following command:

- Dir *.txt

To rename all files in the current directory that end with the extension TXT to end with the extension OLD, type the following command:

- Ren *.txt *.old

To confirm that you renamed the files successfully, type the following at the command prompt:

- Dir

The files that had the extension TXT now have the extension OLD.

DELETING FILES

This section explains how to delete, or remove, a file that you no longer want on your disk. If you don't have very much disk space, deleting files you no longer use is essential.

To delete a file, you will use the del command.

The del command stands for "delete."

- Deleting a File

In this section, you will delete two files using the del command.

Before you begin, make sure your command prompt looks like the following:

- C:\FRUIT>

To delete the PEARCOM and PEAR.HLP files

Delete the PEAR.COM file by typing the following at the command prompt:

- Del pear.com

Delete the PEAR.HLP file by typing the following at the command prompt:

- del pear.hlp

To confirm that you deleted the files successfully, type the following at the command prompt:

- dir

The PEAR.COM and PEAR.HLP files should no longer appear in the list.

- Deleting a Group of Files

In this section, you will use wildcards to delete a group of files.

Before you begin this section, make sure your command prompt looks like the following:

- C:\FRUIT>

To delete files in the current directory that end with the extension OLD by using wildcards

View all files that end with the extension OLD by typing the following at the command prompt:

- dir *.old

A list of all the files that end with the extension OLD appears. Make sure that these are the files you want to delete. When you are deleting files by using wildcards, this step is very important. It will prevent you from deleting files accidentally.

Delete all files ending with OLD by typing the following at the command prompt:

- del *.old

To confirm that all the files with the extension OLD have been deleted, type the following at the command prompt:

- dir

The FRUIT directory should contain no files.

Now that the FRUIT directory is empty, you can delete it by using the rd (remove directory) command that you learned to use in "Deleting a Directory" earlier in this chapter.

- To delete the FRUIT directory

Return to the root directory by typing the following at the command prompt:

- cd \

You can see the FRUIT directory in the directory list by typing the following at the command prompt:

- dir or dir/p

Remove the FRUIT directory by typing the following at the command prompt:

- rd fruit

To verify that the FRUIT directory has been removed, type the following at the command prompt:

- dir or dir/p

The FRUIT directory should not appear in the directory list.

FORMATTING A FLOPPY DISK

When you purchase new floppy disks, you may be required to format them before you can use them. Practice formatting a floppy disk now.

Caution The data on the disk you format will be erased, so make sure you select a disk that does not contain information you may need later.

To format a floppy disk

Type the following at the command prompt:

- format a:

This command specifies that you want to format the disk in drive A.

When you press ENTER, the following message appears:

- Insert new diskette for drive A:
- and press ENTER when ready...

Insert the disk you want to format in drive A label-side up. Then close the drive door or make sure the disk clicks into the drive. When you are ready, press ENTER.

The following message appears:

- Checking existing disk format
- Saving UNFORMAT information

As it formats the disk, MS-DOS displays the percentage of the disk that has been formatted.

When the format is complete, the following message appears:

- Volume label (11 characters, ENTER for none)?

A volume label is a name for your disk. You can give your disk any name you like, as long as it has 11 or fewer characters. For this exercise, type practice and then press ENTER.

Information similar to the following appears:

- 1213952 bytes total disk space
- 1213952 bytes available on disk
- 512 bytes in each allocation unit.
- 2371 allocation units available on disk.
- Volume Serial Number is lE49-15E2 Format another (Y/N)?

If you have another disk to format, press Y. If not, press N.

COMMAND. COM

Let's discuss MS-DOS commands from COMMAND. COM. It's a command processor which works as an interface between you, the user, and DOS. It basically interprets what you have typed at the DOS prompt and processes them. Commands can be categorized into INTERNAL (memory resident) and EXTERNAL (utilities/programs) types.

INTERNAL COMMANDS

Internal commands are memory resident commands. They are resident in the memory when the COMMAND.COM is loaded in the boot up process. Table 1 below shows the list of internal commands.

BREAK	DEL or ERASE	MKDIR or MD	SHIFT
CALL	DIR	PATH	TIME
CHCP	ECHO	PAUSE	TYPE
CHDIR or CD	EXIT	PROMPT	VER
CLS	FOR	REM	VERIFY
Copy	GOTO	RENAME or REN	VOL
CTTY	IF	RMDIR or RD	
DATE	LOADHIGH or LH	SET	

List of Internal Commands.

View the Brief Description of these Commands

- BREAK: Sets or clears extended CTRL+C checking.
- *CALL:* Calls one batch program from another.
- *CHCP:* Displays or sets the active code page number.
- *CHDIR:* Displays the name of or changes the current directory.
- *CD:* Displays the name of or changes the current directory.
- *CLS:* Clears the screen.
- *COPY*: Copies one or more files to another location.
- *CTTY:* Changes the terminal device used to control your system.
- *DATE*: Displays or sets the date.
- *DEL*: Deletes one or more files.
- *ERASE*: Deletes one or more files.
- *DIR*: Displays a list of files and subdirectories in a directory.
- *ECHO*: Displays messages, or turns command echoing on or off.
- *EXIT*: Quits the COMMAND.COM program (command interpreter).
- *FOR*: Runs a specified command for each file in a set of files.

- *GOTO*: Directs MS-DOS to a labelled line in a batch program.
- IF: Performs conditional processing in batch program.
- *LOADHIGH*: Loads a program into the upper memory area.
- *LH:* Loads a program into the upper memory area.
- *MKDIR*: Creates a directory.
- *MD:* Creates a directory.
- *PATH:* Displays or sets a search path for executable files.
- *PAUSE*: Suspends processing of a batch file and displays a message.
- *PROMPT:* Changes the MS-DOS command prompt.
- *REM*: Records comments (remarks) in a batch file or config.sys.
- *RENAME*: Renames a file or files.
- *REN*: Renames a file or files.
- *RMDIR:* Removes a directory.
- *RD:* Removes a directory.
- *SET*: Displays, sets, or removes MS-DOS environment variables.
- *SHIFT*: Changes the position of replaceable parameters in a batch file.
- *TIME*: Displays or sets the system time.
- TYPE: Displays the contents of a text file.
- VER: Displays the MS-DOS version.
- VERIFY Directs MS-DOS to verify that your files are written correctly to a disk.
- *VOL*: Displays a disk volume label and serial number.

EXTERNAL COMMANDS

External commands are MS-DOS utilities/programs. These are the.EXE or.COM programs located on your hard drive. They are normally placed under C:\DOS, the default directory. MS-DOS will load external commands if and only if you instruct to execute them at the DOS prompt and/or in a batch program.

WILD CARD

INTRODUCTION AND USES

Wildcards are characters that can be used to stand-in for unknown characters in file names. In card games, a wildcard is a card that can match up with any other cards. In DOS, wildcard characters can match up with any character that is allowable in a file name.

There are two wildcards in DOS:

- * = matches up with any combination of allowable characters
- ? = matches up with any single allowable character

Of course, since these two characters are used for wildcards, they are not allowable in filenames themselves. A filename like myfile?.txt would not be allowed. If you tried to create a file with this name you would get an error message "Bad file name." But wildcards are very useful in any DOS command which uses a filename as an argument (which is most DOS commands, come to think of it.)

*The asterisk character, *, can stand in for any number of characters. Some examples of this command:*

- c:\>del *.doc

This command would delete every file with the *doc* extension from the root directory of C:. So files like *myfile.doc, testfile.doc,* and *123.doc*would all be deleted.

- C:\>copy ab*.txt a:

This command would copy every file that began with *ab*, and had an extension of *txt*, to the floppy drive A:. So files like *abstract.txt,abalone.txt*, and *abba.txt* would all be copied.

- C:\temp\>del *.*

This is the fastest way to clean out a directory. This command will delete every file in the directory C:\temp\. The first apostrophe covers every filename, and the second one covers every extension. The question mark wildcard, ?, stands in for any single character.

Some examples of this command:

- C:\>del ?.doc

This command would only delete files that had a single

character filename and a *doc* extension from the root directory. So a file like *a.doc* or*1.doc* is history, but a file like *io.doc* is perfectly safe, since it has two characters.

- C:\>copy ab?.txt a:

This command would copy any file with a three-letter name, of which the first two letters were *ab*, and with a *txt* extension, to the floppy drive A:. So files like *abz.txt* and *ab2.txt* would be copied.

You can combine these wildcards in any command as well.

- C:\temp\>del *ab?.do?

This command would be very selective. It would look in the temp directory for files that had anywhere from 1 to 5 beginning characters, followed by *ab* followed by one character, and which had an extension of *do* followed by any one character. It would then delete any such files as matched. Examples of matching files would be *itab3.dox, mearabt.doq,* and *123abc.doc*. But the file *allabon.doc* would not be deleted because it does not match. It has two characters following the letters *ab* in the filename, and the command specified one character in that position.

Attributes

Every file in DOS has four *attributes*.

These are:

- Read-only
- Archive
- System
- Hidden

As we saw in lesson 9, each file has an entry in the directory, and in that entry there are four bits, one each for the four attributes. These attributes are turned on if the bit is set to 1, and turned off if it is set to 0.

The Read-only attribute, if it is set to on, will let you read the contents of a file, but you cannot modify it in any way. If you turn the read-only attribute off, you can modify, delte, or move the file.

The Archive bit is set on when a file is first created, and then set off when the file has been backed-up by a good backup software program. If the file is ever modified, the archive bit is turned back on. That way, the software that does the backup can look at the archive bit on each file to determine if it needs to be backed up.

The System attribute is used to mark a file as a system file. In earlier versions of DOS, files marked "system" were completely off-limits without specialized utilities, but now the attribute serves mostly as a warning.

The Hidden attribute is used to prevent a file from being seen by other commands. If you try to clean out a subdirectory (such as by using the DEL *.* command), then try and remove the subdirectory, and then get an error that the subdirectory is not empty, you have a hidden file in there that was not deleted, even with the wildcards.

You can view the attributes for any file by using the DOS command ATTRIB. If you run the command without any arguments, you will get a listing of all the attributes that are turned on for every file in the subdirectory:

- C:\temp\>attrib

This will give you a list of the files in the C:\temp\ subdirectory, for every attribute that is turned on you will see a letter (A for archive, S for system, H for hidden, and R for read-only) at the beginning of the line.

You can also look at the attributes for any one file by including that filename (with an optional path) as an argument in the command:

- C:\temp\>attrib myfile.txt
- C:\temp\>attrib c:\docs\123.doc

And you can change the attributes for any file by making *the following arguments in the command:*

- +r = makes a file read-only
- -r = removes the read-only status, makes a file editable again
- +a = turns on the archive bit (*i.e.* flags this file as not having been backed up)
- -a = turns off the archive bit (*i.e.* shows this files as having been backed up)
- +s = marks the file as a system file

- -s = removes the system file designation
- +h = makes the file "hidden" to other commands
- -h = reveals the file to other commands
- C:\temp\> attrib -h hidfile.txt
  The file *hidfile.txt* will now be visible to other DOS commands.
- You can chain these together if you wish:
- C:\temp\>attrib -h -r myfile.txt
- This will both reveal the file *myfile.txt* and make it editable and deletable.

DIR with Wildcards

The DIR command is generally used to get a listing of all of the files in given subdirectory. But it can do more. If the DIR command is given without any arguments, it returns a list of all files in the subdirectory. But with a few arguments it becomes a search tool that works much like the Windows Find tool.

For instance, you can use wildcards to search for a file that matches certain characters:

- C:\>dir *.doc

This command would return a list of all the files in the root directory with the DOC extension.

- C:\>dir memo?.*

This command would return a list of all files in the root directory with names that begin with MEMO, have one additional character following in the name, and have any extension at all. You can use all of the DOS Wildcards we discussed in the last lesson to find specific files. This can be very handy in a large directory to check for files, or to make sure before using a DEL command with wildcards that you know exactly what you are deleting. Remember that DOS does not have a Recycle Bin, so when you delete a file it may very well be unrecoverable. (There are DOS utilities to "undelete" a file, but they are uncertain. Better to not make a mistake in the first place.)

DIR with Attributes

You can also use the DIR command with an Attribute

argument to find files that match the attribute selected. The syntax for this is the DIR command, followed by a space, then/ A:, which signals an attribute argument, followed by the specific attribute(s) you want to search for. You can enter as many attributes as you like in order, without leaving a space between them.

There are 10 attributes you can specify:

1. h = hidden
2. -h = not hidden
3. s = system
4. -s = not system
5. a = archivable files
6. -a = already archived files
7. r = read-only files
8. -r = not read-only (*i.e.* editable and deletable) files
9. d = directories only, no files
10. -d = files only, no directories

So, if you wanted to find all the files you not yet backed up, you would use a command like this:

- C:\>dir/a:a

Every file in the root directory with the archive bit set "on" would be returned by this command.

- C:\docs\>dir/a:-ar

This would return every file in the C:\DOCS subdirectory that was read-only and already backed up. If you know about Boolean operators, what happens when you use multiple attributes is that the command is interpreted as a logical "AND" command, which means that every file returned has to satisfy all of the attribute specifications.

- C:\temp\>dir/a:h

This would return every file in the C:\TEMP subdirectory that was marked hidden. Interestingly, if you used a simple DIR command, no hidden files would be displayed. But if you use the command shown above, they are displayed for you quite plainly. Marking a file as hidden in DOS is not a lot of security, in other words. Don't rely on it that way.

Sometimes, particularly in the root directory, you may need to look for the subdirectories you have established. If you use a simple DIR command, you will be presented with several screens of files and subdirectories all mixed up.

But you can do this:

C:\>dir/a:d

This command will return only the subdirectories from the root directory, without displaying any of the files in the root directory.

DIR in Order

You can also display the results of your DIR command in order. The syntax for this is very similar to using attributes. You leave a space after the DIR command, or a space after any other switches, and enter "/O:", followed by a selection, to put things in order.

Here you have 12 possible options

1. N = alphabetical order (by filename)
2. -N = reverse alphabetical order (by filename)
3. E = alphabetical order (by file extension)
4. -E = reverse alphabetical order (by file extension)
5. D = Order by date and time, earliest first
4. -D = Order by date and time, latest first
5. S = By size (increasing)
6. -S-By size (decreasing)
7. C = By DoubleSpace compression ratio lowest to highest (Version 6.0 only)
8. -C = By DoubleSpace compression ratio highest to lowest (Version 6.0 only)
9. G = Group directories before other files
10. -G-Group directories after other files

So, if you wanted to see your directory results grouped by file extension, you might want to try:

C:\>dir/o:e

This will return a list of files put in alphabetical order of file extension. So all the *.DOC files will come before all of the *.EXE files, and they will come before all of the *.TXT files.

But if you are looking for that file you were working on yesterday:

C:\>dir/o:-d

This will return a list of files with the most recent ones at the top of the list.

If you need to clean up your hard drive because you are running out of space:

- C:\>dir/o:-s

This will return a list of files with the largest ones at the top of the list.

DIR with Multiple Arguments

You can use multiple arguments in a DIR command to achieve fairly complex results. Remember that each argument has to be separated from its neighbours by a blank space on each side.

- C:\>dir/a:a/o:d/p

This command would select only those files that have not yet been backed up (/a:a), display them in order by date, beginning with the oldest (/o:d), and display the results on your monitor one page at a time (/p).

So you can really do some slick stuff with the DIR command once you master the use of these arguments and switches. In case you were wondering, anything that modifies a command is an argument. If it has a slash in front, it is a switch. So all switches are also arguments, but some arguments (*e.g.* path) are not switches.

Try out some of these. The best way to get comfortable with these commands is to practice using them.

REDIRECTING INPUT AND OUTPUT IN MS DOS

Placeholders used:

- COMMAND stands for the command line command string, which could be anything from the "*DIR* *.*" command to "*ECHO Hi*"
- SRC stands for Source
- DEST stands for Destination
- STDIN (0) stands for Standard Input or channel 0
- STDOUT (1) stands for Standard Output or channel 1
- STDERR (2) stands for Errors or channel 2

STDIN and *STDOUT* can be various different things, such as:

- NUL = Nothing (usually used for suppressing any output to anywhere)
- CON = Console or Screen
- PRN = Printer (Only works, if a DOS printer is configured on LPT1)
- AUX = Auxiliary
- COM1... COM9 = Serial Ports 1 to 9
- LPT1... LPT9 = Parallel Ports 1 to 9
- *FileName* = a File Name, File Path/Location & File Name
- *Command* = another Command

The character "<" (less than) stands for Input, the character ">" (greater than) stands for Output (with overwrite) and 2x ">" (greater than) = ">>" also stands for Output, but without overwrite (appending).

COMMAND>DEST redirects the Standard Output of *COMMAND* to *DEST* (Overwriting Previous Outputs) COMMAND>>DEST redirects the Standard Output of *COMMAND* to *DEST* (Not Overwriting Previous Outputs) COMMAND<SRC feeds *COMMAND* via the Standard Input from *SRC*

If you redirect the output to a File for example, you maybe noticed that sometimes not everything is being redirected into the file and some output still occurs on the screen. The reason for that is that you only redirect the *STDOUT* channel, but not the *STDERR* channel, which some commands and applications actually use for their error messages output. If you want to redirect the *STDERR* output to the same output channel specified *as DEST*use the following syntax:

COMMAND>DEST 2>&0

COMMAND output ">" redirect to DEST (STDOUT), "space", 2, which stands for STDERR and ">" redirect to "&0", which stands for STDOUT

The basics are clear to most folks, like setting a new environment variable with Set VARNAME = VALUE, returning the current value of *VARNAME* via SET VARNAME or using the *VALUE* of *VARNAME* via%VARNAME% in the batch script code. Also the use of the runtime generated variables%1 ...%X for the command line parameters that were passed to the batch script are basic *BATCH* script knowledge.

As you know, parameter values that include the space (blank) character, must be enclosed in double-quotes (") to avoid that the *BATCH* script will interpret the individual segments before and after a space as separate parameters. For example BATCH.BAT C:\Documents and Settings would result in three (3) parameters in the Batch Script, like:

- %1 = C:\Documents
- %2 = and
- %3 = Settings

You have to enter BATCH.bat "C:\Documents and Settings" instead to have the path only appear as one (1) parameter in the batch, which is accessible via%1. The problem is that%1 will also include the double-quotes, which are not really part of the value that you want to pass. In many cases this does not matter or is even good, if you invoke file commands for example, where the parameter should again be enclosed in double-quotes to work properly.

To remove the enclosing (") (double-quotes) from a parameter, add the character "~" (tilde) after the "%" (per cent) sign.

For example:%~1

This does not work for regular environment variables that were created via the "SET" command.

The following would not work and error out, if you try to execute it:

- SET VAR="VALUE"
- ECHO%~VALUE%

Other characters that require that a parameter value will be enclosed in double-quotes are: &()[]{}^=;!'+,'~

Did you know that%0 also exists?%0 stands for the command itself. In the examples above,%0 would returnBATCH.bat. Note: Calling the script via the command BATCH without the extension ".bat" is also valid, if no other executable with the same base name exists in the same directory or path (*e.g.* a *BATCH.exe* or*BATCH.com*). If the batch file is executed this way,%0 also would not include the extension and simply return the value BATCH.

THE SET COMMAND

Typical use would be this: Set Counter = 0 where the value of "*Counter*" would then be accessible in the batch script (and beyond!) via%Counter%. Using the parameter/*A* indicates that the variable has a numeric value and should also be treated as such. This is important if you want to do arithmetic operations with a variable such as: set/A Counter+=1

This is especially powerful in combination with the "*Delayed Environment Variables Expansion*" feature enabled. See more about this option further down below. set/P VARNAME=Prompt_String

Displays "*Prompt_Sting*", then waits for user input (in *DOS*, not a Windows Input Box) and stores the entered value in the variable *VARNAME* once the user finished his input by pressing the *ENTER* key.

STRING SUBSTITUTIONS

- %PATH:str1=str2% = Expands *PATH* and substitutes any occurrences of *str1* with *str2*
  String Offsets
- %PATH:~10,5% = Expands *Path* and use 5 characters of the value from position 11 (offset) only
  Left & Right String Functions
- %PATH:~0,-2% = Expands *PATH* and uses all but the last 2 characters of the value

Other system environment variables

Other variables than%PATH%, which I used in the previous examples, which are good to know, but also require that *EXTENSIONS* were enabled via the SETLOCAL ENABLEEXTENSIONS command or via cmd.exe parameter.

- %CD% = Path to current directory
- %DATE% = Current Date
- %TIME% = Current Time

- %RANDOM% = Expands to a random number between 0 and 32767
- %ERRORLEVEL% = Returns the current ErrorLevel value
- %CMDEXTVERSION% = Version of the current command processor extensions
- %CMDCMDLINE% = original command line that invoked the command processor

DELAYED ENVIRONMENT VARIABLES EXPANSION

Always disabled by default, but may be enabled/disabled via the/*V* command line switch to *CMD.EXE* or via the command "setlocal enabled delayed expansion" at run-time. Disabled means that variables will be expanded at the time they are parsed, which is bad, if the value of the variable is supposed to change within the batch script itself.

Here is a nice example script to illustrate the different behaviour.

- Set VAR=before
- If "%VAR%" == "before" (
- Set VAR=after
- If "%VAR%" == "after" @echo If you see this, it worked
-)

If you run this, the script should return nothing. The second IF statement never can become true, even though you have the "SET" command right before it that should have changed the variable's value to make the IFstatement true. Why? Because%VAR% was already set to *"before"* and because of that expands to *"before"* throughout the entire script. Now add at the very top the line "setlocal enabledelayedexpansion" and run the script again. Now you should get the text *"If you see this, it worked" back as a result*. Here is another example of the implication of the "set local enabled delayed expansion" statement.

- Set LIST=
- For%%i in (*) do set LIST=!LIST!%%i
- Echo%LIST%

This script will not return the list of all files in the current directory. It will only show one file name of the directory. It would work the same way as if you would have made the FOR command statement to:

- For%%i in (*) do set LIST=%%i

Add "setlocal enabledelayedexpansion" at the top of the script again and run it once more. Another typical use where enabling delayed expansion is crucial, are Counters and other mathematical operations and manipulation of values during the execution of a *BATCH* script.

THE SHIFT COMMAND

The SHIFT Command is probably difficult to get its head around it. The applications are versatile. Shift basically shifts the sequence of parameters to the left. *Parameter 2* becomes *Parameter 1, Parameter 1* disappears and*Parameter 2* would be empty, unless there is another *Parameter 3*. This is hard to grasp, so here is a short sample batch that illustrates this behaviour.

- @echo off
- Call:testfn 1 2
- Goto:EOF
- Testfn
- Echo 1 =%1, 2 =%2
- Echo shift
- Shift
- Echo 1 =%1, 2 =%2

Results:

1 = 1, 2 = 2

shift

1 = 2, 2 =

There are other variables like the ones starting with 2x "%" like%%a or variables that are enclosed in "!" instead of "%", like !VARNAME! instead of%VARNAME%, but that would require me to make this post much longer than it already is. Check the help for the "FOR", "SET" and "CMD" commands to learn more about them.

DOS EDITOR

INTRODUCTION

"MS-DOS Editor" is a Text User Interface and its colour

scheme can be adjusted. It has a multiple document interface in which Windows 9x versions can open up to nine files at a time while DOS versions are limited to a only one file. The screen can be split vertically into two panes which can be used to view two files simultaneously or different parts of the same file. The editor can also open files in "binary mode", where a fixed number of characters are displayed per line, and new lines are treated as any other character. Editor converts Unix new lines to DOS new lines and has mouse support. Some of these features were added only in 1995 (version 2.0), with the release of Windows 95.

MS-DOS Editor is a text editor that comes with MS-DOS (since version 5) and 32-bit versions of Microsoft Windows. Originally (up to MS-DOS 6.22) it was actually QBasic running in editor mode. With DOS 7 (Windows 95), QBasic was removed and MS-DOS Editor became a standalone program.

Editor is sometimes used as a substitute for Notepad on Windows 9x, where Notepad is limited to small files only. Editor can edit files that are up to 65,279 lines and up to approximately 5MB in size. MS-DOS versions are limited to approximately 300KB, depending on how much conventional memory is free. Editor can be launched by typing it into the Run command dialog on Windows, and by typing edit into the command-line interface (usually cmd.exe). Edit is still included in later versions of Windows such as Windows XP and Windows Vista.

CREATING FILES

Text files are files that contain only plain unformatted text (words). Microsoft includes the text editing program edit.com with DOS and Windows. When DOS is installed correctly you can run edit.com at any time by typing Edit at the DOS prompt. You can also create a new file or open an existing file by typing it's name directly afterwards. In order for Edit to work correctly it's location should be specified in the PATH command inside the Autoexec.bat. Some Older versions also require Qbasic.exe in order for it to run properly.

You can make a batch file to automate commands in DOS.

A batch file can be made with any text editor such as Edit or Notepad. It's just a list of DOS commands you would normally type by hand. If you use DOS a lot you may want to create a Batch file that display's a menu of the DOS programs you use the most. Here's how...

First thing you do is create a file named Menu.bat. This file clears the screen with the command cls. Then it echo's your menu to the screen.

This is the file Menu.bat:

- ECHO OFF
- cls
- echo.
- echo Start Menu
- echo ––––––––––––––––––
- echo 1. Doom
- echo 2. Warcraft II
- echo ––––––––––––––––––
- echo Type a Number and press ENTER:

Next you need a batch file for each program in the list. These batch files are named using the number of the menu item for the program you want to run.

This is the file 1.bat:

- CD C:\doom
- doom.exe
- CD\menu.bat

This is the file 2.bat:

- D C:\war2
- war2.exe
- CD\
- menu.bat

How's it work? Put the menu.bat and all the numbered bat's onto C:\. When you type menu at the C:\ prompt the following is displayed on the screen.

Start Menu

––––––––––––––––––

1. Doom

2. Warcraft II

––––––––––––––––––

Type a Number and press ENTER:
C:\

The menu.bat is finished, all it does is display a list of menu items. The C:\ is the normal DOS prompt waiting for your next command. Now if you want to play doom and type 1, your actually starting the batch file named 1.bat. If you'll notice above 1.bat starts by typing CD C:\doom which switches to the doom directory. Next it types doom.exe which starts the game doom. When doom is finished it types CD\ which returns the prompt to C:\. Then it runs the menu.bat file again so the screen is cleared and the menu is displayed again.

To have Menu.bat run automatically when DOS is started add C:\Menu.bat to the bottom of your Autoexec.bat. That way menu.bat will be run automatically when DOS starts.

CONFIG.SYS

The Config.sys file system contains the location of any device drivers or special settings that need to be loaded during start up. You can edit Config.sys using any text editor. Edit.com is provided with DOS for editing text files. You can also use Notepad in Windows95. Below is a basic Config.sys file. Note: before editing Config.sys it's a good idea to make a second copy. You can do that in DOS by typing "copy config.sys config.bak". That will make a second copy named Config.bak.

This is what a basic Config.sys file looks like but yours may be different:

- DEVICE=C:\DOS\HIMEM.SYS
- DEVICE=C:\DOS\EMM386.EXE NOEMS
- DOS=UMB
- LASTDRIVE=G
- DOS=HIGH
- DEVICEHIGH=C:\SB16\DRV\CTMMSYS.SYS
- DEVICEHIGH=C:\PDPACK\CD.SYS/D:CD001

This is what each line does in this example:

- DEVICE=C:\DOS\HIMEM.SYS
- DEVICE=C:\DOS\EMM386.EXE NOEMS

These are the memory managers provided by Microsoft. In this case both Himem.sys and Emm386.exe are located on C: in the DOS folder. The NOEMS following EMM386.EXE tells DOS not to use Expanded Memory. DEVICE= tells DOS this is a normal device driver. On your computer these files maybe located elsewhere.

DOS=UMB

You need this command in order for DOS to use the Upper Memory area. It tells DOS to keep a link between Conventional Memory and Upper memory

LASTDRIVE=G

This line tells DOS G: is the last drive letter used in the computer. This keeps DOS from reserving space for drives that don't exist.

DOS=HIGH

This line tells DOS to put itself into the Upper memory area.

DEVICEHIGH=C:\SB16\DRV\CTMMSYS.SYS

This loads a device driver for a Soundblaster sound card. In this case DEVICEHIGH= is used to put the driver in the Upper memory area so Conventional memory is left free.

DEVICEHIGH=C:\PDPACK\CD.SYS/D:CD001

This is the CD-ROM driver. The/D:CD001 is the name the driver gives the CD-ROM. Normally a floppy disk with an install program will come with the CD and directions on what switchs you can add after the sys file/D is the switch here and CD001 the value that goes with it.

AUTOEXE.BAT

The Autoexec.bat is what's known as a DOS batch file. All batch files have the extension *.bat. You can create your own batch files with any text editor. It's simply a list of typed DOS commands that are carried out 1 line at a time. The Autoexec.bat is special because it's the only *.bat file that automatically runs at the start of DOS.

This is what a basic Autoexec.bat file looks like but yours may be different:

- @ECHO OFF

- PROMPT $p
- SET SOUND=C:\VIBRA16
- SET BLASTER=A220 I5 D1 H5 P330 T6
- SET MIDI=SYNTH:1 MAP:E
- C:\VIBRA16\DIAGNOSE/S
- C:\VIBRA16\MIXERSET/P/Q
- PATH C:\DOS;C:\WINDOWS
- LH C:\MOUSE\MOUSE
- LH C:\DOS\MSCDEX.EXE/D:CD001

This is what each line does in this example:

- @ECHO OFF

This is a batch file command that stops the lines in the batch file from being displayed or echoed to the screen.

- PROMPT $p

This is a batch file command that changes the way the DOS prompt looks. By default the prompt looks like C:\>, after this command it looks like C:\.

- SET SOUND=C:\VIBRA16

This line tells DOS that the directory location for the sound card drivers.

- SET BLASTER=A220 I5 D1 H5 P330 T6

This line tells DOS the hardware settings used by the sound card. Sound Blaster is the leading sound card made by Creative Labs. Most software and other brand sound cards are compatible with it. These settings may present even if you don't have a Soundblaster Sound Card.

- SET MIDI=SYNTH:1 MAP:E

This line contains additional settings for the MIDI portion of the Sound card. MIDI stands for Musical Instrument Digital Interface. It allows the computer to communicate with musical instruments. Normally the sound cards joystick port also doubles as a MIDI port. The Sound Card can usually simulate MIDI sounds internally as well.

- C:\VIBRA16\DIAGNOSE/S

This line runs the Diagnose.exe program provided by the sound card maker. The/S is a switch used to engage certain settings within the program.

- C:\VIBRA16\MIXERSET/P/Q

This line runs the Mixerset.exe program provided by the sound card maker. The/P and/Q are switches used to engage certain settings within the program.

- PATH C:\DOS;C:\WINDOWS

This is a batch file command that sets a path for DOS to search automatically when you type a program name at the prompt.

- LH C:\MOUSE\MOUSE

This line runs the mouse.com program needed to use a mouse in DOS. LH is the abbreviation for LOADHIGH which places the program into the Upper memory area if possible.

- LH C:\DOS\MSCDEX.EXE/D:CD001

This is the Microsoft CD Extension program that allows DOS and Windows to use CD-ROM players. The/D:CD001 matches the name assigned by the CD.SYS line used in the Config.sys file. LH is the abbreviation for LOADHIGH which places the program into the Upper memory area if possible.

EDITING FILES WITH EDITOR

ABOUT EDIT

Edit allows a user to view, create, and/or modify their computer files.

If you are unable to get this program to work, try typing in "path c:\windows\command" if you haveWindows95/98, or type in "path c:\dos" if you have Dos 5.x/6.x/7.x or Windows 3.xand try again. If you still are not able to get edit to work, it may not be on the hard drive; type in dir edit.com/ s at the c:\>. If it says that the file is not found, you may not have this feature. If you are running a MS-DOS version 4.x or lower or you are unable to find edit.com on your hard disk drive, you can also use the below command to create a file.

copy con <name of file>

Once you have entered the above command this will create the file with the name specified. Once you have typed all the lines you wish to be in the file, press and hold CTRL + Z. This should enter ^Z, once on the screen, press enter and one file should be copied.

SYNTAX

EDIT [/B] [/H] [/R] [/S] [/<nnn>] [/?] [file(s)]

/B	Forces monochrome mode.
/H	Displays the maximum number of lines possible for your hardware.
/R	Load file(s) in read-only mode.
/S	Forces the use of short filenames.
/<nnn>	Load binary file(s), wrapping lines to <nnn> characters wide.
/?	Displays this help screen.
[file]	Specifies initial files(s) to load. Wildcards and multiple file specs can be given.

EXAMPLES

- edit c:\autoexec.bat

This would look at the autoexec.bat. However, if the file is not found, you will have a blank blue screen. When editing this or any file, ensure that you know what you are placing in the files improperly editing the file can cause issues with your computer.

Using edit you can also create files; for example, if you wanted to create a file called myfile.txt, you would type:

- edit myfile.txt

This would bring up a blank edit screen, as long as the file is saved upon exit this will create the file myfile.txt.

ADDITIONAL INFORMATION

Edit is only able to open a file with a maximum of 65,280 lines. Because this file is generally used from MS-DOS, it can be a possibility for no mouse support within the file. Below is a listing of Edit's shortcut keys and what they do.

Quick Tip: Simply pressing Alt will allow you to quickly navigate through edit without having to memorize the below commands.

- *Home*: Move cursor to the beginning of the line currently on.
- *End*: Move cursor to the end of the line currently on.

- *Ctrl + Up*: Scroll up one line.
- *Ctrl + Down*: Scroll down one line.
- *PageUp*: Scroll up one screen.
- *PageDown*: Scroll down one screen.
- *Ctrl + PageUp*: Scroll left one screen.
- *Ctrl + PageDown*: Scroll right one screen.
- *Ctrl + Home*: Scroll to the top of the document.
- *Ctrl + End*: Scroll to the bottom of the document.
- *Ctrl + Left*: Move left one word.
- *Ctrl + Right*: Move right one word.
- *Enter*: Starts a new line or moves text after cursor down.
- *Delete (Del)*: Deletes one character that cursor is on or currently selected text.
- *Backspace:* Deletes one character before the cursor.
- *Tab*: Moves cursor or text to next tab stop, or indents line if at first character.
- *Insert*: Switch between insert and overwrite modes.
- *Ctrl + Y*: Deletes the current line.
- *Ctrl + V*: Pastes contents currently within buffer, if any.
- *Ctrl + P*: Allows special characters to be inserted into Edit.
- *Shift*: Using shift in combination with any of the above scrolling or moving commands will highlight text, such as Ctrl + Shift + Right.
- *Ctrl + C*: Copies currently selected text into buffer.
- *Ctrl + X*: Cuts the currently selected text into buffer.
- *Shift + Tab*: Un-indents the currently selected line.
- *Ctrl + Q + F*: Find text.
- *Ctrl + Q + A*: Find and replace text.
- *F3*: Repeat last search.
- *F6*: Switch to the next edit window, if any.
- *Ctrl + F6*: Open new edit window.
- *Ctrl + F4*: Closes second edit window.
- *Ctrl + F8*: Resizes edit window.
- *F1*: Displays help.

4

Windows

WINDOWS OPERATING SYSTEM

INTRODUCTION

Microsoft first started developing the Interface Manager (later renamed Microsoft Windows) in September 1981. While the first prototypes used Multiplan and Word-like menus at the bottom of the screen, the interface was modified in 1982 to utilize pull-down menus and dialogues, as used on the Xerox Star. On November 10, 1983, at the Plaza Hotel in New York City, Microsoft Corporation officially announced Microsoft Windows, a next-generation operating system that would supply a graphical user interface (GUI) and a multitasking environment for IBM computers. This was after the release of the Apple Lisa, and prior to Digital Research announcing GEM, and DESQ from Quarterdeck and the Amiga Workbench, or GEOS/GeoWorks Ensemble, IBM OS/2, NeXTstep or even DeskMate from Tandy.

Windows assured an easy-to-use graphical interface, device-independent graphics and multitasking support. The development was held up several times, however, and the Windows 1.0 arrive at store shelves in November 1985. The selection of applications was thin, however, and Windows sales were moderate.

Windows 1.0 package, included: MS-DOS Executive, Calendar, Cardfile, Notepad, Terminal, Calculator, Clock, Reversi, Control Panel, PIF (Program Information File) Editor,

Print Spooler, Clipboard, RAMDrive, Windows Write, Windows Paint.

Microsoft Windows version 1.0 was viewed as buggy, rough, and sluggish. This bumpy start was made sorrier by a threatened lawsuit from Apple Computers. In September 1985, Apple lawyers warned Bill Gates that Windows 1.0 infringed on Apple copyrights and patents, and that his corporation had stolen Apple's trade secrets. Microsoft Windows had similar drop-down menus, tiled windows and mouse support. Bill Gates and his head counsel Bill Neukom, chose to make an offer to license features of Apple's operating system.

Apple concurred and a contract was drawn up. The key to this is: Microsoft wrote the licensing agreement to include use of Apple features in Microsoft Windows version 1.0 and all future Microsoft software programs. As it turned out, this move by Bill Gates was as intelligent as his decision to purchase QDOS from Seattle Computer Products and his persuading IBM to let Microsoft keep the licensing rights to MS-DOS.

Windows 1.0 fluttered on the market until January 1987, when a Windows-compatible program called Aldus PageMaker 1.0 was brought out. PageMaker was the first WYSIWYG desktop-publishing program for the PC. Later that year, Microsoft released a Windows-compatible spreadsheet called Excel. Other popular and functional software like Microsoft Word and Corel Draw helped advance Windows, yet, Microsoft recognized that Windows required further development.

Microsoft Windows version 2.0 came out in December 1987, and evidenced somewhat more popular than its predecessor. A great deal of the popularity for Windows 2.0 came through its inclusion as a "run-time version" with Microsoft's new graphical applications, Excel and Word for Windows. They could be operated from MS-DOS, executing Windows for the length of their activity, and shutting down Windows upon exit.

Microsoft Windows incurred a major boost about this time when Aldus PageMaker came out in a Windows version, having previously run exclusively on Macintosh. Some computer historians date this, the introduction of a significant and non-Microsoft application for Windows, as the start of the success of Windows.

Versions 2.0x used the real-mode memory model, which held it to a maximum of 1 megabyte of memory. In such a form, it could run under a different multitasker like DESQview, which used the 286 Protected Mode. Subsequently, two new versions were published: Windows/286 2.1 and Windows/386 2.1. Like preceding versions of Windows, Windows/286 2.1 used the real-mode memory model, but was the first version to support the HMA.

Windows/386 2.1 had a protected mode kernel with LIM-standard EMS emulation, the predecessor to XMS which would at last shift the topology of IBM PC computing. All Windows and DOS-based applications at the time were real mode, running over the protected mode kernel by using the virtual 8086 mode, which was new with the 80386 processor.

After Versions 2.0 and beyond were released, Apple began filing suit against IBM for various copyright infringements. In their defence, Microsoft claimed that their licensing agreement actually afforded them the rights to use Apple features. Apple claimed that Microsoft had encroached on 170 of their copyrights. After a four-year court case, Microsoft won.

The courts stated that the licensing agreement gave Microsoft the rights to use all but nine of the copyrights, and Microsoft later convinced the courts that the other nine copyrights shouldn't be covered by copyright law. Bill Gates asserted that Apple had acquired ideas from the graphical user interface developed by Xerox for Xerox's Alto and Star computers.

On June 1, 1993, Judge Vaughn R. Walker of the U.S. District Court of Northern California ruled in Microsoft's favour in the Apple vs. Microsoft & Hewlett-Packard copyright suit. The judge granted Microsoft's and Hewlett-Packard's motions to dismiss the last remaining copyright infringement claims against Microsoft Windows versions 2.03 and 3.0, as well as HP NewWave.

What would have occurred if Microsoft had lost the lawsuit? Microsoft Windows might never have become the predominant operating system that it is today.

FEATURES

Some individuals with disabilities require assistive technology (AT) in order to access computers. Hundreds of Windows AT third-party products are available, making it possible for almost anyone to use Windows® applications, regardless of their disabilities. The Microsoft® Windows® operating systems also provides a core set of basic accessibility features and AT applications, which can be deployed on all computers in a computer lab or classroom without additional cost. These applications provide students with basic accessibility features from any workstation, maximizing the inclusiveness of the learning environment.

It should be noted that the AT applications that are bundled with Windows provide only a minimum level of accessibility, not the full set of features that many users require for equal access to the operating system, educational programs, and other software applications. Therefore, many educational entities deploy the standard set of Windows AT on all workstations by default, but addditionally 1) provide a small number of dedicated workstations that are equipped with commonly requested third party AT, and 2) are prepared to purchase and install additional AT as needed by specific students. It should also be noted that the availability of AT does not itself guarantee accessibility. Software applications must be designed in a way that is compatible with AT and other accessibility features of the operating system. The following is a list of basic accessibility features that are included with Windows XP. Previous versions of Windows also included several of these same features.

Display and Readability

These features are designed to increase the visibility of items on the screen:

- *Font style, colour, and size of items on the desktop*: Using the Display options, choose font colour, size and style combinations.

- *Icon size:* Make icons larger for visibility, or smaller for increased screen space.
- *Screen resolution*: Change pixel count to enlarge objects on screen.
- *High contrast schemes*: Select colour combinations that are easier to see.
- *Cursor width and blink rate*: Make the cursor easier to locate, or eliminate the distraction of its blinking.
- *Microsoft Magnifier*: Enlarge portion of screen for better visibility.

Sounds and Speech

These features are designed to make computer sounds easier to hear or distinguish-or, visual alternatives to sound.

Speech-to-text options are also available.

- *Sound Volume*: Turn computer sound up or down.
- *Sound Schemes:* Associate computer sounds with particular system events.
- *ShowSounds*: Display captions for speech and sounds.
- *Sound Sentry:* Display visual warnings for system sounds.
- *Notification:* Get sound or visual cues when accessibility features are turned on or off.
- *Text-to-Speech*: Hear window command options and text read aloud.

Keyboard and Mouse

These features are designed to make the keyboard and mouse faster and easier to use.

Mouse Options:

- *Double–Click Speed:* Choose how fast to click the mouse button to make a selection.
- *ClickLock*: Highlight or drag without holding down the mouse button.
- *Pointer Speed*: Set how fast the mouse pointer moves on screen.

- *SnapTo:* Move the pointer to the default button in a dialog box.
- *Cursor Blink Rate*: Choose how fast the cursor blinks—or, if it blinks at all.
- *Pointer Trails*: Follow the pointer motion on screen.
- *Hide Pointer While Typing*: Keep pointer from hiding text while typing.
- *Show Location of Pointer*: Quickly reveal the pointer on screen.
- *Reverse the Function of the Right and Left Mouse Buttons:* Reverse actions controlled by the right and left mouse buttons.
- *Pointer Schemes*: Choose size and colour options for better visibility.

Keyboard Options

- *Character Repeat Rate*: Set how quickly a character repeats when a key is struck.
- *Dvorak Keyboard Layout:* Choose alternative keyboard layouts for people who type with one hand or finger.
- *Sticky Keys*: Allow pressing one key at a time (rather than simultaneously) for key combinations.
- *Filter Keys:* Ignore brief or repeated keystrokes and slow down the repeat rate.
- *Toggle Keys*: Hear tones when pressing certain keys.
- *Mouse Keys*: Move the mouse pointer using the numerical keypad.
- *Extra Keyboard Help*: Get Tool Tips or other keyboard help in programs that provide it.

Accessibility Wizard

The Accessibility Wizard is designed to help new users quickly and easily set up groups of accessibility options that address visual, hearing and dexterity needs all in one place. The Accessibility Wizard asks questions about accessibility needs. Then, based on the answers, it configures utilities and settings for individual users. The Accessibility Wizard can be run again at any time to make changes, or changes can be made to individual settings through Control Panel.

INTRODUCTION TO DESKTOP

The windows desktop is the main work area on the computer screen.

It consists of everything you see on the screen, such as:

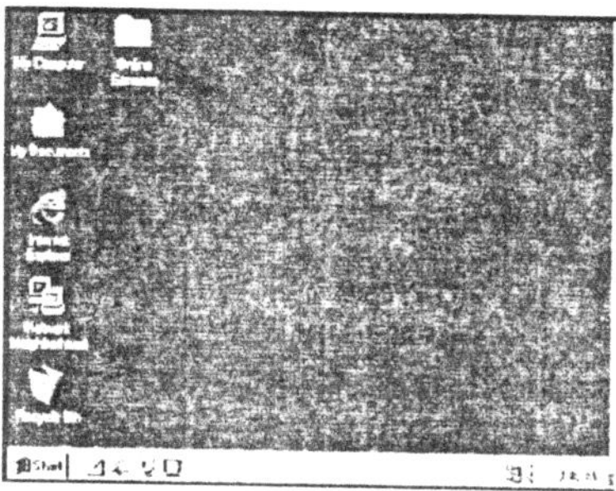

WINDOWS

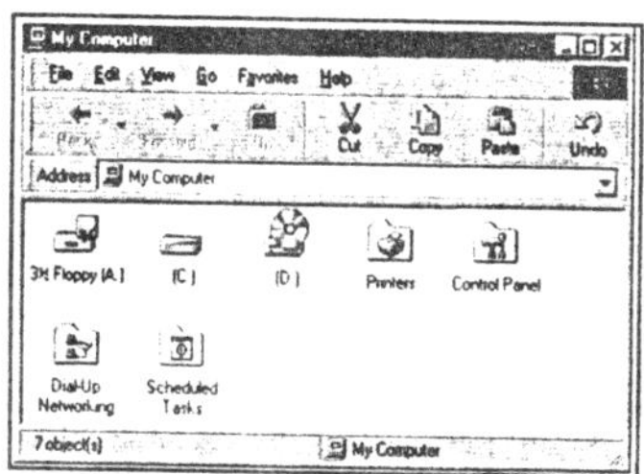

Parts in My Computer Window

Its components are listed from the top down

This is the *Title Bar*. It always gives you the name of the open file or folder.

These buttons are named as minimize, maximize, close

The second button from the left is the restore button. It's job is to return a window to its previous size. It only shows if a window has been maximized.

This is the menu.
There are four tool bars below the menu.
The tool bars are listed here
This is the standard buttons tool bar.

This is the links tool bar.

This is the address bar tool bar.

This is the radio tool bar.

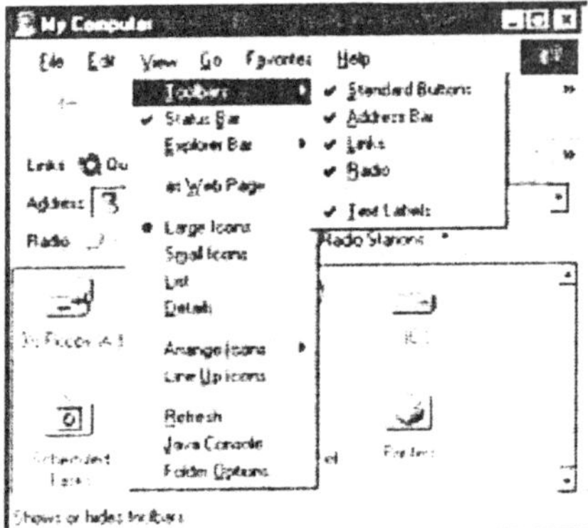

After the tool bars comes the next area of detail as shown below:

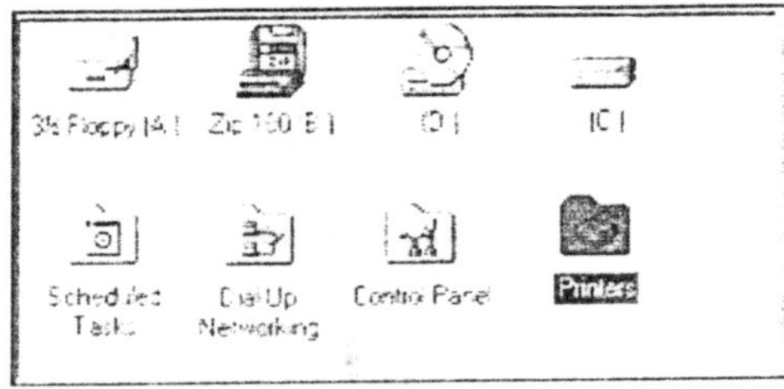

This is the file selection area:

This is the status bar.

DESKTOP ICONS

MY DOCUMENTS

My Documents is also another most important Icon of your Desktop. It shows all Data Files/Folders which you have created and saved while working with your Computer.

To view the My Documents Icon simply Double Click or Right Click on My Documents Icon with the help of Mouse as shown below

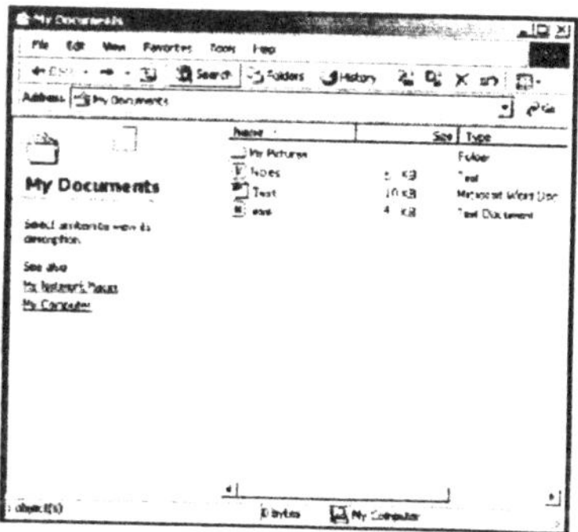

In the Screen you can see the Files and Folders created by you. Another thing to keep in mind that whatever you select and ask for Save in that case your Document will always save in My Document folder. Above.

INTERNET EXPLORER

Internet Explorer is another important Icon on your Desktop Screen. It is an important source for Internet as it helps in connecting your Web Page once your Modem is connected to the Server Computer.

To view the Web Page simply Double Click or Right Click on Internet Explorer Icon with the help of Mouse as shown below:

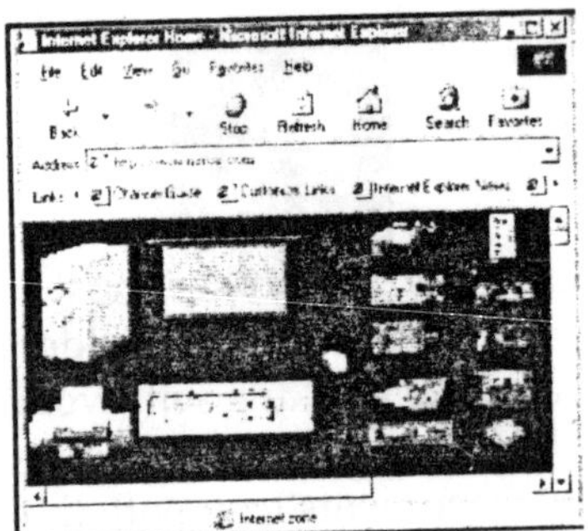

The above screen appears only when your type http://www.nrice.com after opening of your Home Page. For all these purpose the Internet Explorer is very essential

NETWORK PLACE

Network Place or Network Neighbourhood is important Icon on your Desktop Screen. It is used for creating Networking among Computers connecting in LAN. To view what is there inside this Icon simply Double Click or Right Click on Internet Explorer Icon with the help of Mouse as shown below

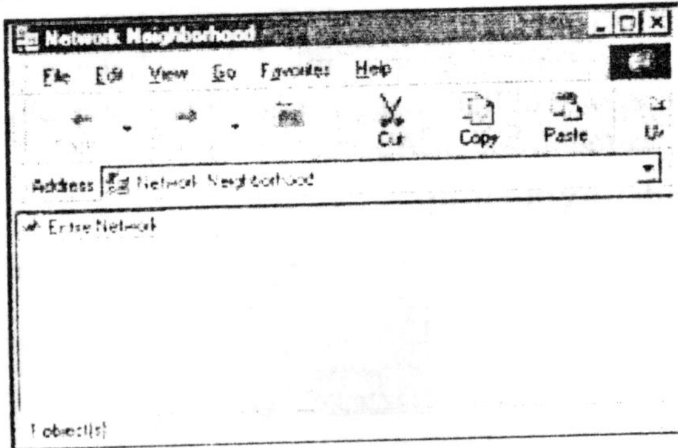

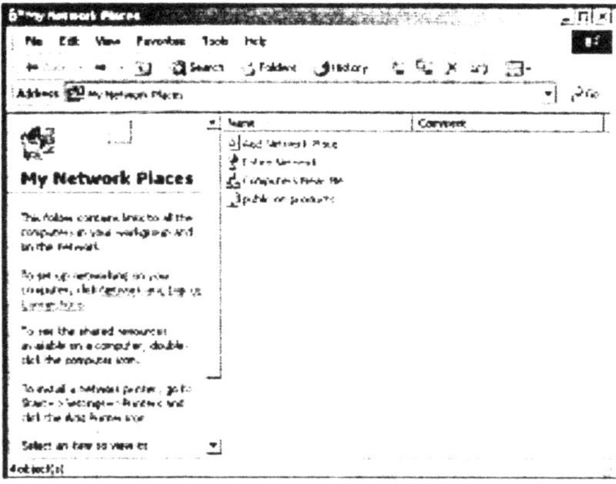

RECYCLE BIN

Recycle Bin is one of the most useful Icon on Main Desktop Screen. It is a box or briefcase which is used for keeping all necessary and dump files/folders what you may or may not require.

If any file or folder is deleted by you, the particular file/ folder gets saved in Recycle Bin. In this you can any time Restore your Deleted files/folders

To view how this box looks from inside just Double Click or Right Click on its Icon with the help of Mouse. After clicking it shown the below screen.

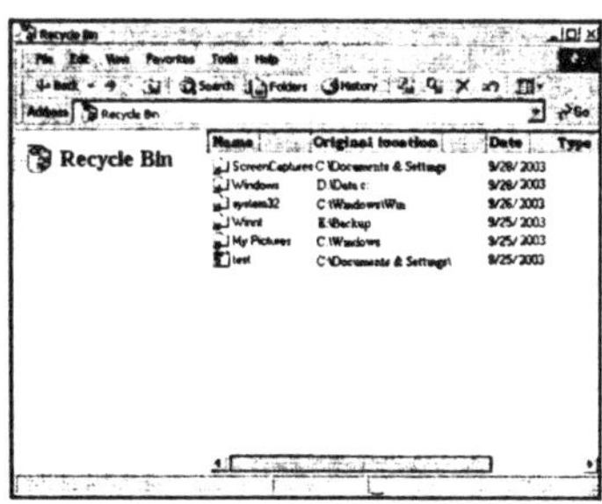

DIALOGUE BOXES

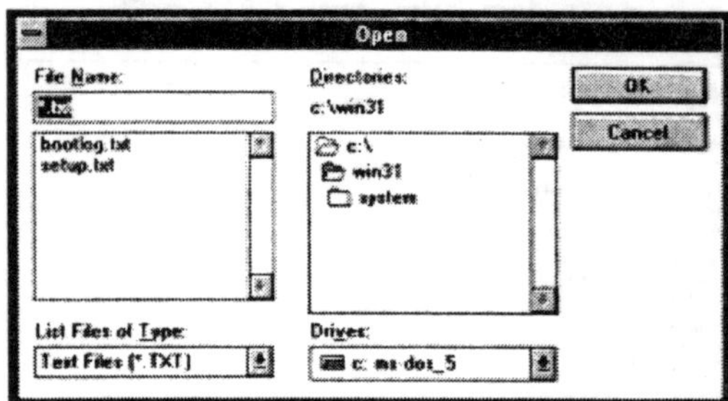

Before you start to work in a desktop environment, take time to learn what a window is, and how it works. Below is a picture of a window and its parts, followed by an explanation of how each part works

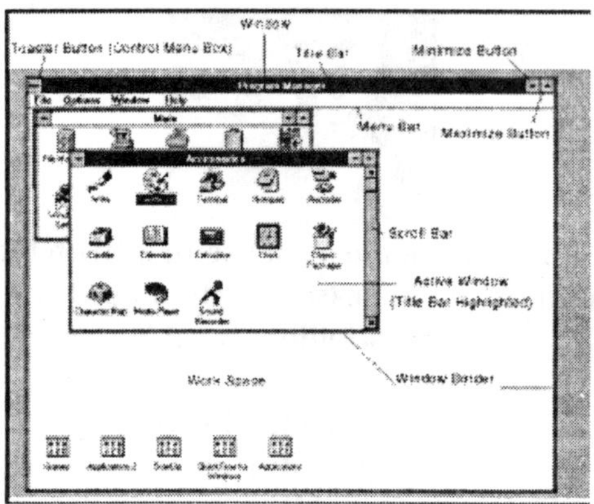

WINDOW:

The most prominent display on the screen. A window is a large square on the screen that represents a "conversation" with the computer. More precisely, windows allow you to command the computer to do things, and to receive information in return.

Changing the Shape

Click on the toaster button once to display the menu. Choose and click on *Size*. When this option is chosen, a four-headed arrow mouse cursor should appear.

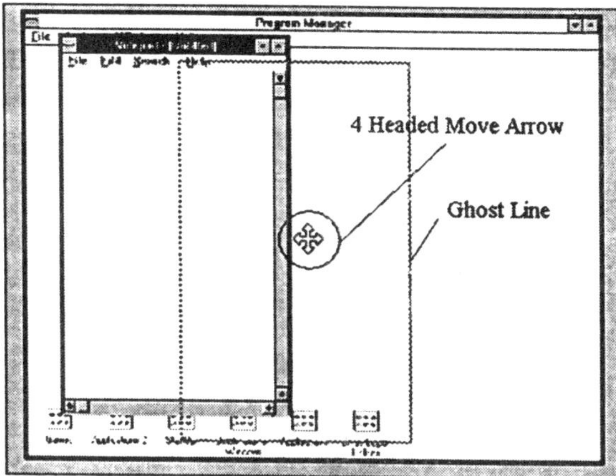

Depress and hold the left mouse button. Move the cursor until the resizing command takes place. (Resizing takes place when the four-headed arrow changes to a two headed arrow and the window is changing its size.)

Release the mouse once you have reached the desired size.

Hint: You can resize both the height and width at the same time when you drag-and-drop on any of the four corners (of course there must be screen space available).

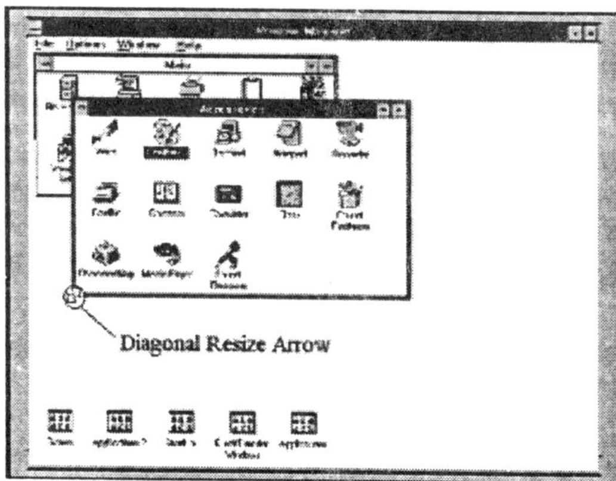

Changing the Position

Click on the toaster button once to display the menu. Choose and click on Move. When this option is chosen, a four headed arrow mouse cursor should appear. Position the mouse

Move the mouse until you have reached the new position (Note the ghost outline as you are moving the window). Before moving the windows

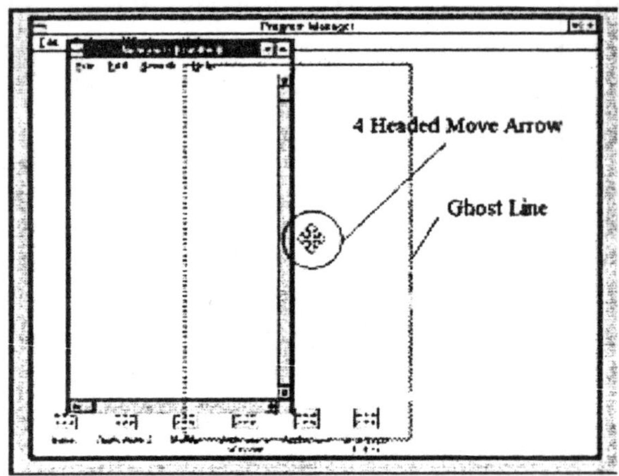

After moving the window Release the left mouse button.

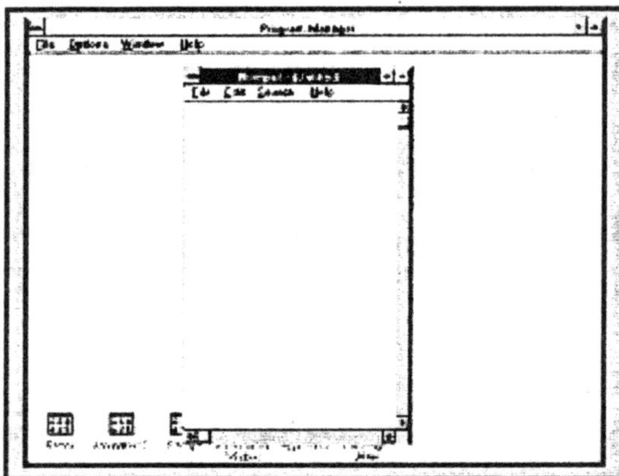

Minimizing, Maximizing, Restoring, and Closing a window

Click on the toaster button once to display the menu. Choose and click on the corresponding command.

Distinguishing a Window's Mode

A large normal window is very similar to a maximized window. Sometimes telling the two apart can be difficult.

There are, however, visual cues that distinguishes a maximized window from a merely big one.

- You can't move or resize a maximized window, but you can restore it.
- You can't restore a normal window, but you can move or maximize it.
- A maximized window has a double-headed arrow in the upper right-hand corner. A normal window has an upward-pointing arrow in the upper right-hand corner.
- A normal window has a very thin border around it, whereas a maximized window does not. Below is a picture which shows the thin border around a normal window.

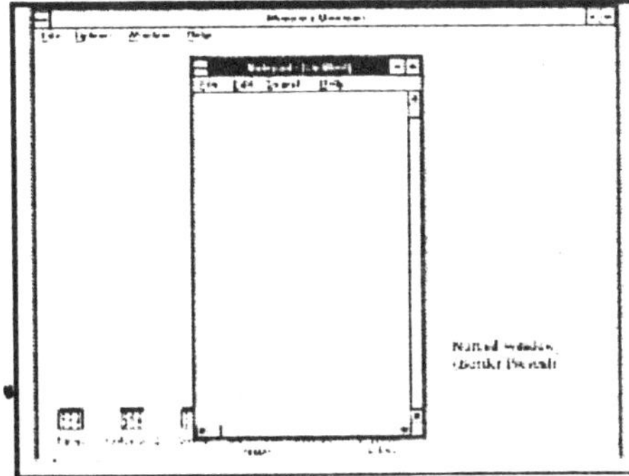

Iconified Window

Iconified windows do not have toaster buttons. To get the standard toaster button menu, click on the icon once. If clicked, a menu should appear above above the icon, which looks like the picture below.

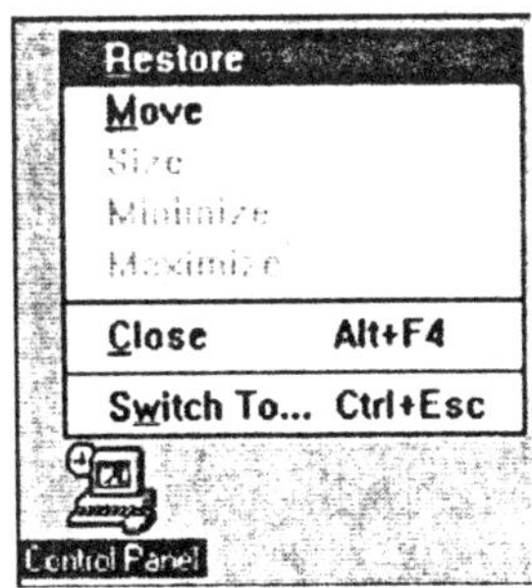

Windows Within a Window

Earlier in this tutorial, we stated that a window is a picture that allows a computer user to operate a program. A second important fact about windows to keep in mind is that different programs have different windows. These differences between mirrors reflect differences between how programs operate—for example, what commands they provide, and how these commands are activated. As a rule, differences between programs manifest themselves as differences between windows in four different ways:

- Different Menus
- Different Toolbars
- Different Status Bars
- Different "Workspaces" (where, by workspace, we mean the main area in the window's frame).

One important difference between workspaces concerns the structure of the workspace. Many programs, like the *Notepad Text Editor* and the*Paintbrush* drawing program, have windows whose workspaces contain a single, monolithic working area.

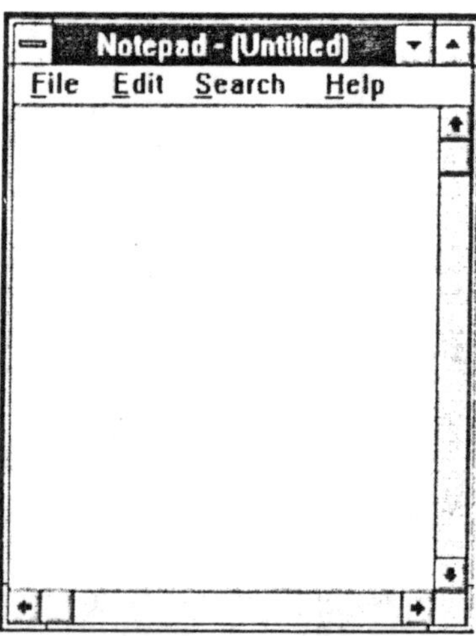

Other programs: Like *Program Manager, File Manager, Word, Access, Excel,* and *PowerPoint*—have windows that, in turn, contain windows. The picture below is an example:

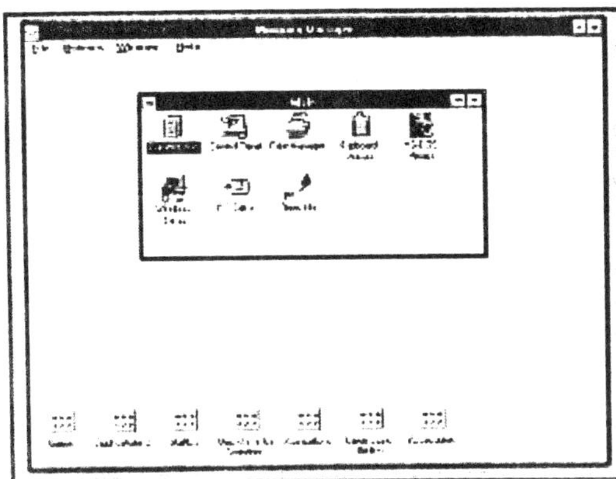

As a rule, a "window that contains windows" represents a program that allows you to shift back and forth between different tasks. In Program Manager, for example, each inner window represents a different program. In Word, each inner window represents a different open document. And, in File Manager, each inner window represents a different part of the file system.

Windows On Top of Windows

These are windows stacked on top of another window(s). They occur when you are working with multiple windows at the same time and do not adjust the windows to share the screen. Here is an example of windows stacked on top of one another:

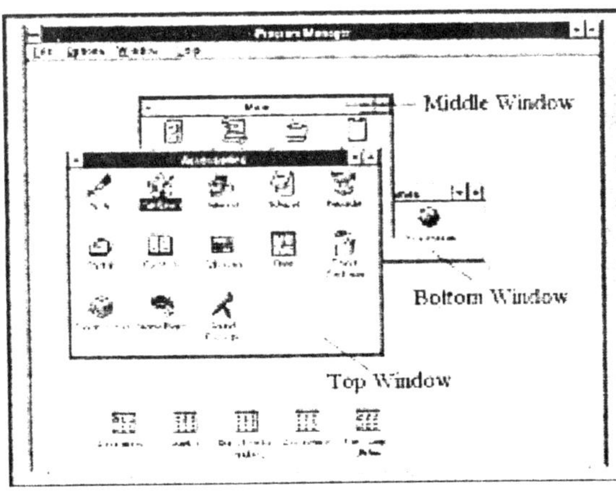

Why Windows on Top of Windows

The concept of dealing with windows stacked on top of windows can be frustrating and confusing. The most frustrating and confusing aspect is keeping track of what windows are open. Since the windows underneath the visible one cannot be seen, you might forget that they are there. This tendency to forget leads to the same applications opened a multiple number of times. When this happens separate instances of the program may conflict.

How to Tell How Many Windows are Open at Once

There is a couple of ways to tell how many windows you have opened at once:

- You can iconify or minimize all the windows you have opened. Once you have iconified all the windows, you can see how many copies of each application are open.
- Another way to tell how many windows are opened is to use "ALT + TAB" command to cycle through the active applications. This method, however, is more difficult since you have to keep track of active applications as you cycle through them.

This feature is located in the upper-left corner of each window. The toaster button allows you to move the window, control its size and close it. The toaster button is most useful when accessed by the keyboard. To find out more about the toaster button, click on the heading.

TITLE BAR

The title bar is at the very top of every window. This part of the window shows the name of the application, document, group, directory, or file.

ACTIVE WINDOW:

This window is special than all the other windows because it allows you work on it. If more than one window is open, the title bar for the active window (the window which you are currently working) has a colour or intensity different from the other title bars. The differencc in the title bar colours allows you to distinguish the active window from all the other windows.

MENU BAR

The menu bar contains the available menus from which you can choose commands. Clicking on any of the choices on the menu bar will bring up a corresponding pulldown menu. Here is an example:

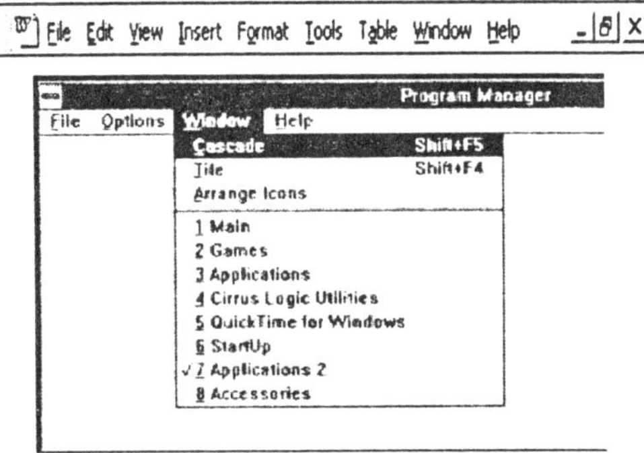

SCROLL BARS

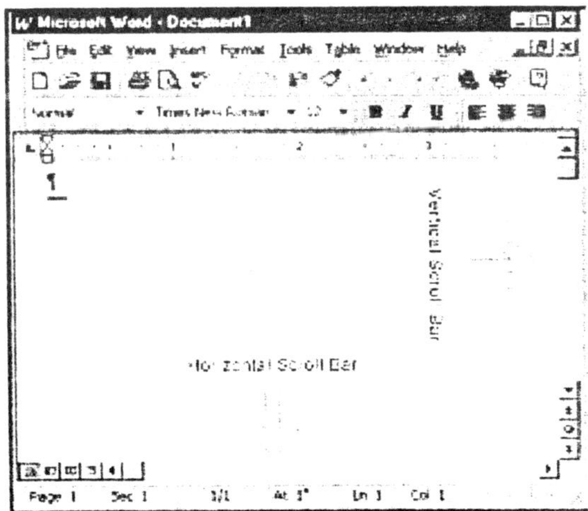

The scroll bars allow you to move through a document

or a list when the entire document or list does not fit in the window or the allotted space. To move up or down a document, click on the up or down scroll arrows.

MAXIMIZE/MINIMIZE BUTTONS

These buttons are located on the upper-right corner of the screen. The maximize button enlarges the active window to fill the entire desktop. The minimize button reduces the active window to an icon.

THE RESTORE BUTTON

This button replaces the maximize button after you enlarge a window. The restore button returns the window to its previous size. Here are some other topics about the button:

WINDOW BORDER

The window border is the outside edge of a window. You can change the size of a window by lengthening and shortening the borders. Click on the title to see more about the window's border.

WORK SPACE

The work space is the area below the menu bar. To find out more about the window's workspace click on the title.

MULTIMEDIA TOOLS

Multimedia authoring tools make it easier to create full scale multimedia projects. Fortunately, there is an assortment of tools available to choose from.

SOUND CARD

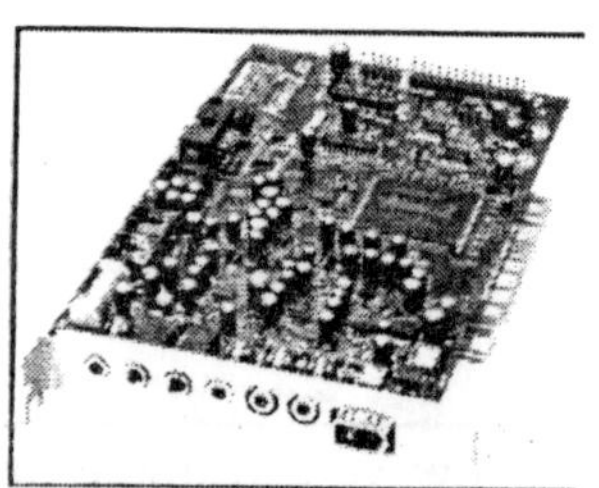

The sound card (also called an *audio card*) is the part of a computer which manages its audio input and ouput. t is usually a controller which can be inserted into an ISA slot (or PCI for more recent ones), but more and more motherboards include their own sound card.

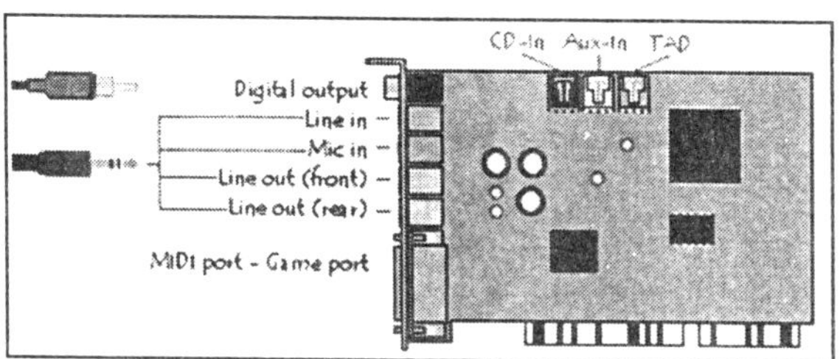

The main components of a sound card are: The specialised processor, called the DSP (*digital signal processor*), which does all the digital audio processing (echo, reverb, vibrato chorus, tremelo, 3D effects, etc.); The digital to analog converter, or DAC for short, which converts the computer's audio data into an analog signal for being sent to a sound system (such as speakers or an amplifier); The analog to digital converter, or ADC for short, which converts an analog *input* signal into digital data which a computer can process;

External input/output connectors:

- On or two standard 3.5 mm line-out jacks, normally light green in colour;
- A line-in jack;
- A microphone input (sometimes called *Mic*), usually a pink-coloured 3.5 mm jack;
- An SPDIF digital output (*Sony Philips Digital Interface,* also known as *S/PDIF* or *S-PDIF* or IEC 958 or *IEC 60958*since 1998). This is an output line which sends digitised audio data to a digital amplifier using a coaxial cable with RCA connectors at the ends.

A MIDI connector, usually gold-coloured, which is used for connecting musical instruments, and can serve as a*game port* for plugging in a controller (like a joystick or gamepad) which has a SUB-D 15-pin connector.

Internal input/output connectors:

A CD-ROM/DVD-ROM connector, with a black socket,

which is used to connect the sound card into a CD-ROM's analog audio output using a CD Audio cable; Auxiliary inputs (AUX-In), with white sockets, used for connecting internal audio sources such as a TV tuner card; Telephone answering device connectors (TAD), which have a green connector.

SPEAKERS

Speakers easily play the most significant role in enhancing your audio experience. So how do they actually manage to reproduce sound from the electrical signals that are fed as input? Devices such as speakers and microphones are technically called transducers. A transducer transforms one form of energy into another. In this case, a speaker converts electrical energy into acoustic energy (sound), in about the same way that a microphone converts acoustic energy into a corresponding electrical signal.

There is more to speakers than just plugging them in and believing that the costly sound system you got is going to take you to new heights. Of course, higher-end systems, with their excellent low-noise amplifiers, filters and impedance matchers reproduce crystal-clear sound even from speakers of the lowest end, but audiophiles know the difference!

We need to dwell into some physics to understand its mechanism. During our school days, we all have played around with the tuning fork during our physics practicals. On striking the tuning fork, we hear a long hum. This sound is created by the compression and rarefaction of air particles, around the vibrating fork arms. When these compressions and rarefactions hit the eardrum, it vibrates, and we perceive sound. In a speaker, this compression and rarefaction is performed by a paper diaphragm that vibrates in accordance with the electrical signal fed to it. The construction of a speaker sheds more light on its functioning. At the base is a powerful ring magnet. In the centre is a voice coil made up of fine wire, wound around a paper cylinder. As we can see in the picture, the voice coil is attached to a spider (an elastic paper sheet that holds the voice coil), such that it always returns to its fixed position under normal conditions. To start off with the functionality of a speaker, the underlying principle is electromagnetism. The basic interaction between an electromagnetic coil and a powerful permanent magnet is what drives the speaker to produce sound. The primary source of sound is a diaphragm. One end of the voice coil is attached to the centre of the paper diaphragm. This diaphragm, in turn, compresses and rarefies the air particles around it, thereby producing sound.

HEADPHONE

One way to test earplugs is to insert an earplug in an ear canal of a person, or of a manikin head with an ear simulator that simulates the acoustic characteristics of the ear and that has a sound detector. Then sound of controlled amplitude is applied to the person or manikin. The amplitude of sound detected by the person or ear simulator is noted in relation to the amplitude of sound applied to the outside of the ear canal, to indicate the effectiveness of the earplug. When a person who is going to wear an earplug wishes to test it, it is desirable that that person test it on him/herself.

One problem encountered when applying sound through an earphone, or headphone, is that the amplitude of sound applied to the outside of the ear may not be sufficiently high over the frequency range of interest. One test used in the industry measures the blocking ability of earplugs at five frequencies: 250 Hz, 500 Hz, 1000 Hz, 2000 Hz and 4000 Hz. It would be desirable if the amplitude of sound output from the headphone were approximately the same at each of these frequencies for a constant electrical power input. It also would be desirable if the headphone were as efficient as possible. Although low speaker output can be compensated for by a higher power input, the speaker output at higher amplitudes will be distorted, and an excessively high electrical input can damage the speaker.

Conventional headphones place the speaker so it lies close to the outer ear. During earplug effectiveness tests, the earplug can touch the headphone grille and prevent the headphone from fully seating on the ear, or disturb the earplug installation, or make the wearer uncomfortable.

In accordance with one embodiment of the invention, a headphone is provided that produces a high sound level (at least 120 dB SPL) at the wearer's ear, over a range of interest of 250 HZ to 4000 HZ, for a 25 mW electrical input to its speaker (by applying one volt RMS). Applicant mounts the speaker of the headphone in a reverse orientation from the usual one, with the front of the speaker diaphragm facing away from the wearer's ear, and with the rear of the speaker which has holes, facing towards the wearer's ear. The holes in the rear of the speaker lie in a circle, and a tube in the headphone frame has an outer end with a diameter that encompasses the ring of holes to direct sound from the holes to the person's ear.

The tube in the headphone frame has a tapered outer end that is enlarged to encompass the ring of holes, with the ear end of the tube being of smaller diameter than the speaker end. The tube in the headphone frame has a length of at least 0.6 inch to accommodate a long projecting end of an earplug in the wearer's ear.

The novel features of the invention are set forth with particularity in the appended claims. The invention will be best understood from the following description when read in conjunction with the accompanying drawings.

CD \ DVD ROM

CD-ROM drives are necessary today for most programs. A single CD can store up to 650 MB of data (newer CD-Rs allow for 700 MB of data, perhaps more with "overburn"). Fast CD-ROM drives have been a big topic in the past, but all of today's CD-ROM drives are sufficiently fast. Of course, it's nice to have the little bits of extra speed. However, when you consider CD-ROM drives are generally used just to install a program or copy CDs, both of which are usually done rarely on most users' computers, the extra speed isn't usually very important. The speed can play a big role if you do a lot of CD burning at high speeds or some audio extraction from audio CDs (*i.e.* converting CDs to MP3s). CD-R/RW (which stands for Recordable/ReWritable) drives (aka burners, writers) allow a user to create their own CDs of audio and/or data. These drives are great for backup purposes (backup your computer's hard drive or backup your purchased CDs) and for creating your own audio CD compilations (not to mention other things like home movies, multimedia presentations, etc.).

DVD-ROM drives can store up to 4 GB of data or about 6 times the size of a regular CD (not sure on the exact size, but suffice to say it's a very large storage medium). DVDs look about the same and are the same size as a CD-ROM. DVD drives can also read CD-ROM drives, so you don't usually need a separate CD-ROM drive. DVD drives have become low enough inprice that there isn't much point in purchasing a CD-ROM drive instead of a DVD-ROM drive. Some companies even make CD burner drives that will also read DVDs (all in one). DVD's most practical use is movies. The DVD format allows for much higher resolution digital recording that looks much clearer than VCR recordings.

DVD recordable drives are available in a couple of different formats-DVD-R or DVD+R with a RW version of each. These are slightly different discs and drives (although some drives support writing to both formats).

5

Unix and Linux

UNIX

WHAT IS UNIX?

UNIX is an operating system which was first developed in the 1960s, and has been under constant development ever since. By operating system, we mean the suite of programs which make the computer work. It is a stable, multi-user, multi-tasking system for servers, desktops and laptops. UNIX systems also have a graphical user interface (GUI) similar to Microsoft Windows which provides an easy to use environment. However, knowledge of UNIX is required for operations which aren't covered by a graphical program, or for when there is no windows interface available, for example, in a telnet session.

TYPES OF UNIX

There are many different versions of UNIX, although they share common similarities. The most popular varieties of UNIX are Sun Solaris, GNU/Linux, and MacOS X. Here in the School, we use Solaris on our servers and workstations, and Fedora Linux on the servers and desktop PCs.

THE UNIX OPERATING SYSTEM

The UNIX operating system is made up of three parts; the kernel, the shell and the programs.

The Kernel

The kernel of UNIX is the hub of the operating system: it

allocates time and memory to programs and handles the filestore and communications in response to system calls.

As an illustration of the way that the shell and the kernel work together, suppose a user types rm myfile (which has the effect of removing the file myfile). The shell searches the filestore for the file containing the program rm, and then requests the kernel, through system calls, to execute the programrm on myfile. When the process rm myfile has finished running, the shell then returns the UNIX prompt% to the user, indicating that it is waiting for further commands.

The shell

The shell acts as an interface between the user and the kernel. When a user logs in, the login program checks the username and password, and then starts another program called the shell.

The shell is a command line interpreter (CLI). It interprets the commands the user types in and arranges for them to be carried out. The commands are themselves programs: when they terminate, the shell gives the user another prompt (% on our systems).

The adept user can customise his/her own shell, and users can use different shells on the same machine. Staff and students in the school have the tcsh shell by default. The tcsh shell has certain features to help the user inputting commands.

Filename Completion-By typing part of the name of a command, filename or directory and pressing the [Tab] key, the tcsh shell will complete the rest of the name automatically. If the shell finds more than one name beginning with those letters you have typed, it will beep, prompting you to type a few more letters before pressing the tab key again.

History: The shell keeps a list of the commands you have typed in. If you need to repeat a command, use the cursor keys to scroll up and down the list or type history for a list of previous commands.

Files and Processes

Everything in UNIX is either a file or a process. A process

is an executing program identified by a unique PID (process identifier). A file is a collection of data. They are created by users using text editors, running compilers etc.

Examples of files:

- A document (report, essay etc.)
- The text of a program written in some high-level programming language
- Instructions comprehensible directly to the machine and incomprehensible to a casual user, for example, a collection of binary digits (an executable or binary file);
- A directory, containing information about its contents, which may be a mixture of other directories (subdirectories) and ordinary files.

The Directory Structure

All the files are grouped together in the directory structure. The file-system is arranged in a hierarchical structure, like an inverted tree. The top of the hierarchy is traditionally called root (written as a slash/)

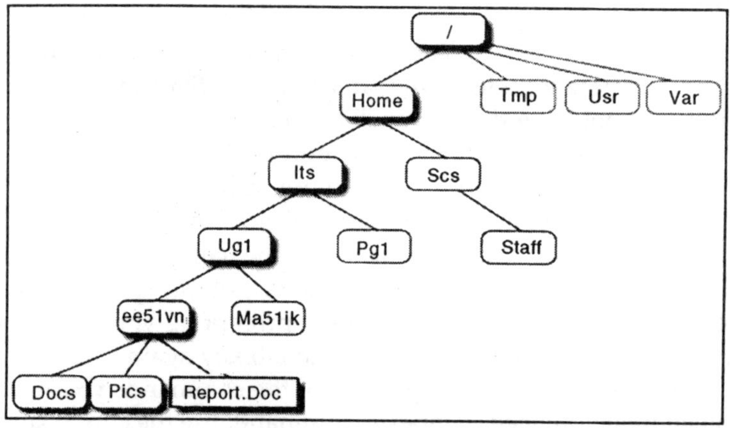

In the diagram above, we see that the home directory of the undergraduate student "ee51vn"contains two sub-directories (docs and pics) and a file called report.doc.

The full path to the file report.doc is "/home/its/ug1/ee51vn/report.doc"

Starting an UNIX Terminal

To open an UNIX terminal window, click on the "Terminal" icon from the drop-down menus.

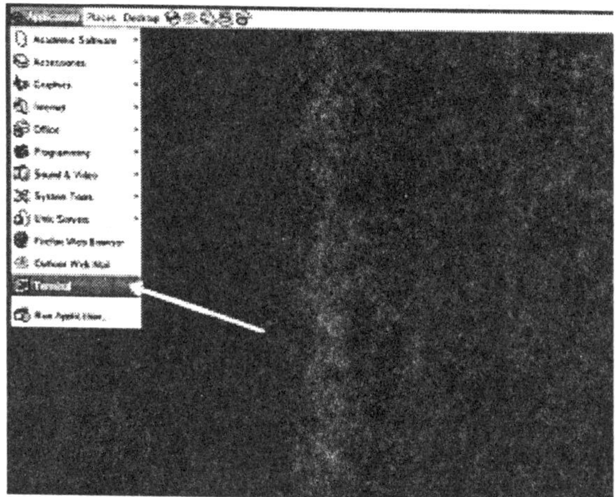

An UNIX Terminal window will then appear with a% prompt, waiting for you to start entering commands.

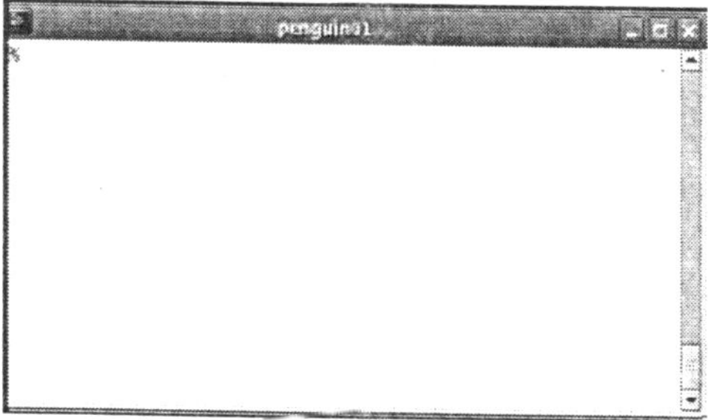

UNIX SYSTEM

Listing Files and Directories

When you first login, your current working directory is your home directory. Your home directory has the same name as your user-name, for example, ee91ab, and it is where your personal files and subdirectories are saved.

To find out what is in your home directory, type:

- % ls

The ls command lists the contents of your current working directory.

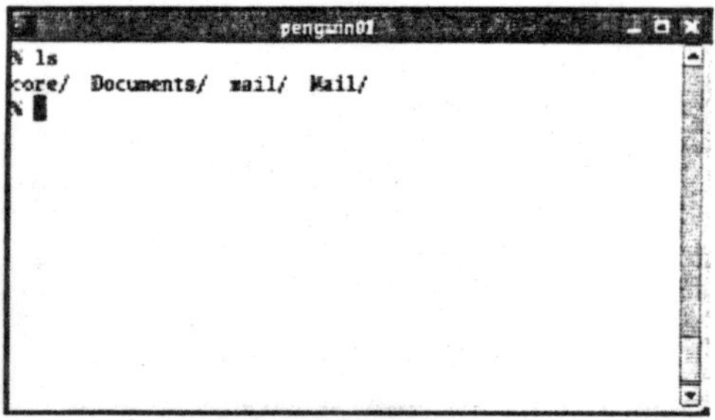

There may be no files visible in your home directory, in which case, the UNIX prompt will be returned. Alternatively, there may already be some files inserted by the System Administrator when your account was created.

ls does not, in fact, cause all the files in your home directory to be listed, but only those ones whose name does not begin with a dot (.) Files beginning with a dot (.) are known as hidden files and usually contain important program configuration information. They are hidden because you should not change them unless you are very familiar with UNIX!!!

To list all files in your home directory including those whose names begin with a dot, type:

- % ls -a

As you can see, ls -a lists files that are normally hidden.

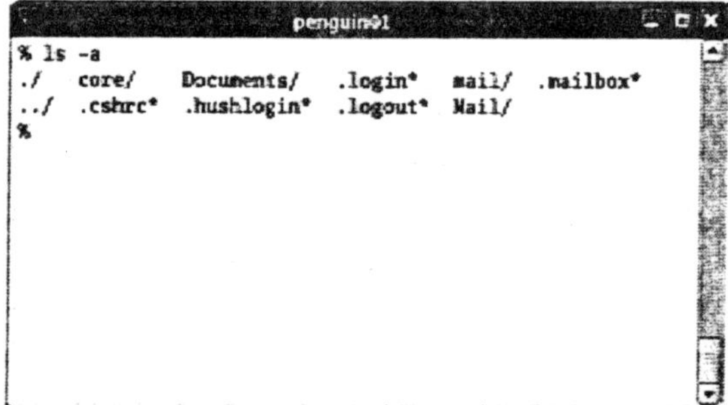

is an example of a command which can take options: -a is an example of an option. The options change the behaviour of the command. There are online manual pages that tell you which options a particular command can take, and how each option modifies the behaviour of the command. (See later in this tutorial)

Making Directories

- *mkdir (make directory)*: We will now make a subdirectory in your home directory to hold the files you will be creating and using in the course of this tutorial. To make a subdirectory called unixstuff in your current working directory type
- % *mkdir unixstuff*: To see the directory you have just created, type
- % ls

Changing to a Different Directory

cd (change directory)

The command cd *directory* means change the current working directory to '*directory*'. The current working directory may be thought of as the directory you are in, *i.e.* your current position in the file-system tree.

To change to the directory you have just made, type,

- % cd unixstuff

Type ls to see the contents (which should be empty) Exercise 1a Make another directory inside the unixstuff directory called backups

The Directories. and..

Still in the unixstuff directory, type

- % ls -a As you can see, in the unixstuff directory (and in all other directories), there are two special directories called (.) and (..) The current directory (.) In UNIX, (.) means the current directory, so typing
- % cd.

Note: There is a space between cd and the dot means stay where you are (the unixstuff directory). This may not seem very useful at first, but using (.) as the name of the current directory will save a lot of typing, as we shall see later in the tutorial. The parent directory (..)

(..) means the parent of the current directory, so typing

- % cd.. will take you one directory up the hierarchy (back to your home directory). Try it now.
  Note: Typing cd with no argument always returns you to your home directory. This is very useful if you are lost in the file system.

Pathnames

Pathnames enable you to work out where you are in relation to the whole file-system. For example, to find out the absolute pathname of your home-directory, type cd to get back to your home-directory and then type

- % pwd The full pathname will look something like this -
- /home/its/ug1/ee51vn which means that ee51vn (your home directory) is in the sub-directory ug1 (the group directory),which in turn is located in the its sub-directory, which is in the home sub-directory, which is in the top-level root directory called "/".

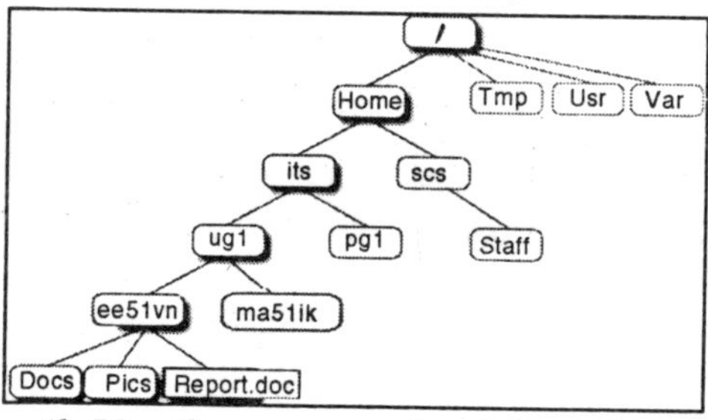

Exercise 1b Use the commands cd, ls and pwd to explore the file system. (Remember, if you get lost, type cd by itself to return to your home-directory)

More About Home Directories and Pathnames

Understanding pathnames First type cd to get back to your home-directory, then type

- % ls unixstuff to list the conents of your unixstuff directory.
  Now type:
- % ls backups

You will get a message like this - backups: No such file or directory

The reason is, backups is not in your current working directory. To use a command on a file (or directory) not in the current working directory (the directory you are currently in), you must either cdto the correct directory, or specify its full pathname. To list the contents of your backups directory, you must type

- % ls unixstuff/backups ~ (your home directory) Home directories can also be referred to by the tilde ~ character. It can be used to specify paths starting at your home directory. So typing
- % ls ~/unixstuff will list the contents of your unixstuff directory, no matter where you currently are in the file system.
  What do you think
- % ls ~
  would list?
  What do you think
- % ls ~/..
  would list?

Summary

Command	Meaning
ls	list files and directories
ls -a	list all files and directories
mkdir	make a directory
cd *directory*	change to named directory
cd	change to home-directory
cd ~	change to home-directory
cd..	change to parent directory
pwd	display the path of the current directory

UNIX FILES SYSTEM

Copying Files

cp (copy) cp *file1 file2* is the command which makes a copy of file1 in the current working directory and calls it file2

What we are going to do now, is to take a file stored in an open access area of the file system, and use the cp command to copy it to your unixstuff directory.

First, cd to your unixstuff directory.

- % cd ~/unixstuff Then at the UNIX prompt, type,
- % cp/vol/examples/tutorial/science.txt.

Note: Don't forget the dot. at the end. Remember, in UNIX, the dot means the current directory. The above command means copy the file science.txt to the current directory, keeping the name the same.

Exercise 2a Create a backup of your science.txt file by copying it to a file called science.bak

Moving Files

mv (move) mv *file1 file2* moves (or renames) file1 to file2

To move a file from one place to another, use the mv command. This has the effect of moving rather than copying the file, so you end up with only one file rather than two. It can also be used to rename a file, by moving the file to the same directory, but giving it a different name. We are now going to move the file science.bak to your backup directory. First, change directories to your unixstuff directory (can you remember how?). Then, inside theunixstuff directory, type

- % mv science.bak backups/. Type ls and ls backups to see if it has worked.

Removing files and Directories

rm (remove), rmdir (remove directory) To delete (remove) a file, use the rm command. As an example, we are going to create a copy of thescience.txt file then delete it.

Inside your unixstuff directory, type:

- % cp science.txt tempfile.txt
- % ls
- % rm tempfile.txt
- % ls

You can use the rmdir command to remove a directory (make sure it is empty first). Try to remove thebackups directory. You will not be able to since UNIX will not let you remove a non-empty directory. Exercise 2b Create a directory called tempstuff using mkdir, then remove it using the rmdir command.

Displaying the Contents of a file on the Screen

clear (clear screen) Before you start the next section, you may like to clear the terminal window of the previous commands so the output of the following commands can be clearly understood.

At the prompt, type

- % clear: This will clear all text and leave you with the% prompt at the top of the window. cat (concatenate) The command cat can be used to display the contents of a file on the screen.
  Type:
- % cat science.txt As you can see, the file is longer than than the size of the window, so it scrolls past making it unreadable. less The command less writes the contents of a file onto the screen a page at a time. Type
- % less science.txt Press the [space-bar] if you want to see another page, and type [q] if you want to quit reading. As you can see, less is used in preference to cat for long files. head The head command writes the first ten lines of a file to the screen.

First clear the screen then type

- % head science.txt
  Then type
- % head -5 science.txt What difference did the -5 do to the head command? tail

The tail command writes the last ten lines of a file to the screen.

Clear the screen and type

- % tail science.txt

Q. How can you view the last 15 lines of the file?

Searching the Contents of a file

Simple searching using less: Using less, you can search

though a text file for a keyword (pattern). For example, to search throughscience.txt for the word 'science', type

- % less science.txt then, still in less, type a forward slash [/] followed by the word to search
- /science As you can see, less finds and highlights the keyword. Type [n] to search for the next occurrence of the word. grep (don't ask why it is called grep) grep is one of many standard UNIX utilities. It searches files for specified words or patterns. First clear the screen, then type
- % grep science science.txt As you can see, grep has printed out each line containg the word science. Or has it ???? Try typing
- % grep Science science.txt The grep command is case sensitive; it distinguishes between Science and science. To ignore upper/lower case distinctions, use the -i option, *i.e.* type
- % grep -i science science.txt To search for a phrase or pattern, you must enclose it in single quotes (the apostrophe symbol). For example to search for spinning top, type
- % grep -i 'spinning top' science.txt

Some of the other options of grep are:

- -v display those lines that do NOT match
- -n precede each matching line with the line number
- -c print only the total count of matched lines Try some of them and see the different results. Don't forget, you can use more than one option at a time. For example, the number of lines without the words science or Science is
- % grep -ivc science science.txt wc (word count)

A handy little utility is the wc command, short for word count. To do a word count on science.txt, type,

- % wc -w science.txt

To find out how many lines the file has, type,

- % wc -l science.txt

Summary

Command	Meaning
cp *file1 file2*	copy file1 and call it file2
mv *file1 file2*	move or rename file1 to file2
rm *file*	remove a file
rmdir *directory*	remove a directory
cat *file*	display a file
less *file*	display a file a page at a time
head *file*	display the first few lines of a file
tail *file*	display the last few lines of a file
grep *'keyword' file*	search a file for keywords
wc *file*	count number of lines/words/characters in file

UNIX REDIRECTIONAL

Redirection

Most processes initiated by UNIX commands write to the standard output (that is, they write to the terminal screen), and many take their input from the standard input (that is, they read it from the keyboard). There is also the standard error, where processes write their error messages, by default, to the terminal screen.

We have already seen one use of the cat command to write the contents of a file to the screen.

Now type cat without specifing a file to read

- % cat

Then type a few words on the keyboard and press the [Return] key. Finally hold the [Ctrl] key down and press [d] (written as ^D for short) to end the input.

What has happened? If you run the cat command without specifing a file to read, it reads the standard input (the keyboard), and on receiving the 'end of file' (^D), copies it to the standard output (the screen). In UNIX, we can redirect both the input and the output of commands.

Redirecting the Output

We use the > symbol to redirect the output of a command.

For example, to create a file called list1containing a list of fruit, type

- % cat > list1

Then type in the names of some fruit.

Press [Return] after each one.

- pear
- banana
- apple
- ^D {this means press [Ctrl] and [d] to stop}

What happens is the cat command reads the standard input (the keyboard) and the > redirects the output, which normally goes to the screen, into a file called list1

To read the contents of the file, type

- % cat list1

Exercise 3a Using the above method, create another file called list2 containing the following fruit: orange, plum, mango, grapefruit. Read the contents of list2 Appending to a file The form >> appends standard output to a file. So to add more items to the file list1, type

- % cat >> list1

Then type in the names of more fruit

- peach
- grape
- orange
- ^D (Control D to stop)

To read the contents of the file, type

- % cat list1

You should now have two files. One contains six fruit, the other contains four fruit. We will now use the cat command to join (concatenate) list1 and list2 into a new file called biglist. Type,

- % cat list1 list2 > biglist

What this is doing is reading the contents of list1 and list2 in turn, then outputing the text to the filebiglist

To read the contents of the new file, type

- % cat biglist

Redirecting the Input

We use the < symbol to redirect the input of a command.

The command sort alphabetically or numerically sorts a list. Type

- % sort

  Then type in the names of some animals.

Press [Return] after each one.

- dog
- cat
- bird
- ape
- ^D (control d to stop)

The output will be

- ape
- bird
- cat
- dog

Using < you can redirect the input to come from a file rather than the keyboard. For example, to sort the list of fruit, type

- % sort < biglist

  T!he sorted list will be output to the screen.

  To output the sorted list to a file, type,

- % sort < biglist > slist

  Use cat to read the contents of the file slist

Pipes

To see who is on the system with you, type,

- % who

One method to get a sorted list of names is to type,

- % who > names.txt
- % sort < names.txt

This is a bit slow and you have to remember to remove the temporary file called names when you have finished. What you really want to do is connect the output of the who command directly to the input of the sort command. This is exactly what pipes do. The symbol for a pipe is the vertical bar |

For example, typing

- % who | sort

will give the same result as above, but quicker and cleaner.

To find out how many users are logged on, type

- % who | wc -l

Exercise 3b Using pipes, display all lines of list1 and list2 containing the letter 'p', and sort the result.

Summary

Command	Meaning
command > file	redirect standard output to a file
command >> file	append standard output to a file
command < file	redirect standard input from a file
command1 | command2	pipe the output of command1 to the input of command2
cat file1 file2 > file0	concatenate file1 and file2 to file0
sort	sort data
who	list users currently logged in

UNIX CONVENTIONS

Wildcards

The * wildcard The character * is called a wildcard, and will match against none or more character(s) in a file (or directory) name.

For example, in your unixstuff directory, type,

- % ls list* This will list all files in the current directory starting with list.... Try typing
- % ls *list This will list all files in the current directory ending with....list The ? wildcard The character ? will match exactly one character. So ?ouse will match files like house and mouse, but not grouse. Try typing
- % ls ?list

Filename Conventions

We should note here that a directory is merely a special type of file. So the rules and conventions for naming files apply also to directories.

In naming files, characters with special meanings such as/

* &%, should be avoided. Also, avoid using spaces within names.

The safest way to name a file is to use only alphanumeric characters, that is, letters and numbers, together with _ (underscore) and. (dot).

Good filenames	Bad filenames
project.txt	project
my_big_program.c	my big program.c
fred_dave.doc	fred & dave.doc

File names conventionally start with a lower-case letter, and may end with a dot followed by a group of letters indicating the contents of the file. For example, all files consisting of C code may be named with the ending.c, for example, prog1.c. Then in order to list all files containing C code in your home directory, you need only type ls *.c in that directory.

Getting Help

On-line Manuals: There are on-line manuals which gives information about most commands. The manual pages tell you which options a particular command can take, and how each option modifies the behaviour of the command. Type man *command* to read the manual page for a particular command.

For example, to find out more about the wc (word count) command, type,

- % man wc
  Alternatively
- % whatis wc gives a one-line description of the command, but omits any information about options etc.
  Apropos
  When you are not sure of the exact name of a command,
- % apropos keyword
  will give you the commands with keyword in their manual page header. For example, try typing
- % apropos copy

Summary

Command	Meaning
*	match any number of characters
?	match one character
man command	read the online manual page for a command
whatis command	brief description of a command
apropos *keyword*	match commands with keyword in their man pages

UNIX FILE SYSTEM

File System Security (access rights)

In your unixstuff directory, type

- % ls -l (l for long listing!)

You will see that you now get lots of details about the contents of your directory, similar to the example below.

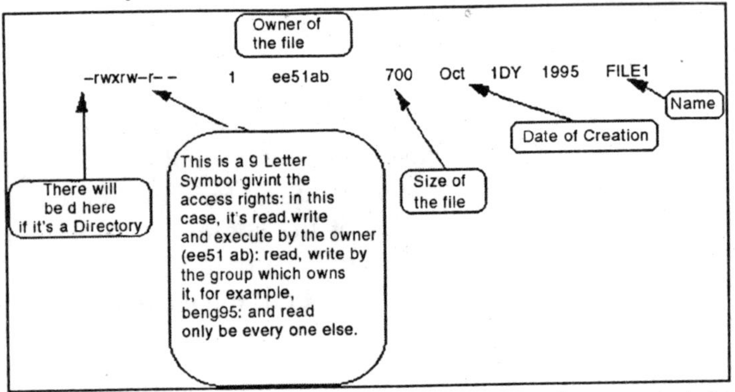

Each file (and directory) has associated access rights, which may be found by typing ls -l. Also, ls -lg gives additional information as to which group owns the file (beng95 in the following example):

- -rwxrw-r— 1 ee51ab beng95 2450 Sept29 11:52 file1

In the left-hand column is a 10 symbol string consisting of the symbols d, r, w, x, -, and, occasionally, s or S. If d is present, it will be at the left hand end of the string, and indicates a directory: otherwise-will be the starting symbol of the string. The 9 remaining symbols indicate the permissions, or access rights, and are taken as three groups of 3.

- The left group of 3 gives the file permissions for the user that owns the file (or directory) (ee51ab in the above example);
- The middle group gives the permissions for the group of people to whom the file (or directory) belongs (eebeng95 in the above example);
- The rightmost group gives the permissions for all others.

The symbols r, w, etc., have slightly different meanings depending on whether they refer to a simple file or to a directory.

Access rights on files.

- r (or -), indicates read permission (or otherwise), that is, the presence or absence of permission to read and copy the file
- w (or -), indicates write permission (or otherwise), that is, the permission (or otherwise) to change a file
- x (or -), indicates execution permission (or otherwise), that is, the permission to execute a file, where appropriate

Access rights on directories.

- r allows users to list files in the directory;
- w means that users may delete files from the directory or move files into it;
- x means the right to access files in the directory. This implies that you may read files in the directory provided you have read permission on the individual files.

So, in order to read a file, you must have execute permission on the directory containing that file, and hence on any directory containing that directory as a subdirectory, and so on, up the tree.

Some examples

-rwxrwxrwx	a file that everyone can read, write and execute (and delete).
-rw———	a file that only the owner can read and write-no-one else can read or write and no-one has execution rights (*e.g.* your mailbox file).

Changing Access Rights

chmod (changing a file mode)

Only the owner of a file can use chmod to change the permissions of a file.

The options of chmod are as follows

Symbol	Meaning
u	user
g	group
o	other
a	all
r	read
w	write (and delete)
x	execute (and access directory)
+	add permission
-	take away permission

For example, to remove read write and execute permissions on the file biglist for the group and others, type

- % chmod go-rwx biglist

This will leave the other permissions unaffected. To give read and write permissions on the file biglist to all,

- % chmod a+rw biglist

Exercise 5a: Try changing access permissions on the file science.txt and on the directory backups

Use ls -l to check that the permissions have changed.

Processes and Jobs

A process is an executing program identified by a unique PID (process identifier). To see information about your processes, with their associated PID and status, type

- % ps

A process may be in the foreground, in the background, or be suspended. In general the shell does not return the UNIX prompt until the current process has finished executing.

Some processes take a long time to run and hold up the terminal. Backgrounding a long process has the effect that the UNIX prompt is returned immediately, and other tasks can be carried out while the original process continues executing.

Running background processes: To background a process, type an & at the end of the command line. For example, the command sleepwaits a given number of seconds before continuing. Type

- % sleep 10

This will wait 10 seconds before returning the command prompt%. Until the command prompt is returned, you can do nothing except wait.

To run sleep in the background, type

- % sleep 10 &

[1] 6259

The & runs the job in the background and returns the prompt straight away, allowing you do run other programs while waiting for that one to finish. The first line in the above example is typed in by the user; the next line, indicating job number and PID, is returned by the machine. The user is be notified of a job number (numbered from 1) enclosed in square brackets, together with a PID and is notified when a background process is finished. Backgrounding is useful for jobs which will take a long time to complete. Backgrounding a current foreground process.

At the prompt, type:

- % sleep 1000

You can suspend the process running in the foreground by typing ^Z, *i.e.*hold down the [Ctrl] key and type [z]. Then to put it in the background, type

- % bg

Note: do not background programs that require user interaction *e.g.* vi

Listing Suspended and Background Processes

When a process is running, backgrounded or suspended, it will be entered onto a list along with a job number. To examine this list, type

- % jobs

An example of a job list could be

- Suspended sleep 1000
- Running netscape

- Running matlab
  To restart (foreground) a suspended processes, type
- % fg%*jobnumber*
  For example, to restart sleep 1000, type
  % fg%1

Typing fg with no job number foregrounds the last suspended process.

LINUX

FUNDAMENTAL OF LINUX

If you truly enjoy working with computers, Linux is the operating system of your dreams. It is more fun than any other computer operating system around. Linux is a computer hobbyist's paradise.

However, the reason why Linux is truly revolutionary is that it is Open Software. Our science and technology work owing to the free availability of information, peer review, public critique, and the capablitiy to pick up ideas and modify or extend them. Open Software is an implementation of the scientific method into the field of software development. The freedom to pick-up, modify and extend, that comes with the Linux licence, offers a promise that the software development under Linux licence will continue in the way that science does.

The making of horseshoes, good glass, or measuring time were once closely guarded trade secrets. Science and technology exploded 500 years ago thanks to the sharing of knowledge by the means of printing, and thus breaking the monopoly of the few on the know-how. Why were the science and technology relatively stagnant before the printing era? Because the "trade secret" approach to growth has its limits: the development continues until the rate of learning equals the rate of forgetting.

Moving the know-how to the public domain (printed on paper) shifted the position of the equilibrium to a higher level, which, after 500 years of turbulent development, we are still to achieve. For interested, I can present equations, borrowed from chemical equilibrium field, that describe this in a more formal way. The main point is that printing increased the audience, and allowed passing information across space and time. In the early days of printing, many of those who dared to share were assassinated for revealing "trade secrets." Linux is for the computer age what Gutenberg was for writing. Hopefully there will be no assassinations this time:-). Linux does clash, violently at times, with those who claim the "ownership" of information, trying to push time back 500 years.

Open Source Linux has also implications for computer security. Imagine a plane based on secret "scientific laws" and built to an unreviewed design, a plane at internals of which nobody but the manufacturer could inspect. Would you believe that this new, unique, completely proprietary plane, obviously built by clever and well-financed marketers in their basement, is any safer than one built in the open world, under the eyes of thousands of critical engineers and curious hobbyists with no association to the manufacturer?.

Then why would you trust a secret computer program? Open-source Linux is ideally suited for a mission-critical application—its security and power are based on robust solutions which are reviewed with no restrictions whatsoever, and continuously improved upon. Linux is quite different from MS Windows, so do not expect that if you can get around MS Windows, then Linux will be straightforward for you. You may need to learn.

On the other hand, if you come from UNIX, Linux will be easy for you. If you don't know much about computers or you don't enjoy them, chances are Linux administration is not for you. If you don't know your hardware, Linux installation may be a challenge.

BENEFITS OF LINUX

Linux can give you:

- A modern, very stable, multi-user, multitasking environment on your inexpensive PC hardware, at no (or almost no) monetary cost for the software. Linux is a rich and powerful platform—don't think of it as a "poor people" operating system. Out-of-box Linux has as much capability as MS Windows NT with $5000 in software add-ons, is more stable, and requires less powerful hardware for comparable tasks.

- Standard platform. Linux is VERY standard—it is essentially a POSIX compliant UNIX. (Yes, Linux is a best-of-the-breed UNIX. The word "UNIX" is not used in conjunction with Linux because "UNIX" is a registered trademark of "The Open Group".) Linux includes all the tools and utilities typically associated with UNIX, plus more, significantly more than even the most expensive commercial UNIX implementations. To run Linux software, UNIX vendors these days implement "Linux compatiblity layers" into their platforms.
- Unsurpassed computing power, portability, flexibility, and customizibility. A Linux cluster recently (April 1999) beat a Cray supercomputer in a standard benchmark. Linux is most popular on Intel-based PCs (price of the hardware), but it runs very well on numerous other hardware platforms, from toy-like to mainframes. One distribution (Debian) expresses the idea like this: "Linux, The Universal Operating System." Linux can be customised to perform almost any computing task.
- Advanced graphical user interface. Linux uses a standard, network-transparent X-windowing system with a "window manager" (typically KDE or GNOME). The graphical desktop under Linux can be made to look like MS Windows (or probably ANY other graphical user interface of your choice).
- Dozens of excellent, free, general-interest desktop applications. These include a range of web browsers, e-mail programs, word processors, spreadsheets, bitmap and vector graphics programs, file managers, audio players, CD writers, some good games, etc.
- Thousands of free applets, tools, and smaller programs. "Small is beautiful" goes well with Linux

philosophy. The small Linux tools and applets often work in tandem to perform more complex tasks.

- Hundreds of specialized applications built by researchers around the world (astronomy, information technology, chemistry, physics, engineering, linguistics, biology...). In many fields, Linux seems like "the only" operating system in existence (try to find out what your friend astronomer runs on her computer). The software in this category is typically not very easy to use, but if you want the power, it is the best software that humanity has in these areas.
- Scores of top-of-the line commercial programs including all the big databases (*e.g.*, Oracle, Sybase, but no Microsoft's). Many (most?) of these are offered free for developers and for personal use.
- A truly great learning platform. If you are a parent, you should be really glad your daughter/son does Linux--s/he will surely learn something of lasting value. If you are a teacher, you should consider the installation of Linux at your school. "It is indeed a strange world when educators need to be convinced that sharing information, as opposed to concealing information, is a good thing". You select Linux if you care to provide education, not training. The better the university, the greater the chance their computer department uses Linux in teaching. For example, under Linux, you can immediately begin modifying and compiling for yourself a spreadsheet application which is in every bit as advanced and capable as MS Excel. Linux puts you right on the cutting edge (in technology, project management, QA, methodology of science). Many teachers won't use Linux in schools because they are lacking in computer education themselves.
- Excellent networking capability built into your operating system. You think you don't need a network? Once you try home networking, you will

never be able to live without it! How about connecting the two or more computers that you have at home and sharing your hard drives, CDROM(s), sound card(s), modem, printer(s), etc.? How about browsing the net on two or more machines at the same time using a single Internet connection? How about playing a game with your son over your home network? Even your old 386 with Win3.11 may become useful again when connected to your Linux Pentium server and when it is able to use your network resources. All necessary networking software comes with standard Linux, free, just setup is required. And it is not second-rate shareware--it is exactly the same software that runs most of the Internet (the Apache software runs more than 50% of all Internet web servers and Sendmail touches some 70% of all e-mail). The pleasure of home networking is something I was able to discover only owing to Linux.

- Connectivity to Microsoft, Novel, and Apple proprietary networking. Reading/writing to your DOS/MS Windows and other disk formats. This includes "transparent" use of data stored on the legacy MS Windows partition of your hard drive(s).
- State-of-the-art development platform with many best-of-the-kind programming languages and tools coming free with the operating system. Access to all the operating system source codes, should you require it, is also free. The "C" compiler that comes standard with Linux can compile code for more platforms than (probably) any other compiler on earth. Perl, Python, Guile, Tcl, Ruby, powerful "shell" scripting, and even assembler tools also come as standard with Linux.
- Freedom from viruses, "backdoors" to your computer, software manufacturer "features," invasion of privacy, forced upgrades, proprietary file formats, licensing and marketing schemes, product

registration, high software prices, and pirating. How is this? Linux has no viruses worth mentioning because it is too secure an operating system for the viruses to spread with any degree of efficiency. The rest follows from the open-source and non-commercial nature of Linux: Linux evolved itself by "bazaar-like" mechanisms to encapsulate the best computing practices, code legibility and correctness, security, flexibility, usefulness, coolness, and performance.

- The operating platform that is guaranteed "here-to-stay." Since Linux is not owned, it cannot possibly be put out of business. The Linux General Public License (GPL) insures that development/maintenance will be provided as long as there are Linux users. There are a great number of highly-educated Linux users and tens of thousands of actively developed projects.
- A platform which will technically develop at a rapid pace. This is insured by the modern, open-software development model which Linux implements: "build-on-the-back-of-the-previous-developer" and "peer-review-your-code" (as opposed to the anachronistic closed-software model: "always-start-from-scratch" and "nobody-will-see-my-code"). Even if the current "Linux hype" died out, Linux will develop as it did before the media hype started. Open source development does have its peculiarities: the development appears rather slow (vertically) but it proceeds on a very wide front, dangerous security bugs are fixed almost upon discovery, there are typically several alternatives for a program of similar functionality. Linux depth cannot be overestimated.

DIFFERENCES BETWEEN LINUX AND UNIX

Command-line-wise, almost none, although this has been changing (for better or worse). Linux has a much larger market appeal and following than any commercial UNIX. GUI-wise there are also no major differences—Linux, as most other UNIXes, uses an X-Windowing system.

The major differences:

- Linux is free, while many UNICES (this is supposed to be the plural of UNIX), are very expensive. The same for applications—many good applications are available on Linux free. Even the same commercial application (if you wanted to buy one) typically costs much more for a commercial UNIX than for Linux.
- Linux runs on many hardware platforms, the commodity Intel-x86/IBM-spec personal computers being the most prominent. In contrast, a typical UNIX is proprietary-hardware-bonded (and this hardware tends to be much more expensive than a typical PC clone).
- With Linux, you are in charge of your computer, whereas on most UNICES you are typically confined to be an "l-user" (some administrators pronounce it "loser").
- Linux feels very much like DOS/Win in the late 80s/90s, but is much sturdier and richer, while a typical UNIX account feels like a mainframe from the 60s/70s.
- Some UNICES may be more mature in certain areas (for example, security, some engineering applications, better support of cutting-edge hardware). Linux is more for the average Joe who wants to run his own server or engineering workstation.

DIFFERENCES BETWEEN LINUX AND MS WINDOWS

Mouse-click-wise, almost none, once Linux is properly installed. Linux installation can be a challenge though, whereas MS Windows comes, most likely, pre-installed with your computer.

The major differences:

- Linux is free, whereas MS Windows costs money. Same for applications. If MS Windows or Office comes preinstalled with the computer it is unlikely it is free. Ask in the store to take it off your computer (your run Linux) and you are likely to obtain a discount, at least in smaller stores.

- Linux file formats are free, so you can access them in a variety of ways. On MS Windows, the common practice is to make you lock your own data in secret formats that can only be accessed with tools leased to you at the vendor's price. How corrupt (or incompetent?) must be the politicians who lock our public records into these formats! "What we will get with Microsoft is a three-year lease on a health record we need to keep for 100 years" [http://news.bbc.co.uk/hi/english/health/newsid_1694000/1694372.stm].
- With Linux, you are unlikely to violate any licence agreement—all the software is happily yours. With MS Windows you likely already violate all kinds of licenses and you could be pronounced a computer pirate if only a smart lawyer was after you (don't worry, most likely none is after you).
- MS Windows tries to be the "lowest-common-denominator" operating system (for better or worse), whereas Linux is built for more sophisticated, feature-hungry computer users (for better or worse).
- MS Windows is based on DOS; Linux is based on UNIX. MS Windows Graphical User Interface (GUI) is based on Microsoft-owned specifications. Linux GUI is based on an industry-standard network-transparent X-Windowing system.
- Linux beats Windows hands down on network features, as a development platform, in data processing capabilities, and as a scientific workstation. MS Windows desktop has a more polished appearance, smoother general business applications, and many more games for kids (these are not better games though—Linux games tend to be more sophisticated).
- Linux is more feature-rich than you could imagine.

Heard on the Internet: "Two big products came from the University of California: UNIX and LSD. And I don't think it's a coincidence." MS Windows is simpler.

LINUX IS A GOOD

The Linux community has repeatedly been labeled "religious zealots" by journalists whose well-established computer magazines received massive feedback after they had published highly unfair articles on Linux. So yes, the Linux community is numerous, literate, and willing to express its opinions. And many computer journalists/magazines know that Linux means less money for them (users pay less for their computing and the associated advertisement, while expecting more). Does this explain the "zealots"?

Face it, you salespeople pretending to be journalists. There is hardly any integrity left in the computing press. How many words on Linux did your PC Magazine (or any other IT magazine) publish by 1999-01-01? Wasn't Linux at least an interesting technology by that time? It surely was, yet you conspired to keep your readership in the dark, selling your journalistic integrity for a few dollars.

And now, after Linux has surfaced in the mainstream (non-computer) media, you keep writing misleading articles about it saying "yah, but it will/cannot/may...." whatever (trying the "fear, uncertainty and doubt" tactics to kill it). And adding "Microsoft is already...", continuing to write about the vapourware and the future paradise in the face of the increasingly stealthy, unstable, pricey, architecturally unsound computer platform, whose greatest achievement has been exhorting unheard-of-before money by denying interoperatibility, and killing any existing or proposed standard (by "embracing" and then proprietary-extending it). Whom do you serve? Surely not your readers.

I worded it as strongly as I could. Am I a zealot? Or am I just trying to voice my disapproval for the self-serving actions of the computer "powers-that-be"? You think "self-serving" is OK in business? How pathetic must your business be then!

I always thought that business was a social contract in which we exchange good values, for a mutual benefit. As I read history, societies use to hang/guillotine/electrocute those members who really persisted in their self-serving business. Well, times have changed. A bit for the better, a bit for the worse:))

To be fair, there seems to be a number of hard-core devotees around any computer program/platform, and Linux might have accummulated a fair share of them. Oh, well, you may be religious about whatever you like.

COMPARISON OF LINUX WITH MS-DOS AND WINDOWS

LINUX VS MS-DOS

DOS was the first operating system I learned to use. I remember a test by my tutor in which one had to create a hierarchical set of directories. This probably sounds trivial to anyone familiar with graphical user interfaces, but then the scenario was very different. It even looks ancient by today's standards. Windows 95 hadn't been released at that time, and Linux was unheard of in India. I liked DOS much better than Windows 3.1, which looked quite flimsy and unstable, not to mention that it was a big memory hog. DOS is quite different from Linux in many ways.

DOS does not provide any graphical user interface and you have to learn at least a dozen commands with its numerous options to do some basic tasks likc copying a file or moving between the directories. Even a minor spelling mistake can result in a "Bad command or file name" error.

DOS does not support the concept of multi-users; each and every user has to customise the system according to his need every time he wants to work on it. It was also not a multitasking system. This meant that you could not check out the value of a calculation when typing a letter without closing that application first.

DOS also does not have any in built security features. This was acceptable as long as you did not want a networking system. There was other variants of MS-DOS, like PC-DOS from IBM and some others, which tried to add the missing features. Some of the deficiencies have been resolved using third party utilities but basic limitations like the arcane 640kb-memory limit and single-tasking were not acceptable to many.

Now in case you are wondering why anyone would care to use DOS, I will point out some advantages. Basically DOS has had very different goals from that of Linux. It was a very cheap system (as far as cost is concerned) and it was quite usable with its minimalist set of features. It was a simple system to work with. There weren't too many complications to worry about if you didn't want to develop anything on it. It was arguably the world's most popular operating system and it had a comfortable number of applications for common tasks.

Files and Directories

The files in Linux can be very long, up-to 255 characters like Windows, and they do not always have extensions. The executable files are identified through an attribute rather than the extension. File extensions are less important to Linux than for DOS and Windows, since Linux usually identifies files by a unique identification code called the magic number that depends on the file type.

Directories are similar to that of DOS and follow a hierarchical structure. The path names are separated by forward slashes (/)in Linux whereas DOS and Windows uses back slashes (\).

For example:

- % cd/mnt/cdrom A/denotes the root and.. stands for the parent directory, similar to DOS. In bash shells, the ~ symbol maybe used to jump to the home directory quickly.

For example:

- % cd ~

Linux Shell

Several of the DOS commands have Linux equivalents.

The Linux shell is similar to the DOS command line but is far more powerful, and I found that it was also more workable with features like colour highlighting and friendlier navigation capabilities, depending on the particular shell you are using.

Most Linux distributions come with the Bash (Bourne Again SHell) as the default. There are several others, like the Korn shell and the C shell. They are usually similar. It's recommended that you learn to work with one shell completely before trying out the others. Things usually get complicated if you want to run shell scripts, which are similar to batch files (files with the.bat extension) under DOS.

Running DOS Programs Under Linux (DOS Emulation)

There is a DOS emulator called dosemu www.dosemu.org for Linux that is capable of running DOS programs under the Linux operating system. This software is still under development; you may wish to try it out though. It is known to be fairly usable at least for some applications. If you are looking for Linux just to use DOS programs for free then try using FreeDOS www.freedos.org. That should be much better than Linux.

LINUX VS. WINDOWS

As I have said before Windows is more or less similar to Linux. When people are introduced to Linux they are at first intimidated by the system. It has different kinds of graphical interfaces and things don't always work as they are expected to. When users look at me in a puzzled manner I demonstrate in some easy ways how common tasks like changing the desktop wallpaper or playing a song is similar to Windows. The problem with this kind of approach is that the users complain very soon that Linux doesn't offer them much more than Windows does:-).

I agree with them to a certain extent on this. There are some limitations to what you can expect from an operating system. You just can't expect Linux to work like a 3D-shooter game or something. Of course, there are many differences in the shell, the choice of user interfaces and the philosophy and goals of the operating system. Linux is developed as a open system in which the source code of the core Linux system (kernel) is available for anyone for free but how this could affect the end user is difficult to explain initially.

The user interface is probably the first thing you notice when you begin to use the Linux system. Windows offers a single, monolithic user interface, which is more or less the same across all the versions. In contrast, Linux has two major desktop environments called KDE and Gnome. KDE has a built-in window manager, while Gnome is supported by many, such as Sawfish and Enlightenment.

The decision of choosing one among the desktop environments and windows managers is left to you. Some of them can run efficiently in a system with low amounts of memory and some of them are designed to look like a game console. KDE would be more similar to Windows, and Gnome with the Enlightenment window manager was fancy enough for me. Try out some of the popular ones before making the decision. Let's take a look at Windows in more detail so that you can clearly make out the differences.

Versions of Windows

Windows has two major series, a desktop oriented series (Windows 9x) And a network oriented series Windows.There are also other versions like Windows CE for embedded systems.

Bibliography

Aaron, E.: *Programming with Java: A Primer*, N.J.: Scarecrow Press, 2004.

Boston, M.A.: *ASP.Net and VB.Net Web Programming*, Buckingham: Open University Press, 2006.

Chris, B.: *Web Programming Building Internet Applications*, Boston: Allyn and Bacon, 2008.

Christopher, A.: *Open Source Linux Web Programming*, Beverly Hills: Sage Publications, 2002.

Deven, N.: *A Complete Guide to Internet and Web Programming*, CA: Sage Publications, 2000.

Ellen, P.: *Programming the Web using XML*, New York: Oxford University Press, 1998.

George, K.: *Web Programming: Techniques for Integrating Python, Linux*, MA: Sinauer Associates, 1999.

James, S.: *Programming Web Services with SOAP*, NJ: Princeton University Press, 2001.

Jerry, A.: *Professional Visual Basic 6 Web Programming*, New York: St. Martin's Press, 2003.

Jon, D.: *Beginning Web Programming with HTML, XHTML, and CSS*, N.J: Scarecrow Press, 2004.

Lynn, T.: *Programming the Web with Visual Basic Net*, New York: Oxford University Press, 1998.

Maximiliano, F.: *Programming the Mobile Web*, NJ: Princeton University Press, 2001.

Michael, J.: *A Web-based Introduction to Programming: Essential*

Algorithms, New York: Springer-Verlag, 2007.

Moller, A.: *An Introduction to XML and Web Technologies*, New York: Falmer Press, 2005.

Rashim, M.: *Java Web Services Programming*, New York: Springer-Verlag, 2007.

Simon, S.: *Programming Web services with XML-RPC*, IL: F.E. Peacock Publishers, 2008.

Toby, S.: *Programming the Semantic Web*, NY: Pergamon Publications, 1997.

Index

L

M

O

P

Q

S

T

U

V

W